BY THIS
STANDARD

BY THIS STANDARD

The Authority of God's Law Today

Greg L. Bahnsen

Institute for Christian Economics
Tyler, Texas

Cover design by George Grant
Cover illustration by Randy Rogers

Published by
Institute for Christian Economics
P.O. Box 8000
Tyler, Texas 75711

This book is affectionately
dedicated to my parents

Robert and Virginia Bahnsen

who first taught me
respect for the law

TABLE OF CONTENTS

PROLOGUE

by Gary North

The book which you have before you is a kind of lawyer's brief. It is tightly reasoned, yet clear. It covers the basic outline of the New Testament's case for the continuing validity of Old Testament law. Argument by argument, Dr. Bahnsen refutes the supposed biblical arguments against the continuing validity of the law of God.

That there is today an *unrecognized* crying need for a book such as this one testifies to the theological deprivation that the church of Jesus Christ has suffered for almost two millennia since the death of her Founder. Nevertheless, that such a book should now appear at what seems to be the final crisis of the humanist era of Western civilization indicates that the timing is near-perfect. The thinking of at least a minority of American church leaders has begun to shift. There is a market for this book (in my entrepreneurial view) which did not exist two decades ago. Indeed, this market barely existed as recently as five years ago. Fundamental changes in perspective have taken place within the American Christian community, and are now accelerating—changes that Christian news media recognize even less clearly than the secular press does.

There are numerous reasons for this shift in perspective. In the United States, the most important historical incident in this shift was the decision of the United States Supreme Court to strike down state laws against abortion, the infamous *Roe v. Wade* decision of 1973. That decision made philosophy a life-and-death issue. It brought to the forefront the inescapable reality of a philosophical position that Dr. Bahnsen and other defenders of biblical law have long argued, namely, that *there is no such thing as neutrality.* The issue of abortion has graphically illustrated the truth of this conclusion. Either the unborn child is left alone to mature in the womb, or else it is executed—in this case, by a state-licensed medical professional. (It is illegal, at present, to commit an abortion for a fee unless you are a licensed physician; to do so would involve practicing medicine without a license, and the Supreme Court would uphold your being sent to jail for such a crime against humanity—"humanity" being defined as an exceedingly profitable medical monopoly.) There is no third possibility, no neutral zone between life and death, except for the rare case of an aborted child who somehow survives the executioner initially, and is born alive in the abortionist's office. This medical possibility has created havoc for humanism's legal theorists.[1] It has been called by one medical authority "the ultimate complication." Once out of the womb, must the abortionist regard the baby as a legal person, or can he legally destroy it?

A legal dilemma such as this one can only arise in a civilization which has turned its back on God and His law. Humanist lawyers need humanistic principles of "casuistry" — the application of permanent general laws to concrete cases — in order to deal with such dilemmas, just as surely as Christian legal thinkers need biblical principles of casuistry. Yet Christian casuistry has been ridiculed by secular historians. We should not forget: it is never a question of casuistry vs. no casuistry; it is always a question of *which kind of casuistry?*

What has become clear to a growing minority of Christians with respect to the "medical and social neutrality" of abortion is also becoming clearer with respect to such social evils as pornography, inflation, officially neutral tax-supported education ("values clarification"), homosexuality, globalism, the New World Order, New Age humanism, and contemporary Western theories of national defense (mutually assured destruction, or MAD). When the principle of neutrality is exposed as fraudulent in one area, it tends to become increasingly suspect in other areas, especially political areas. Thus, step by step, a radically defective heritage of Christian pietism and retreatism is being overcome.

---

1. Franky Schaeffer, *Bad News for Modern Man: An Agenda for Christian Activism* (Westchester, Illinois: Crossway Books, 1984), pp. 3-6.

Biblical Law and Evangelism

As Christians rediscover that at one time in American history, this was a Christian nation, and Western civilization was once Christian civilization, the question then arises: *What makes a Christian society appear visibly different from any other kind of society?* The answer today is exactly what it was in Moses' day: *ethics.* In Moses' day, as today, ethical systems were at war with each other, and a God-given and man-enforced ethical system was required as a form of international evangelism. As we read in Deuteronomy 4:

> Behold, I have taught you statutes and judgments, even as the Lord my God commanded me, that ye should do so in the land whither ye go to possess it. Keep therefore and do them; for this is your wisdom and your understanding in the sight of the nations, which shall hear all these statutes, and say, Surely this great nation is a wise and understanding people. For what nation is there so great, who hath God so nigh unto them, as the Lord our God is in all things that we call upon him for? And what nation is so great, that hath statutes and judgments so righteous as all this law, which I set before you this day? (vv. 5-7).

God is glorified when His law is enforced by those who honor Him. Similarly, God is outraged when men turn their backs on His law, for in doing so, they turn their backs on the social and legal restraints that alone keep man from destroying himself and the creation. Someone has called God's law a "user's manual" for the creation, but it is more than this: it is a user's manual for life. God's laws, when imparted to men redeemed by grace through faith in Christ, are the laws of life.

Faith without works is dead (James 2:20). Christians without faithful works are equally dead, and therefore unfaithful. The question is: How do we test the faithfulness of any man's works, or any civilization's works? In short: *By what standard?*

Apologetics

Dr. Bahnsen studied apologetics (the philosophical defense of the faith) and theology under Dr. Cornelius Van Til, the eloquent defender of the absolute sovereignty of God and the absolute sovereignty of the Bible. No Christian philosopher in the history of the church has ever attacked the myth of neutrality more confidently or more effectively than Dr. Van Til. When R. J. Rushdoony wrote a book on Van Til's thought, he titled it, *By What Standard?* This was appropriate, for it has been Van Til, more than anyone in church history, who has thrown down the challenge to self-proclaimed autonomous man to defend his standards apart from God, while Van Til has continued to defend the Bible in terms of the Bible. There is no philosophical strategy that can work, and there is no strategy that ever has worked, except this one: to challenge the lost in terms of the revelation of God in His Bible. The autonomous Emperor has no clothes. Covenant-breakers have no internally self-consistent philosophical response. By what standard can man know anything truly? By the

Bible, and *only* the Bible, Van Til answered—in volume after erudite volume.

Dr. Bahnsen is certainly a spiritual and intellectual heir of Van Til, as Van Til recognized early in Dr. Bahnsen's seminary career. Dr. Bahnsen is a trained philosopher and a rigorous logician; indeed, he writes more precisely than Van Til. There is a price to pay for this precision, however, both for the author and his readers. The author suffers from a narrower market, and readers must think precisely in order to follow the arguments. Not that many readers are sufficiently self-disciplined to take up the challenge.

It is not that Dr. Bahnsen's exposition is difficult to follow; it is that one must pay attention in order to follow him. This requires *pre*viewing and *re*viewing. It also requires readers to remember the outline of the arguments that have been presented in earlier sections. (Read and reread pages 345-47.) Dr. Bahnsen requires of his readers the ability and willingness to pay attention, not a high IQ. His glossary provides definitions for technical terms. Use it.

His performance in this book is admittedly unexciting. He considers the standard arguments that have been used against the idea of the continuing validity of biblical law, and he exposes them, one by one, as illogical, anti-biblical, and productive of great harm. He shows not only that these arguments are wrong logically but also that they are wrong morally. He wraps his opponents in an exegetical net. The more they struggle, the more ensnared they become. He never names them, but you can hear them screaming anyway.

His performance could also be compared to a man who "milks" a poisonous snake: he operates methodically, without visible emotion, and precisely. Eventually, the snake is rendered harmless. Temporarily. Until the poison is again manufactured by its system. Then it's another round of "milking," with yet another argument being squeezed dry of logical and biblical content, until the snake is exhausted. On and on it goes, until the snake finally dies or has its fangs extracted. To appreciate the technician's efforts, however, the observer must recognize the danger of the poison and the seriousness of the operation. The observer also should not be surprised that from start to finish, there is a lot of outraged hissing going on.

What is notable about Dr. Bahnsen's previous writings on biblical law has been the dearth of published criticism. *Theonomy in Christian Ethics* appeared in 1977, and it received considerable verbal criticism. Murmurings might better describe the response. But there was not much published criticism, and what there was cannot be described as a serious threat to Dr. Bahnsen's case. A few critical essays appeared, but only one was of any academic significance, Dr. Meredith Kline's, and Dr. Bahnsen's subsequent response ended the debate.[2] Whenever I reread the

---

2. Meredith G. Kline, *Westminster Theological Journal,* vol. XLI, No. 1 (Fall 1978); Greg. L. Bahnsen, "M. G. Kline on Theonomic Politics: An Evaluation of His Reply," *Journal of Christian Reconstruction*, VI, No. 2 (Winter 1979-80). The latter volume is available from Chalcedon Foundation, P.O. Box 158, Vallecito, California 95251.

two essays, I am reminded of that 5-second "underground" cartoon, "Bambi Meets Godzilla." Bambi is skipping through the forest, when a giant reptilian foot squashes him. End of cartoon. In the case of Dr. Kline, end of debate. There was no rematch. (The most amusing aspect of this historic confrontation is that "Bambi" initiated it.)

Bullies and Weaklings

This book's introduction to the question of the continuing validity of Old Testament law is not definitive. It is only an introduction. It should not be regarded as a final statement of the theonomic position. *Theonomy in Christian Ethics* is an extended defense of the case which is presented in this book. Rushdoony's *Institutes of Biblical Law*, James Jordan's *Law of the Covenant*, and my own economic commentary on the Bible, *The Dominion Covenant*, are also examples of how biblical law can be successfully applied to contemporary social issues and policy-making.

There are those in the Christian community who will immediately reject Dr. Bahnsen's thesis, but their voices are growing increasingly shrill because of their desperation. They are under siege: from Bahnsen on their right and from secular humanism on their left. Their numbers are thinning even more rapidly than their hair. A younger generation of Christian activists is in no mood to take seriously lame traditional excuses for not challenging humanist civilization in the name of biblical principles. These younger men are tired of being pushed around by God-haters. More significantly, they have begun to recognize that the church is not culturally impotent, and God's law does not lead to impotence.

Unlike the comic book advertisement for Charles Atlas's "dynamic tension" program, where the 200-pound bully kicks sand in the face of the 98-pound weakling, Christians in the twentieth century have been the 200-pound weaklings who have been pushed around by 98-pound bullies. Like Samson without his hair, Christians without God's law are impotent, and have been regarded by Philistines throughout the ages as drudges to be misused and humiliated publicly, if the opportunity presents itself. What Dr. Bahnsen is proposing is that we flex our muscles and knock the pillars out from under humanism's temple. But this time, we should push from the outside of the arena, not pull from the inside. When it comes to social collapse, let the Philistines of our day be inside. Let *us* pick up the pieces.

The much-abused traditional slogan, "we're under grace, not law," is increasingly recognized by intelligent Christians as an ill-informed and even perverse theological defense of a perverse cultural situation: "We're under a God-hating humanist legal structure, not God's law, and there's nothing we can do about it." But there *is* something Christians can do about it: they can start studying, preaching, and rallying behind biblical law.

It is unlikely that antinomian critics of biblical law can be successful much longer in withstanding the pressures of our era. A growing minority of Christian leaders now recognize that they must come up with *valid social alternatives to a collapsing humanist civilization*—a humanist order which they now seek to embarrass and even destroy, if possible—if they are to escape the fate of those who now live under the self-declared sovereignty of self-proclaimed autonomous man.

The Bus Will Crash, Unless. . . .

There is an old political maxim that says: "You can't fight something with nothing." The wisdom of this maxim has been demonstrated for over half a century: Christians have been impotent to stop the drift into social disintegration. Now at last they are feeling the cultural pressure. *Their* children are at last being visibly assaulted by the perversions of this age. *Their* churches are now being threatened by some federal bureaucracy. They are now becoming aware of the fact that they can no longer remain as silent participants in the back of humanism's bus, unless they are willing to go over the cliff. They are slowly beginning to understand that they can't get off this speeding bus, although a theology of "back door escape" has been popular until quite recently. But "Rapture fever" is steadily cooling. So there is now only one alternative: they must persuade the other passengers to allow them to take over at the wheel.

Christians alone possess a valid road map: the law of God. This map is rejected by the present driver, and if the other passengers (including confused and psychologically defeated Christians) continue to assent to this driver, then the bus will crash. It may even explode.

The humanists' free ride at the wheel is coming to an end. They are going to have to fight for continuing political control. There are millions of Christians in the back of humanism's bus who are not impressed by the driver's skills any more. They may not have all the answers yet, but they are getting restless. And then along comes Dr. Bahnsen with his road map. We paid our taxes, too, he argues, and we should prepare ourselves to challenge the humanists' control over the driver's seat.

This book is a preliminary defense of the continuing reliability of the road map which God's people were given at Sinai. More than this: it is a defense of the idea that *there is only one road map which is accurate*. There are many, many other maps that are being sold to Christians and humanists alike, but they all have one thing in common: they are inaccurate. It is astounding that a majority of Christians in our day have implicitly and even explicitly claimed that *any* road map is adequate, and that Christians can live tolerably well under the political and social administration of institutions governed by various humanist law-orders. Anything will do, we are told; we can learn to live with any social order, except one. Only one is categorically rejected by an older generation of Christian social thinkers as invalid in New Testament times: God's law.

Christians' Inferiority Complex

Why have so many Christians, especially theologians and professors at Christian colleges, proclaimed such a monstrous social philosophy, a philosophy of "anything is politically acceptable except the Old Testament"? I believe that one reason above all is at the root of the problem: *Christians have been afraid to exercise dominion.* They have been bullied into submission by professional humanist guilt-manipulators who have persuaded Christians that Christianity, when applied to politics, has led to tyranny and war. As an example, they cite the 800-year-old story of the medieval crusades, where a few thousand professional soldiers went off to fight the Muslims. And who is complaining loudly today about the evil Crusades? Defenders of humanism whose various representatives have launched twentieth-century wars and revolutions in which as many as 150 million people died from 1901 until 1970.[3]

These same critics have complained repeatedly about the Roman Catholic Church's burning of the occult magician Bruno[4] or Calvin's approval of the burning of unitarian Servetus (with the enthusiastic approval of the Catholics, who were also after him, and who tipped Calvin off when Servetus came into Geneva), four centuries ago. Compare these two events with the atrocities of Stalin, who killed 20 to 30 million Russians in his purges in the 1930's, including a million Communist Party members,[5] plus

---

3. Gil Eliot, *Twentieth Century Book of the Dead* (New York: Scribners, 1972).

4. That Bruno was an occultist rather than a scientist is proven conclusively in Miss Frances A. Yates' *Giordano Bruno and the Hermetic Tradition* (New York: Vintage, [1964] 1969).

5. Robert Conquest, *The Great Terror: Stalin's Purges of the Thirties* (New York: Collier, [1968] 1973), p. 710.

an additional ten million who died unnatural deaths during the famines produced by his forced collectivization of agriculture.[6] Then there is the continuing atrocity of the Soviet Union's concentration camp population, which has probably included about one-third of the Soviet population over the years, with at least one percent of the entire population in the camps at any given time.[7]

This slaughter took place in the 1930's without any significant criticism in the prestige liberal humanist press for the next twenty years. Malcolm Muggeridge, a reporter for the *Manchester Guardian* in this era, says in the first volume of his autobiography that Western reporters and liberals knew what Stalin was doing; they approved of his ruthlessness. Even in our day, some apologists still exist. ("Stalin, despite certain excesses, was a progressive force in his day, and we must understand that it is not easy to bring a backward society into technological maturity, blah, blah, blah.") Yet these same ideologues taunt Christians about the Salem witch trials in the 1690's, in which all of 20 people were executed, and which never happened again. In one year, Mao's policies killed 30 million Chinese.[8] Spare Christians the guilt trips, please.

Christians have until recently been humbled into

---

6. Paul Johnson, *Modern Times: The World from the Twenties to the Eighties* (New York: Harper & Row, 1982), p. 272.

7. Vladimir Bukovsky, *To Build a Castle: My Life as a Dissenter* (New York: Viking, 1978), p. 318.

8. Stephen Mosher, *Broken Earth: The Rural Chinese* (New York: Free Press, 1983), pp. 263-64.

submission by state-licensed, profit-seeking medical psychopaths who tell us that abortion is a morally valid way to control population growth and to solve marital and financial difficulties. A renewed interest in biblical law will "unhumble" Christians soon enough. It already has.

People may ask: Wouldn't biblical law lead to tyranny? I answer: Why should it? God designed it. God mandated it. Was Israel a tyranny? Or was Egypt the real tyranny, and Babylon? *Tyranny was what God visited upon His people when they turned their backs on biblical law.*

But to be practical about it, I cannot imagine a successful modern tyranny that is financed by less than ten percent of national income. I can easily imagine many tyrannies that are coercively financed by five to seven times the tithe. So can you. In this bloody humanist century, this takes very little imagination. A history book is all it takes. Or a subscription to the *New York Times*.

Pipers and Tunes

He who pays the piper calls the tune. The humanists have taxed our money away from us in order to hire pipers to play their tunes. But they weren't satisfied with direct taxation; they debased the money, and the pipers are in revolt. Now they are borrowing the money (with the "full faith and credit" of the federal government) to keep the pipers playing, but when those who lend the money finally run out of patience and faith, the piper-payers will be in big, big trouble. So will their pipers.

When that day comes, Christians had better be ready with the biblical answer: voluntary charity, the tithe to finance the church, and all levels of civil government combined limited by Constitutional law to under ten percent of the people's income. The state is not God, and is therefore not entitled to a tithe. Christians will pay the pipers voluntarily, and pipers will play our tunes. Humanists can only cough up enough money to pay pipers when they have stolen the money with the ballot box, by means of the politics of guilt and pity, and the politics of envy. The gospel of Christ, when accompanied by faith in biblical law, destroys the psychological foundations of political guilt, pity, and envy. The humanists' political end is in sight, and they are outraged. Psalm 2 tells us what God thinks of their outrage, and how much good it does them.

Conclusion

I will put it bluntly: no theologian of repute (or even disrepute) has successfully challenged Dr. Bahnsen's defense of biblical law during the last eight years. I will go farther: no theologian or Christian social thinker in our generation is capable of successfully challenging Dr. Bahnsen's general thesis, because it is correct. I will take it one step farther: we will not see any prominent Christian philosopher even attempt it, because enough of them know what happened to Meredith Kline: he was cut off at the knees in full view of anyone who bothered to read Dr. Bahnsen's response. Nobody is excited about the prospects of going up against Dr. Bahnsen in print. It leads to excessive humiliation.

Yet if someone from at least one modern theological camp does not respond, and respond soon — dispensationalist, neo-evangelical, Reformed, Roman Catholic, or Eastern Orthodox — then the intellectual battle is very nearly won by the theonomists. It does no good for defenders of an older world-and-life view to pretend that they can safely ignore a brilliant case presented for any new position, let alone the biblical position. If the establishment theologians remain silent for another eight years, the theonomists will have captured the minds of the next generation of Christian activists and social thinkers. Once the younger activists and intellectuals are won over, the fight is in principle over. To the victors will go the spoils: the teaching positions, the satellite T.V. networks, and shelf space in the Christian bookstores — and maybe even secular bookstores, until they finally go bankrupt or go Christian.

Now, who will be the sacrificial lamb? Who wants to attempt to prove in print that this little book is the work of a heretic, or an incompetent? Who will be the person to try to prove that this book's thesis cannot be sustained by an appeal to the New Testament? Who will then go on to refute *Theonomy in Christian Ethics?* A lot of very bright young men are waiting to hear from you, and then to hear from Dr. Bahnsen.

Stay tuned for "Bambi Meets Godzilla, Part II."

FOREWORD

"But that's what the *Old* Testament said! We live in New Testament times."

Whether spoken out loud or not, this is the reaction that many Christians have to any suggestion that we should conform to some requirement of the law of God. A common working assumption is that New Testament believers are not expected by God to live according to Old Testament stipulations. It is erroneously thought that their ethical attitude and standard should be limited to the New Testament, almost as though the Old Testament is now nothing but a historical curiosity — rather than a revelation which is still profitable for "instruction in righteousness" (2 Tim. 3:16-17). This book is written to stimulate Scripture-guided reflection on the question of whether the Old Testament law is still binding as a moral standard today. Such a question can prove controversial, and one will find there exists a large number of different answers posed for it. This book is by no means the last word on the subject, and it is not intended to be so. But it *is* a word which strives diligently to be faithful to the full scope of Biblical teaching about the law of God. Hopefully the reader will find the book helpful in organizing issues, presenting convincing proposals, and forcing him or her to check all opinions by the written word of God.

The various chapters which make up this book were first composed as short articles, most of which appeared in my monthly newsletter, *Biblical Ethics* (published by the Institute for Christian Economics of Tyler, Texas). These studies ran from September, 1978 to July, 1982. Their order of appearance has been slightly changed for book form, and in some cases more than one month's material has been combined into single chapters for this book. The "Biblical Ethics" series — and now this book — aimed to distill for a wider reading audience the more extensive discussions of the validity of God's law which can be found in my book, *Theonomy in Christian Ethics* (2nd ed., Nutley, New Jersey: Craig Press, 1984). *Theonomy* sets forth the basic position which it seems to me the New Testament takes toward the Old Testament law.

The present book is an attempt to set forth a *summary* of *Theonomy,* as well as of the forthcoming book, *Debate Over God's Law,* a detailed rebuttal of the published criticisms of *Theonomy.* It does not aim for the depth of coverage or minute detail of argumentation which characterizes these other publications. It is anticipated that this will render the present publication more useful for a broader audience of readers—those who have, as Christians, a natural interest in the questions of Biblical ethics. After becoming familiar with the position regarding God's law which is presented herein, readers who have a greater interest in the subject, or who have more questions about it, or who might have further challenges to raise regarding what is said, should get hold of my other book.

My prayer is that through these books Christians will become convinced of the wisdom and authority of God's commandments, learning to say from the heart: "O how love I thy law!" (Ps. 119:97).

*   *   *   *   *   *   *   *   *

As I send this book to press, I wish to express my gratitude to a number of people who have made the publication possible and helped me in its production. I extend thanks to Dr. Gary North of the Institute for Christian Economics for initiating this project and underwriting its costs, like a "Theophilus" of the modern age. I also want to thank R. E. McMaster, whose generous contribution helped to finance the publication of this book. I am grateful to my friends in the Sovereign Grace Reformed Church (Ashland, Ohio) who have faithfully supported my teaching ministry while these studies were being composed. Those who have criticized theonomic ethics are to be thanked for helping me to show the common misunderstandings or errors about the theonomic position which called for attention in a book such as this. In preparing the text for publication, I have been greatly aided by the editorial and proofreading efforts of Mr. Doug Jones and my lovely wife, Cathie. Their insights and corrections have been a service to both me and the reader. Finally, I want to thank my parents, to whom this book is dedicated, for the patient and nurturing love which led me to see life and conduct, not in terms of arbitrary opinion, but in terms of reliable guiding principles.

Rev. Greg L. Bahnsen
M.Div., Th.M, Ph.D.
Covenant Community Church
Placentia, California

1

SPECIFICATION OF PURPOSE AND POSITION

"Over against the autonomous ethical philosophies of men, where good and evil are defined by sinful speculation, the Christian ethic gains its character and direction from the revealed word of God."

Throughout the history of the Christian church, believers have asked what their attitude should be toward the commandments of God that are revealed in the Old Testament. A large variety of positions have been taken regarding God's law — stretching all the way from saying that there have been *no changes* in how the law should be observed (so that, for instance, animal sacrifices would be continued) to saying that *everything has been changed* because of the change of dispensation (so that the Christian ethic is totally restricted to the New Testament). Between the two extreme poles numerous other positions or attitudes (some pro-nomian, some antinomian) can be found, with subtle variations distinguishing one school of thought from another in many cases. Against the background of this welter of opinions, it would be well to specify and summarize the position regarding God's law which is taken in these chapters.

The Basic Thesis

Fundamental to the position taken herein is the conviction that God's special revelation — His written word — is necessary as the objective standard of morality for God's people. Over against the autonomous ethical philosophies of men, where good and evil are defined by sinful speculation, the Christian ethic gains its character and direction from the revealed word of God, a revelation which harmonizes with the general revelation made of God's standards through the created order and man's conscience.

When we explore what the Bible teaches about the character of God, the salvation accomplished by Christ, the work of the Holy Spirit in making us holy in heart and conduct, or the nature of God's covenantal dealings with men, we see why the believer should take a positive attitude toward the commandments of God, even as revealed in the Old Testament. Indeed, the Bible teaches that we should *presume continuity* between the ethical standards of the New Testament and those of the Old, rather than abbreviating the validity of God's law according to some preconceived and artificial limit.

Because He did not come to abrogate the Old Testament, and because not one stroke of the law will become invalid until the end of the world, Jesus declared: "Therefore, whosoever breaks one of these least commandments and teaches men so, shall be called least in the kingdom of heaven" (Matt. 5:17-19). Given this instruction, our attitude must be that all Old Testament laws are presently our obligation *unless* further revelation from the Lawgiver shows that some change has been made.

The *methodological* point, then, is that we presume our obligation to obey any Old Testament commandment unless the New Testament indicates otherwise. We must assume continuity with the Old Testament rather than discontinuity. This is *not* to say that there are *no changes* from Old to New Testament. Indeed, there are—important ones. However, the word of God must be the standard which defines precisely what those changes are for us; we cannot take it upon ourselves to assume such changes or read them into the New Testament. God's word, His direction to us, must be taken as continuing in its authority until God Himself reveals otherwise. This is, in a sense, the heart of "covenant theology" over against a dispensational understanding of the relation between Old and New Testaments.

To this methodological point we can add the *substantive conclusion* that the New Testament does not teach any radical change in God's law regarding the standards of *socio-political morality*. God's law as it touches upon the duty of civil magistrates has not been altered in any systematic or fundamental way in the New Testament.

Consequently, instead of taking a basically antagonistic view of the Old Testament commandments for society and the state, and instead of taking a smorgasbord approach of picking and choosing among those laws on the basis of personal taste and convenience, we must recognize the continuing obligation of civil magistrates to obey and enforce the relevant laws of the Old Testament, including the penal sanctions specified by the just Judge of all the earth. As with the rest of God's law, we must presume continuity of binding authority regarding the socio-political commandments revealed as standing law in the Old Testament.

Discontinuity (Change) Has Not Been Denied

What has been said above is simply that the *presumption* should be that an Old Testament law is binding in the New Testament. This does not in any way preclude or reject many radical differences between the Old and New Testaments. Changes do indeed come through the course of redemptive history, so that there certainly are exceptions to the general continuity that characterizes the relation between Old and New Covenants. God has the right to make alterations for the New Age. In the transition to this New Age we observe that advances are made over the Old Covenant, with some laws laid aside and some laws observed in a new fashion.

Given the progress of revelation, we must be committed to the rule that *the New Testament should interpret the Old Testament for us;* the attitude of Jesus and the Apostles to the Mosaic law, for instance, must be determinative of the Christian ethic. Thus a simplistic equation between Old and New Testament ethics—one that abstractly absolutizes the New Testament teaching about continuity with the Old Testament (not recognizing qualifications revealed elsewhere)—is not advanced by the position taken here. What *is* maintained is that our obligation to God's Old Testament law should be interpreted and qualified by the New Testament *Scripture, not* by relative human opinion which can cite no Biblical warrant for departing from God's stipulations.

It should be recognized that certain aspects of the Old Covenant are not authoritative today. For instance, in addition to the standing laws by which the Jews were always to live, God gave certain *localized imperatives* to them—commands for specified use in one concrete situation, not principles with the continuing force of law from generation to generation. An example would be the command to go to war and gain the land of Palestine by the sword; this is not an enduring requirement for us today.

Likewise, there were *cultural details* mentioned in many of God's laws so as to illustrate the moral principle which He required (for example, the distinction between accidental manslaughter and malicious murder was illustrated in terms of a flying axhead). What is of permanent moral authority is the *principle* illustrated, and not the cultural detail used to illustrate it. Thus we ought not to read the case laws of the Old Testament as binding us to the literal wording utilized (for example, flying sickle blades and faulty car brakes are *also* covered by the law dealing with the flying axhead).

In addition to localized imperatives and cultural details of expression, we would note that certain *administrative details* of Old Testament society are not normative for today (for example, the type or form of government, the method of tax collecting, the location of the capitol). These aspects of Old Testament life were not prescribed by standing law, and they do not bind us today.

Other discontinuities with Old Testament life and practices would pertain to the typological foreshadows in the Old Testament — replaced according to the New Testament with the realities they typified. For instance, we have the ceremonial laws of sacrifice which served during the Old Testament as "weak and beggarly" shadows of the perfect sacrifice of Christ which was to come. We can also think here of the provisions regarding the land of Palestine. With the coming and establishment of that kingdom typified by the "promised land," and with the removal of special kingdom privileges from the Jews by Christ, the laws regulating aspects of the land of Canaan (for example, family plots, location of cities of refuge, the levirate institution) have been laid aside in the New Testament as inapplicable.

Other examples could perhaps be given, but enough has been said by now to demonstrate the point that the position taken herein is *not* that every last detail of Old Testament life must be reproduced today as morally obligatory, but simply that our *presumption* must be that of *continuity* with the *standing* laws of the Old Testament (*when* properly, contextually interpreted).

We need to be sensitive to the fact that interpreting the Old Testament law, properly categorizing its details (for example, ceremonial, standing, cultural), and making modern day applications of the authoritative standards of the Old Testament is *not an easy or simple task*. It is not always readily apparent to us how to understand an Old Testament commandment or use it properly today. So the position taken here does not make everything in Christian ethics a simple matter of looking up obvious answers in a code-book. Much hard thinking— exegetical and theological homework—is entailed by a commitment to the position advocated in these studies.

What Is NOT Being Attempted or Advocated

The aim of these studies is to set forth a case in favor of the continuing validity of the Old Testament law, including its socio-political standards of justice. It is advocated that we should presume the abiding authority of any Old Testament commandment until and unless the New Testament reveals otherwise, and this presumption holds just as much for laws pertaining to the state as for laws pertaining to the individual. As already noted, such a presumption does not deny the reality of some discontinuities with the Old Testament today; it simply insists that such changes be warranted by Biblical teaching, not by untrustworthy personal feeling or opinion.

So then, the position taken here does not pretend to be a *total* view of Christian ethics, touching on its many facets. Only one perspective in Christian ethics is taken up—namely, the normative perspective dealing with the question of standards for conduct. Motivational and consequential perspectives (touching on inner character and goal in ethics) are not equally treated, nor is the vital area of producing and maintaining moral behavior.

Moreover, the one aspect of ethics which is the focus of attention in these studies, the question of law, is presented with a view toward *avoiding* certain serious *errors* that can be made about God's law. Obedience to God's law is not the way a person gains justification in the eyes of God; salvation is not by meritorious works but rather by grace through faith. And while the law may be a pattern of holy living for sanctification, the law is not the dynamic power which enables obedience on the part of God's people; rather, the Holy Spirit gives us new life and strength to keep God's commands. The externalistic interpretation of God's law which characterized the Pharisees is also repudiated herein; the demands made by God extend to our hearts and attitudes so that true obedience must stem from a heart of faith and love. It is not found simply in outward conformity to (part of) His law.

What these studies present is a position in Christian (normative) *ethics*. They do *not* logically commit those who agree with them to any particular school of *eschatological* interpretation. Premillennialists, amillennialists, and postmillennialists can all harmonize this normative perspective with their views of history and God's kingdom. While the author has definite views in eschatology, they are not the subject matter of these studies either explicitly or implicitly.

It can be added that the ethical position taught here is of a *foundational* character. It deals with a fundamental issue, the validity of God's law, and does not answer all questions about detailed application of God's law to our modern world. The specific interpretation of God's commandments is not taken up and discussed at length. Indeed, those who agree with the foundational conclusion of these studies — that God's law is binding today unless Scripture reveals otherwise — may very well disagree among themselves over particular matters in interpreting what God's law demands at this or that point, or that may disagree over how these demands should be followed today. These studies do not aim to settle all such matters. They simply argue that God's law cannot be ignored in making decisions in Christian ethics. To say this, is *not to endorse every abuse* that has been or is being made by believers regarding the requirements set forth in the Old Testament commandments.

Furthermore, it should be observed that these studies do not advocate the imposition of God's law *by force* upon a society, as though that would be a way to "bring in the kingdom." God's kingdom advances by means of the Great Commission — evangelism, preaching, and nurture in the word of God — and in the power of God's regenerating and sanctifying Spirit. While these studies take a distinctive position regarding the law of God and the modern state, they do not focus upon a *method* of *political change*. The concern is rather with the *standard* of political justice.

Thus it might be well to avert misconceptions here by repudiating any thought of the church taking up the sword in society, any thought of rebellion against the powers that be, and likewise any thought of mindless submission to the *status quo* in one's society. Our commitment must be to the transforming power of God's word which reforms all areas of life by the truth. Ignoring the need for socio-political reform or trying to achieve it by force both contradict the church's reformational responsibilities.

Errors pertaining to the socio-political use of God's law can be discarded in advance here. Not all sins are crimes, and thus the civil magistrate is *not* obligated to enforce the *entire* law of God. Rulers should enforce only those laws for which God revealed social sanctions to be imposed (not matters of private conscience or personal piety). It is obvious that not all political leaders are *in fact* seeking to guide their deliberations and actions by the revealed law of God. What these studies contend is that magistrates *ought* to submit to the law of God for socio-political affairs: they will answer to God ultimately for their disobedience to His standards.

Of course, when magistrates do come to the decision to enforce the commandment(s) of God in a particular area — whether because they have personally been converted or whether they simply see the wisdom and justice of those laws as unbelievers — they are obliged to do so in a proper and fair manner. The Christian does not advocate *ex post facto* justice whereby offenders are punished for offenses committed prior to the civil enactment of a law prohibiting their actions. Nor does the Christian advocate the punishment of criminals who have not been convicted under the full provisions of *due process* in a court of law. Those who believe that God's law for society ought to be obeyed must be concerned that all of God's laws for society be obeyed, touching not only the punishment of offenders but their just treatment and conviction as well.

Finally we must distance ourselves from the mistaken impression that because these studies pay attention to a particular subsection of Christian theology and ethics they intend to portray that area of the truth as more important than other areas of Biblical teaching. All discussion will of necessity narrowly consider one topic instead of another, for not everything can be discussed simultaneously. To write about the virgin birth, for instance, is not to offer a slight to the doctrine of Christ's coming again; it is merely to take up one of many important matters of Christian theology.

Likewise, to set forth a position regarding the validity of God's Old Testament law and to argue that its standards of political justice bind us today (so that civil magistrates ought to enforce the law's penal sanctions) is to focus attention on just one aspect of the total picture of Christian theology and ethics. It is not to say that the most important emphasis in our lives and thinking should be the Old Testament law of Moses. It is not to say that political ethics is more vital than personal ethics or that the cultural mandate is more crucial than the evangelistic mandate of the church. And it most certainly is not to contend that capital punishment is the most significant topic in Christian ethics or even in Christian social ethics.

By taking up a study of the Mosaic law and the validity of its penal sanctions we are simply pointing out that these are aspects of Biblical teaching — indeed aspects which serve a beneficial purpose and as such are included in God's revealed word — and should not be misunderstood or ignored in deciding what the whole Bible has to say to us about our lives, conduct, and attitudes. By paying attention to the question of God's law in Christian ethics we are simply being consistent with the Reformed conviction that our Christian beliefs should be guided by *sola Scriptura* and *tota Scriptura* — only by Scripture and by *all* of Scripture.

2

GOD'S WORD IS OUR NORM

"Will your life be founded upon the sure rock of God's word, or the ruinous sands of independent human opinion?"

Day by day we make decisions on how to act, we form attitudes and cultivate emotions, we set goals for ourselves and try to attain them. We do these things individually, as well as in various groups: our family, friends, church, community, occupation, state. In all of these contexts the kind of people we are, the kind of goals we have, and the kind of rules we observe in decision-making are ethical matters. All human behavior and character is subject to appraisal according to moral value; every one of our attainments (whether they be aims that are fulfilled or character traits that are developed) and every one of our actions (whether they be mental, verbal, or bodily behavior) expresses an unspoken code of right and wrong. *All of life is ethical.*

But there are many moral values which are recommended to us. There are numerous implicit codes of right and wrong. We go through every day in the midst of a plurality of ethical viewpoints which are in constant competition with each other. Some people make pleasure their highest value, while others put a premium on health. There are those who say we should watch out for ourselves first of all, and yet others tell us that we should live to be of service to our neighbor. What we hear in advertisements often conflicts with the values endorsed in our church. Sometimes the decisions of our employers violate laws established by the state. Our friends do not always share the code of behavior fostered in our family. Often we disagree with the actions of the state. All of life is ethical, but making ethical decisions can be confusing and difficult. Every one of us needs a moral compass to guide us through the maze of moral issues and disagreements that confront us every moment of our lives.

To put it another way, making moral judgments requires a *standard* of ethics. Have you ever tried to draw a straight line without the aid of a standard to follow, such as a ruler? As good as your line may have seemed initially, when you placed a straight-edge up to it, the line was obviously crooked. Or have you ever tried to determine an exact measurement of something by simple eyeball inspection? As close as you may have come by guessing, the only way to be sure and accurate was to use a proper standard of measurement, such as a yardstick. And if we are going to be able to determine what kinds of persons, actions, or attitudes are morally good, then we will need a standard here as well. Otherwise we will lead crooked lives and make inaccurate evaluations. What should our ethical standard be? What yardstick should we use in making decisions, cultivating attitudes, or setting goals for ourselves and the groups in which we move? How does one know and test what is right and wrong?

"Yardsticks" for Civilization

In ancient Greece and Rome the city or state was taken as the ultimate authority and yardstick in ethics. Caesar was lord over all when moral questions were raised. Over against the totalitarian, divinized state the early church proclaimed the Lordship of Jesus Christ. The "ruling authorities" (Rom. 13:1) were told that "all authority in heaven and earth" resided in the resurrected Messiah (Matt. 28:18). Accordingly the apostle John portrayed the political "beast" of Revelation 13 as requiring that his own name be written on men's foreheads and hands (vv. 16-17), thereby symbolizing that the state's law had replaced the law of God, which was to be written on the forehead and hand (cf. 6:8). That is why those who stand in opposition to the beast are described as "those who keep the commandments of God and the faith of Jesus" (Rev. 14:1, 12). God's people insist that the state does not have ultimate ethical authority, for God's law is the supreme standard of right and wrong.

The medieval church, however, came to foster two yardsticks of ethics: a standard for religious ethics found in the revealed scriptures, and a standard for natural ethics found in man's reason as it examined the world. Of course that left some ethical decisions or evaluations independent of the word of God, and those religious issues which remained under the umbrella of the Bible were ultimately decided by the Pope. Thus the medieval world was ripe for tyranny in both a secular state and despotic church.

Over against this, the Reformers challenged the traditions of men and reasserted the full authority of God's word, declaring *sola Scriptura* and *tota Scriptura* (only Scripture and all of Scripture). The final standard of faith and practice, the yardstick for all of life (personal as well as social morality), was the Bible. That is why the Puritans strove to let God's word form their lifestyle and regulate their behavior in every sphere of human endeavor. A holy God required them to "be holy in all your conduct" (I Peter 1:15), and the standard of holy living was found in God's holy law (Rom. 7:12). Accordingly the Puritans even took God's law as their yardstick for civil laws in the new land to which they eventually came, and we have enjoyed the fruits of their godly venture in this country for three centuries now. The attitude of the Reformers and Puritans is nicely summarized in Robert Paul's painting which hangs in the Supreme Court Building, Lausanne, Switzerland; it is entitled "Justice Instructing the Judges" and portrays Justice pointing her sword to a book labeled "The Law of God."

Autonomy

Nevertheless, with the coming of the alleged "Enlightenment," the yardstick of ethics progressively shifted from the law of God in the Bible to human laws fostered by independent reason and experience. A neutral or critical attitude toward the inspired Scripture undermined its recognized authority over all of life, and modern ethics has come to be characterized by an autonomous spirit — an attitude of "self-law." The yardstick of ethics would be found within man or his community. Bishop Butler located it in man's conscience, Kant in man's reason, and Hegel in the Absolute state.

The one thing shared by all schools of modern ethics is an antipathy to taking moral direction from the Bible, for to do so is viewed as outdated, ignorant, unreasonable, prejudicial, undemocratic, and impractical. Being uncomfortable and irritated by the holy requirements of God's law for every aspect of human conduct, "modern" men reject this shackle upon their personal liberty and desires, and they ridicule its provisions for social justice. The predictable result in Western culture is the tension between an unrestrained, tyrannical state on the one hand and the liberated, unrestrained individual on the other. Statism and anarchy pull against each other. The immoral policies of the state are matched by the immoral lives of its citizens.

In earlier ages this kind of situation was redressed by the church as it served the function of preservative "salt" in the earth (Matt. 5:13). But today vast numbers of theologians have thrown away the biblical yardstick of ethics and have substituted something else for it. The outcome has been the loss of any respectable, vigorous, reforming ethic in the contemporary church. "Thus said the Lord" has been reduced to "it seems to me (or us)." Bonhoeffer said that "God is teaching us that we must live as men who can get along very well without Him."[1] Not only does Frank Sinatra sing out modern man's testimony for Western culture, "The record shows I took the blows, and did it *my* way," but the German theologian Wolfhart Pannenberg delivers the modern church's response: "The proclamation of imperatives backed by divine authority is not very persuasive today."[2] The Bible no longer directs all of life because its requirements are deemed stifling and are viewed in advance as unreasonable.

Men repudiate the "interference" in their lives represented by God's commandments. This attitude of lawlessness (1 John 3:4) unites all men because of their sin (Rom. 3:23). Even theologians today pretend to be ethical authorities in their own right who know better than the Bible what is right and wrong. In *Christian Ethics and Contemporary Philosophy* Graeme de Graaff says, "There is no room in morality for commands, whether they are the father's, the schoolmaster's or the priest's. There is still not room for them when they are God's commands."[3] The leading

---

1. Dietrich Bonhoeffer, *Letters and Papers From Prison* (London: SCM Press, 1953), p. 164.

2. Wolfhart Pannenberg, *Theology and the Kingdom of God* (Philadelphia: Westminster Press, 1969), pp. 103-104.

3. Graeme de Graaff, "God and Morality," in *Christian Ethics*

advocate of situation ethics in our day, Joseph Fletcher, tersely concludes that "Law ethics is still the enemy." And these lawless attitudes continue to filter down to the local level. A "liberated" woman writes in *The Reformed Journal* (1975): "I thank God that as a reformed Christian I worship a God of grace and not a God of rules."

The Biblical Attitude

By contrast the biblical attitude is expressed by the apostle John when he says, "The love of God is this, that we keep His commandments; and His commandments are not burdensome" (1 John 5:3). Believers in Jesus Christ do not wish to live as a law-unto-themselves, unfettered by external divine requirements. They welcome and love the biblical standard of right and wrong — no matter what it may stipulate for any aspect of life. God's holy law is not a burden to them, and they are not constantly searching for substitutes which will be more pleasing to the autonomous attitude of their age. They do not prefer self-law to God's law, for they recognize that it is impossible to draw straight lines and make accurate measurements in ethics without the infallible yardstick of God's word.

All of life is ethical, I have said. And all ethical judgments require a dependable standard of right and wrong. Jesus said, having just declared that He will eternally reject all those who practice lawless-

---

and Contemporary Philosophy, ed. Ian T. Ramsey (London: SCM Press, 1966), p. 34.

ness, "Therefore everyone who hears these words of Mine and does them may be compared to a wise man, who built his house upon the rock" (Matt. 7:24-27). Will your life be founded upon the sure rock of God's word or the ruinous sands of independent human opinion? Will your ethical decisions be crooked and inaccurate, following foolish and lawless standards, or will you wisely employ the yardstick of God's revealed word?

3

THE ENTIRE BIBLE IS TODAY'S STANDARD

"God expects us to submit to His every word, and not pick and choose the ones which are agreeable to our preconceived opinions."

All of life is ethical, and all of the Bible is permeated with a concern for ethics. Unlike the organization of an encyclopedia, our Bible was not written in such a way that it devotes separate sections exclusively to various topics of interest. Hence the Bible does not contain one separate, self-contained book or chapter that completely treats the subject of ethics or moral conduct. To be sure, many chapters of the Bible (like Exodus 20 or Romans 13) and even some books of the Bible (like Proverbs or James) have a great deal to say about ethical matters and contain very specific guidance for the believer's life. Nevertheless, there will not be found a division of the Bible entitled something like "The Complete List of Duties and Obligations in the Christian Life." Instead, we find a concern for ethics carrying through the whole word of God, from cover to cover — from creation to consummation.

This is not really surprising. The entire Bible speaks of God, and we read that the living and true God is holy, just, good, and perfect. These are attributes of an ethical character and have moral implications for us. The entire Bible speaks of the works of God, and we read that all of His works are performed in wisdom and righteousness — again, ethical qualities. The world which God has created, we read, reveals God's moral requirements clearly and continuously. History, which God governs by His sovereign decree, will manifest His glory, wisdom and justice. The apex of creation and the key figure in earthly history, man, has been made the image of this holy God and has God's law imbedded in his heart. Man's life and purpose take their direction from God. Every one of man's actions and attitudes is called into the service of the Creator — motivated by love and faith, aimed at advancing God's glory and kingdom. Accordingly the entire Bible has a kind of ethical focus.

Moreover the very narrative and theological plot of the Bible is governed by ethical concerns. From the outset we read that man has fallen into sin — by disobeying the moral standard of God; as a consequence man has come under the wrath and curse of God — His just response to rebellion against His commands. Sin and curse are prevailing characteristics, then, of fallen man's environment, history, and relationships.

To redeem man, restore him to favor, and rectify his wayward life in all areas, God promised and provided His own Son as a Messiah or Savior. Christ lived a life of perfect obedience to qualify as our substitute, and then He died on the cross to satisfy the justice of God regarding our sin. As resurrected and ascended on high, Christ rules as Lord over all, bringing all opposition into submission to His kingly reign. He has sent the Spirit characterized by holiness into His followers, and among other things the Holy Spirit brings about the practice of righteousness in their lives. The church of Christ has been mandated to proclaim God's good news, to advance His kingdom throughout the world, to teach Christ's disciples to observe everything He has commanded, and to worship the Triune God in spirit and in truth. When Christ returns at the consummation of human history He will come as universal judge, dispensing punishment and reward according to the revealed standard of God's word. On that day all men will be divided into the basic categories of covenant-keepers and covenant-breakers; then it will be clear that all of one's life in every realm and relationship has reflected his response to God's revealed standards. Those who have lived in alienation from God, not recognizing their disobedience and need of the Savior, will be eternally separated from His presence and blessing; those who have embraced the Savior in faith and submitted to Him as Lord will eternally enjoy His presence in the new heavens and earth wherein righteousness dwells.

It is easy to see, then, that everything the Bible

teaches from Genesis to Revelation has an ethical quality about it and carries ethical implications with it. There is no word from God which fails to tell us in some way what we are to believe about Him and what duty He requires of us. Paul put it in this way: "Every scripture is inspired by God and *profitable* for doctrine, for reproof, for correction, for *instruction in righteousness,* in order that the man of God may be perfect, thoroughly furnished unto every good work" (2 Tim. 3:16-17). If we disregard any portion of the Bible we will—to that extent—fail to be thoroughly furnished for every good work. If we ignore certain requirements laid down by the Lord in the Bible our instruction in righteousness will be incomplete. Paul says that every single scripture is profitable for ethical living; every verse gives us direction for how we should live.

The *entire* Bible is our ethical yardstick for every part of it is the word of the eternal, unchanging God; none of the Bible offers fallible or mistaken direction to us today. Not one of God's stipulations is unjust, being too lenient or too harsh. And God does not unjustly have a double-standard of morality, one standard of justice for some and another standard of justice for others. Every single dictate of God's word, then, is intended to provide moral instruction for us today, so that we can demonstrate justice, holiness, and truth in our lives.

It is important to note here that when Paul said that "every scripture is inspired by God and profitable" for holy living, the New Testament was not as yet completed, gathered together, and existing as a published collection of books. Paul's direct reference was to the well known *Old Testament* scriptures, and indirectly to the soon-to-be-completed New Testament. By inspiration of the Holy Spirit, Paul taught New Testament believers that every single Old Testament writing was profitable for their present instruction in righteousness, if they were to be completely furnished for every good work required of them by God.

Not one bit of the Old Testament has become ethically irrelevant, according to Paul. That is why we, as Christians, should speak of our moral viewpoint, not merely as "New Testament Ethics," but as "Biblical Ethics." The New Testament (2 Tim. 3:16-17) requires that we take the Old Testament as ethically normative for us today. Not just selected portions of the Old Testament, mind you, but "every scripture." Failure to honor the whole duty of man as revealed in the Old Testament is nothing short of a failure to be *completely* equipped for righteous living. It is to measure one's ethical duty by a broken and incomplete yardstick.

The Whole Bible

God expects us to submit to His every word, and not pick and choose the ones which are agreeable to our preconceived opinions. The Lord requires that we obey everything He has stipulated in the Old and New Testaments — that we "live by every word that proceeds from the mouth of God" (Matt. 4:4). Our Lord responded to the temptation of Satan with those words, quoting the Old Testament passage in

Deuteronomy 8:3 which began "All the command-ments that I am commanding you today you shall be careful to do" (8:1).

Many believers in Christ fail to imitate His atti-tude here, and they are quite careless about observ-ing every word of God's command in the Bible. James tells us that if a person lives by and keeps every precept or teaching of God's law, and yet he or she disregards or violates it in one single point, that person is actually guilty of disobeying the whole (James 2:10). Therefore, we must take the *whole* Bible as our standard of ethics, including every point of God's Old Testament law. Not one word which proceeds from God's mouth can be invalidated and made inoperative, even as the Lord declared with the giving of His law: "Whatever I command you, you shall be careful to do; you shall not add to nor take away from it" (Deut. 12:32). The entire Bible is our ethical standard today, from cover to cover.

But doesn't the coming of Jesus Christ change all that? Hasn't the Old Testament law been either cancelled or at least reduced in its requirements? Many professing believers are misled in the direction of these questions, despite God's clear requirement that nothing be subtracted from His law, despite the straightforward teaching of Paul and James that every Old Testament scripture — even every point of the law — has a binding ethical authority in the life of the New Testament Christian.

Perhaps the best place to go in Scripture to be rid of the theological inconsistency underlying a negative attitude toward the Old Testament law is to the very words of Jesus himself on this subject, Matthew 5:17-19. Nothing could be clearer than that Christ here denies twice (for the sake of emphasis) that His coming has abrogated the Old Testament law: "Do not think that I came to abolish the law or the prophets; I did not come to abolish." Again, nothing could be clearer than this: not even the least significant aspect of the Old Testament law will lose its validity until the end of the world: "For truly I say to you, until heaven and earth pass away, not the slightest letter or stroke shall pass away from the law." And if there could remain any doubt in our minds as to the meaning of the Lord's teaching here, He immediately removes it by applying His attitude toward the law to our behavior: "Therefore whoever annuls one of the least of these commandments and teaches others so, shall be called least in the kingdom of heaven." Christ's coming did not abrogate anything in the Old Testament law, for every single stroke of the law will abide until the passing away of this world; consequently, the follower of Christ is not to teach that even the least Old Testament requirement has been invalidated by Christ and His work. As the Psalmist declared, "Every one of Thy righteous ordinances is *everlasting*" (Ps. 119:160).

So then, all of life is ethical, and ethics requires a standard of right and wrong. For the Christian that yardstick is found in the Bible — the *entire* Bible, from beginning to end. The New Testament believer repudiates the teaching of the law itself, of the Psalms, of James, of Paul and of Jesus Himself when the Old Testament commandments of God are ignored or treated as a mere antiquated standard of justice and righteousness. "The word of our God shall stand forever" (Isa. 40:8), and the Old Testament law is part of every word from God's mouth by which we must live (Matt. 4:4).

4

THE SCOPE OF TRUE OBEDIENCE

"Obedience must be from the heart, and yet obedience must not be restricted to the heart."

A number of common moral mistakes are made by believers, even after they come to the realization that God holds them accountable to His revealed commandments. Among those mistakes two can be focused upon here as the root of many other misconceptions. On the one hand, people often fail to see that God's law requires obedience from the heart. On the other hand, people make the mistake of thinking that it is sufficient if their obedience is restricted to matters of the heart. Both of these errors — opposite in character but equal in destructive force — are addressed by God's word, showing us the full dimensions of true obedience to the Lord.

Obedience from the Heart

In Matthew 5:20 Jesus taught something which must have been shocking to His hearers. He said,

"Except your righteousness shall exceed that of the scribes and Pharisees, you shall by no means enter into the kingdom of heaven." The shocking thing about this was that the scribes and Pharisees had a reputation, one which they themselves were anxious to promote, for a deep commitment to obeying even the minor details of the law. But the fact of the matter was that the Pharisees were *far* from living up to the true demands of God's commandments. They had distorted the law's requirements, reading them in a perverse, self-justifying, and externalistic fashion.

In the Sermon on the Mount Jesus exposed the shallow obedience of the Pharisees for what it was, pointing out that God is not satisfied with anything short of full, heart-felt obedience to His law as comprehensively interpreted. By contrast, the Pharisees had appealed to the law in a way calculated to escape God's true and original demands, placing a hypocritical veneer of "piety" upon all of their actions.

The Pharisees made a religious show of adhering to the law, but Christ saw that it was a mere facade. He said to them, "You hypocrites, Isaiah was right when he prophesied of you, saying 'These people honor me with their lips, but their hearts are far from me. In vain do they worship me, teaching as their doctrines the precepts of men' " (Matt. 15:7-9). The Pharisees actually overlooked the weightier matters of the law, such as justice, mercy, and faith (Matt. 23:23-24). They were blind guides who trimmed down the requirements of God's law so that it could be made to appear conformable to their cultural traditions. "And He answered and said unto them, 'Why do you also transgress the command ment of God for the sake of your tradition? For God said. . . . But you say. . . . So you have made void the word of God for the sake of your tradition' " (Matt. 15:3-6, 14).

So it is quite possible to take an avid interest in the commandments of God and still have a heart that is far from the Lord — still have a lifestyle which is anything but pleasing to God since our attitudes and motives are out of line with the moral guidance of Scripture. We can take a concern for the fine details of the law, and we should, but not in such a way that we miss the main point in it all: namely, the display of such godly attitudes as are mentioned listed in "the fruit of the Spirit" — love, joy, peace, patience, kindness, goodness, faithfulness, meekness, and self-control, *against which there is no law* (Galatians 5:22-23).

Back in the Sermon on the Mount (Matthew 5:20ff.), after Christ declared that only a righteous ness exceeding that of the scribes and Pharisees would gain entrance into the kingdom of heaven, He went on to deliver a series of illustrations of how the scribes and Pharisees held to a diminished under standing of God's requirements. He set their ap proach to various commandments over against His own interpretation of God's demands, thereby re storing the full measure of God's purpose and re quirements to the Old Testament law. His illustra tions began with words like these: "You have heard it said by those of old . . . , but I say unto you." In such sayings Jesus was not personally dissenting from the law of God but from the Pharisaical understanding and undervaluating of the law of God.

After all, if the Pharisees really were living up to the law, and Jesus added to the law's demand, then His *ex post facto* condemnation of the Pharisees for not living up to His additions would be quite unfair! Rather, Jesus indicted the Pharisees for not living up to what God originally required. "You have heard it said by those of old" refers to the rabbinic interpretations of the law passed down from one generation to another; the scribes commonly appealed to the traditional interpretations of the ancient rabbis as a way of teaching the law. The amazing thing to the crowds who heard Jesus, though, was that he taught as one having authority in Himself, and not as one of the scribes, always appealing to others (Matt. 7:28-29).

The problem with the scribal or Pharisaical understanding of the Old Testament law was that it was trite and externalistic. Jesus had to point out, in accord with Old Testament teaching (for example, Prov. 6:16-18, 25), that hatred and lust were the root sins of murder and adultery (Matt. 5:21-30). When God commanded that His people not kill and not commit adultery, He did not merely require abstaining from the outward acts of assault and fornication; His requirement went to the heart, requiring that our thoughts, plans, and attitudes be free from violence and unchastity as well.

True obedience to the law, then, stems from a heart that is right with God, a heart that seeks to please the Lord—not simply by outward conformity but by pure attitudes as well. We see, then, why the "obedience" of the Pharisees was not acceptable in God's eyes. They were not truly obeying the law in its comprehensive demand, inward as well as outward. Any obedience which we are to render to God's law today which is going to be pleasing to God, therefore, must be better than externalistic, hypocritical, self-righteous Pharisaism. It must be obedience from the heart.

Obedience Not Restricted to the Heart

A man who refrains from physical adultery while cherishing lustful thoughts is self-deceived if he thinks that he has obeyed the Lord's commandment. On the other hand, a man who thinks that he has a pure attitude and motive, even though he engages outwardly in an act which transgresses God's law, is just as self-deceived. God's law does *not* place a premium upon inwardness and attitudes of the heart *at the expense* of overt obedience to His requirements! When it comes to obeying the Lord, it is *not simply* "the thought that counts."

Situational ethicists, who say a man can act out of love to God and love to his neighbor when he commits adultery with his neighbor's wife, still stand condemned by God and His word on the final day. This should be obvious to most born-again Christians. They know that "walking by the Spirit" means that, unlike those in "the flesh" (in the sinful nature), they can keep the law of God (Rom. 8:5-10); it is "the ordinance of the law" which is "fulfilled in us who walk not after the flesh but after the Spirit" (v. 4).

Those who have hearts made right with God, those who have been given a new heart by God, those who wish from the heart to please God, will seek to walk according to God's commandments (Jer. 31:33; Ezk. 11:19-20; 36:26-27). A proper heart attitude should lead to proper outward conduct as well. Obedience cannot be restricted to the heart. Jesus not only wanted the Pharisees to realize the *inward* values of mercy and faith; He did not want them to leave undone the minor *outward* matters of tithing garden vegetables (Matt. 23:23).

Just as obedience cannot be restricted to the heart in the sense of forgetting the need for outward conformity to God's stipulations, it can likewise be said that obedience—if it is genuine Biblical obedience—cannot be restricted to a concern for our own personal conduct. Full obedience embraces an interest in the obedience of those around me to the laws of God. The Christian must assume the responsibility to exhort those in his home, church, society, etc. to keep the commandments of the Lord. David wrote, "restore unto me the joy of thy salvation, and uphold me with thy free Spirit. *Then will I teach transgressors thy ways,* and sinners will be converted unto thee" (Ps. 51:13). The Great Commission laid upon the church by Christ calls for us to teach the nations *whatsoever Christ has commanded* (Matt. 28:18-20). Anything less than this concern for the obedience of those around us is disloyalty to the Lord and fails to qualify as true obedience to his law. John Murray wrote:

The least of God's commandments, if they bind us, bind others. We must resist the virulent poison of individualism which tolerates in others the indifference and disobedience which we cannot justify in ourselves. . . . The moment we become complacent to the sins of others then we have begun to relax our own grip on the sanctity of the commandments of God, and we are on the way to condoning the same sin in ourselves.[1]

Heart-felt obedience to God's law will lead us to promote obedience to that same law on the part of others.

True saints have indignation for those who break God's law (Ps. 119:53), and they are not ashamed to promote that law publicly (v. 13). If they would keep silent in the face of disobedience, then they would become culpable for the sins they witness. As Psalm 50:18 says, "When you saw a thief, then you consented with him" by keeping your peace. Ephesians 5:11 exhorts the believer *to reprove* the unfruitful works of darkness. Scripture, then, is quite clear in teaching that the requirement of full obedience to God's commands extends to the active promoting of obedience to those commands in others.

The Scripture-guided believer is in a position to offer genuine counsel and help to others and to his society; he knows the purity of God's law. He is "able to admonish" (Rom. 15:14), and so to be quiet in the

---

1. *Principles of Conduct* (Grand Rapids, Michigan: Eerdmans, 1957), p. 154.

face of transgressions would be a guilty silence. Christ directed His followers that they were to be "the light of the world"—which is impossible if our light is placed under a basket (Matt. 5:14-15). Consequently, true Christian obedience to the law of God will take us beyond a concern for ourselves to a concern for the obedience of those around us. Churches which preach (either intentionally or by default) "moral individualism" are failing to proclaim the whole counsel of God. The sins of our society cannot be ignored or swept under the church carpet.

This short study does not by any means touch upon every facet of obedience to God's commandments, but it does point out two very important aspects of genuine obedience. We see how *far-reaching* God's demands are when we keep in mind that obedience must be from the heart, and yet that obedience must not be restricted to the heart.

5

THE COVENANT'S UNIFORM STANDARD OF RIGHT AND WRONG

> "My covenant I will not violate, nor will I alter the utterance of My lips" (Psalm 89:34).

If something was sinful in the Old Testament, it is likewise sinful in the age of the New Testament. Moral standards, unlike the price of gasoline or the changing artistic tastes of a culture, do not fluctuate. In the United States, there was a time when driving your car at 65 miles per hours was permissible; now any speed above 55 is illegal. But God's laws are not like that: just today, unjust tomorrow. When the Lord makes a moral judgment, He is not unsure of Himself, or tentative, or fickle. Unlike human lawmakers, God does not change His mind or alter His standards of righteousness: "My covenant I will not violate, nor will I alter the utterance of My lips" (Ps. 89:34). When the Lord speaks, His word stands firm forever. His standards of right and wrong do not change from age to age: "All His precepts are trustworthy. They are established forever and ever, to be performed with faithfulness and uprightness" (Ps. 111:7-8).

Accordingly Jesus spoke with unmistakable clarity when He said, "It is easier for heaven and earth to pass away than for one stroke of the law to fail" (Luke 16:17). The coming of God's righteous Son surely could do nothing to change the righteous character of God's laws, even the least of them, for then they would be exposed as unjust and less than eternal in their uprightness. So Christ issues this severe warning: "Whoever annuls one of the least of these commandments and so teaches others shall be called least in the kingdom of heaven" (Matt. 5:19). The advent of the Savior and the inauguration of the New Age do not have the effect of abrogating the slightest detail of God's righteous commandments. God has not changed His mind about good and evil or what constitutes them.

We can be very glad that God sticks by His word in this way. The authority of His word for human life is as permanent as that word by which He created and governs the world (cf. Ps. 19:1-14; 33:4-11). If God's word to us were not as stable as this, if He were subject to moods and changed His mind from time to time, then we could not rely on anything He told us. If God's law has a fluctuating validity, then so might His promises! If we say that a commandment given by God in the Old Testament is no longer a standard of righteousness and justice for today, then we can equally anticipate that a promise of salvation given by God in the New Testament will in some future day no longer be a permanent guarantee of His favor toward us. But praise the Lord that His word is stable! He never lets us down as did our human parents and human rulers with commands that are unfair and promises that are not kept.

Whatever God says endures and cannot be emptied of validity (cf. John 10:35). God's gracious salvation and the justice of His law shall not be abolished but endure forever:

> Hearken unto me, my people; and give ear unto me, O my nation: for a law shall proceed from me, and I will make my judgment to rest for a light of the people. My righteousness is near; my salvation is gone forth, and mine arms shall judge the people; the isles shall wait upon me, and on mine arm shall they trust. Lift up your eyes to the heavens and look upon the earth beneath: for the heavens shall vanish away like smoke, and the earth shall in like manner: but my salvation shall be forever, and my righteousness shall not be abolished. Hearken unto me, ye that know righteousness, the people in whose heart is my law; fear ye not the reproach of men, neither be ye afraid of their revilings. For the moth shall eat them up like a garment, and the worm shall eat them like wool: but my righteousness shall be forever, and my salvation from generation to generation (Isa. 51:4-8).

The righteous law of God which condemns our

sin is as permanent as the good news from God which promises salvation from sin's judgment.

Covenant: Unity and Diversity

It is important to remember this, especially when some would tell us that the coming of the New Testament does away with our obligation to the Old Testament's commandments (or many of them anyway). The division of the Bible into two "Testaments" is better understood in the biblical sense as two "Covenants." Prior to the coming of Christ men lived under the Old Covenant which anticipated the Messiah and His work of salvation; after the coming of Christ and His saving work we live under the New Covenant (cf. Lk. 22:20; 1 Cor. 11:25).

Within the "Old Covenant" scriptures we find a few particular covenants, such as those made with Abraham and with Moses. The Abrahamic covenant is often characterized in terms of promise, and the Mosaic covenant is remembered for its strong element of law. Now some people would say that New Covenant believers are under the Abrahamic covenant of promise today, but not the Mosaic covenant with its laws. However, that is far from the outlook of the scriptural writers. In Galatians 3:21 Paul addresses this question to those who speak of being under one or the other covenant: "Is the law contrary to the promises of God?' And his inspired answer is "May it never be!" The fact is that all of the covenants of the Old Covenant (that is, all of the Old Testament covenants) are unified as parts of the one overall covenant of grace established by God. Paul spoke of Gentiles who were not part of the Old Covenant economy which included the Abrahamic, Mosaic, and Davidic covenants as "strangers to the covenants of the promise" (Eph. 2:12).

There were many, progressively revealed aspects to the single promise of God in the Old Testament: many administrations of the one overall covenant of grace. Thus the various covenants of the Old Covenant were all part of one program and plan. Not only were they harmonious with one another, but they are unified with the New Covenant which was promised in Jeremiah 31 and is enjoyed by Christians today (cf. Heb. 8:6-13). There is *one* basic covenant of grace, characterized by anticipation in the Old Covenant and by realization in the New Covenant (cf. John 1:17). Given the unity of God's covenant throughout history and the Bible, then, is it true that Christians living under the New Covenant are not obliged to keep the Old Covenant law (the commandments of the Old Testament, especially those given by Moses)? Every covenant established by God—even the Abrahamic (Gen. 17:1)—not only declares His gracious work on behalf of His people, but lays down stipulations which they are to observe as a sign of fidelity and love to Him. For instance, the giving of the law at Sinai (Ex. 20-23) was preceded by God's gracious deliverance of Israel from bondage (cf. Ex. 19:4; 20:2). God identified Himself as Lord of the covenant and rehearsed his gracious dealings with His people (Deut. 1-4), and then with that foundation and background He delivered His

law (Deut. 5ff.). The failure of the Mosaic generation can be called a failure in *obedience* (Heb. 6:4),
but this was identical with a failure of *faith* (Heb.
3:9). The righteousness of the Mosaic *law* was always to be sought *by faith,* not works (Rom. 9:31-32).

We see illustrated here that even the Mosaic covenant characterized by law is a *gracious* covenant.
The law which we read in the Old Testament is a
provision of God's grace to us (Ps. 19:29, 62-64).
Every covenant carries stipulations which are to be
kept, as we have seen. But prior to that we saw that
all of the covenants of God are unified into one overall Covenant of Grace, fully realized with the coming of Christ in the New Covenant. So if there is *one
covenant* enjoyed by the people of God throughout the
ages, then there is *one moral code* or set of stipulations
which govern those who would be covenant-keepers.
Therefore, we must answer that of course New Testament believers are bound to the Old Testament
law of God. His standards, just like His covenant,
are unchanging.

The Newness of God's Covenant

This perspective is confirmed by the word of
God. When we inquire as to what is *new* about the
New Covenant under which Christians now live, we
must allow the Lord to define the proper answer. We
cannot read into the idea of a "new Covenant" just
anything we wish or can imagine. The revealed *terms*
of the New Covenant are given to us in both Jeremiah 31:33-34 and Hebrews 8:8-12, and when we
look at them we find that the New Covenant is far

from suppressing or changing the law or moral standard by which God's people are to live! Just the opposite is true. Contrary to those who think that the Mosaic law is not applicable to the New Testament believer, Scripture teaches us: "This is the covenant that I will make with the house of Israel after those days, says the Lord: I will put my laws into their minds and I will write them upon their hearts" (Heb. 8:10).

The establishment of the New Covenant does *not* imply the abrogation of the Mosaic law or its depreciation in any sense! The idea of a new law is ruled out altogether, for it is the *well known* law of God which He says He will write upon the hearts of New Covenant believers. Unlike the Old Covenant where God found fault with the people for *breaking* His commandments (Heb. 8:8-9), the New Covenant will give internal strength for keeping those very commandments. It will write the law on believers' hearts, for out of the heart are the issues of life (Prov. 4:23). The Holy Spirit of God will indwell the heart of believers, writing God's law therein, with the result that they will live according to the commandments. "I will put My Spirit within you and cause you to walk in My statutes, and you will be careful to observe My ordinances" (Ezk. 36:27). As Paul writes in Romans 8:4, those who now walk according to the Spirit have the requirement of *the law* fulfilled within them. America's twentieth-century orthodox Protestant leader J. Gresham Machen said, "The gospel does not abrogate God's law, but it makes men love it with all their hearts."[1]

Psalm 89:34 was cited above: "My covenant I will not violate, nor will I alter the utterance of My lips." God's covenant law is one unchanging moral code through Old and New Testaments. Once God has spoken His law and expressed His righteous standards He does not alter it. Indeed He pronounces a warning and curse upon anyone who would dare tamper with his stipulations in the slightest. Times may change, human laws may be altered, but God's law is an eternally just and valid standard of right and wrong.

One of the requirements of his law, which reflects His holy character, is the prohibition of using a double-standard (Deut. 25:13-16; Lev. 19:35-37). It is ungodly to use one measure or yardstick with some people, and then use an altered measure with others. "Divers weights and divers measures, both of them are alike abomination to the Lord" (Prov. 20:10). Accordingly God requires that we have but *one standard* or moral judgment, whether it be for the stranger or the native (Lev. 24:22; Deut. 1:16-17; cf. Num. 15:16). He abhors a double-standard of right and wrong, and we can be sure that He does not judge in such a fashion. Something that was sinful in the Old Testament is likewise sinful for us in the New Testament, for God's standards are not subject to fluctuation from age to age. He has one uniform standard of right and wrong.

---

1. J. Gresham Machen, *What is Faith?* (Grand Rapids, Michigan: Eerdmans, 1925), p. 192.

6

THE FATHER'S UNCHANGING HOLINESS AND LAW

"God's permanent requirement over all of life is God-imitating holiness. In all ages, believers are required to display, throughout their lives, the holiness and perfection of their God."

There is a sense in which the aim of every man's life is to be like God. All men are striving to imitate God in one way or another. Of course not all attempts to be like God are honored by the Lord and rewarded with His favor, for there is a radical difference between submitting to the Satanic temptation to be like God (Gen. 3:5) and responding to Christ's injunction that we should be like God (Matt. 5:48). The first is an attempt to replace God's authority with one's own, while the second is an attempt to demonstrate godliness as a moral virtue.

The basic character of godly morality was made manifest in the probation or testing placed upon

Adam and Eve in the garden. God had granted them permission to eat of any tree of the garden, save one. They were forbidden to eat of the tree of the knowledge of good and evil, but *not* because its fruit was injected with some literal poison. This was rather a test of whether they would live solely under the authority of God's word to them. God had forbidden it. Would they, despite their empirical research and personal desires, submit to his command on His simple say-so? Would they do their duty on the sheer basis that it was their duty? Or would they evaluate the command of God on the basis of some external standard of reasonableness, practicality, and human benefit?

The outcome of the story is all too well known. Satan beguiled Eve, denying what God had told her. She was led to assume the authoritative, neutral position of determining for herself whether God's "hypothesis" or Satan's "hypothesis" was true. Satan implied that God's commands were harsh, too stringent, unreasonable. He in effect condemned the supreme, absolute, and unchallengeable authority of God. He went on to suggest that God is in fact jealous, prohibiting Adam and Eve from eating of the tree lest they become like Him — lest they become rivals to Him in determining what is good and evil.

Thus our first parents were led to seek a lifestyle which was not bound by law from God; thus they were tempted into deciding for themselves what would count as good and evil. Law would not be laid down to them by God, for they would lay it down for themselves. Demonstrating sin's lawlessness (1 John

3:4) they became "like God"—law-givers of their own making and authority. God's law, which should have been their delight, became burdensome to them.

Jesus and God's Law

By contrast, the second Adam, Jesus Christ, lived a life of perfect obedience to the laws of God. When Satan tempted Him to depart from the path of utter obedience to God's commands, the Savior replied by quoting from the Old Testament law: you are not to tempt the Lord your God, you are to worship and serve Him alone, and you are to live by every word that proceeds from His mouth (Matt. 4:1-11). Here we have the very opposite of Adam and Eve's response to Satan. Christ said that the attitude which is genuinely godly recognizes the moral authority of God alone, does not question the wisdom of His dictates, and observes every last detail of his word. This is man's proper path to God-likeness. To live in this fashion displays the image or likeness of God that man was originally intended to be (Gen. 1:27), for it is living "in righteousness and true holiness" (Eph. 4:24). Genuine godliness, as commanded in the Scripture, is gained by imitating the holiness of God on a creaturely level—not by audacious attempts to redefine good and evil in some area of life on your own terms.

Jesus concluded His discourse on God's law in the Sermon on the Mount by saying, "Therefore you are to be perfect as your heavenly Father is perfect" (Matt. 5:48). Those who are not striving to become rivals to God by *replacing* His commands according to their own wisdom will rather endeavor to *reflect* His moral perfection by obeying all of His commands. John Murray has said,

> We cannot suppress the generic character of this statement, 'Ye therefore shall be perfect as your heavenly Father is perfect.' It covers the whole range of divine perfection as it bears upon human behavior, and it utters the most ultimate consideration regulative of human disposition and conduct. The reason of the biblical ethic is God's perfection; the basic criterion of ethical behavior is God's perfection; the ultimate goal of the ethical life is conformity to God's perfection. . . . And shall we say that this standard can ever cease to be relevant? It is to trifle with the sanctities which ever bind us as creatures of God, made in his image, to think that anything less than perfection conformable to the Father's own could be the norm and the goal of the believer's ethic.[1]

God expects of His people nothing less than full conformity to his holy character in all of their thoughts, words, and deeds. They must emulate His perfection in every aspect of their lives. As Murray says, this standard of ethics ever binds the believer and never ceases to be relevant. This standard is just as authoritative and valid today as it was in the Old Testament.

---

1. John Murray, *Principles of Conduct* (Grand Rapids, Michigan: Eerdmans, 1957), p. 180.

The Holiness of God

According to the Old Testament ethic, God's holiness is the model for human conduct: "You shall be holy, for I the Lord your God am holy" (Lev. 19:2). This is also the precise model of moral conduct for the New Testament believer: ". . . but like the Holy one who called you, be holy yourselves also in all your behavior; because it is written, 'You shall be holy, for I am holy' " (1 Peter 1:15-16). There has been no alteration or reduction of the standard of moral behavior between the Old and New Testaments. God's *permanent* requirement over all of life is God-imitating holiness. In all ages, believers are required to display, throughout their lives, the holiness and perfection of their God. They ought to be like God, not in the Satanic sense which amounts to lawlessness, but in the biblical sense which entails submission to God's commands.

Obviously, if we are to model our lives on the perfect holiness of God, we need Him to tell us what the implications of this would be for our practical behavior. We need a perfect yardstick by which to measure holiness in our lives. The Bible teaches us that the Lord has provided this guide and standard in his *holy law* (cf. Rom. 7:12). The law is a transcript of the holiness of God on a creaturely level; it is the ultimate standard of human righteousness in any area of life, for it reflects the moral perfection of God, its Author.

The intimate relation which the law bears to the very person of God is indicated by the fact that it was originally written by the finger of God (Deut. 9:10) and deposited in the ark of the covenant which typified the throne and presence of God in the Holy of Holies (Deut. 10:5). Moreover, this law must be acknowledged to have a very special place or status because it has the exclusive qualities of God himself attributed to it. According to Scripture, God alone is holy (Rev. 15:4) and good (Mark 10:18). Yet God's law is likewise designated holy and good (Rom. 7:12, 16; 1 Tim. 1:8), and obedience to it is the standard of human good (Deut. 12:28; Ps. 119:68; Micah 6:8). God is perfect (Deut. 32:4; Ps. 18:30; Matt. 5:48), and the law which He has laid down for us is accordingly perfect (Ps. 19:7; James 1:25). Every statute revealed by God authoritatively defines the holiness, goodness, and perfections which God's people are to emulate in every age.

The Puritan Heritage

The Puritans were zealous to live in the moral purity which reflects God's own. Consequently they upheld the honor and binding quality of every command from God. The feeling of Thomas Taylor was typical of them: "A man may breake the Princes Law, and not violate his Person; but not Gods: for God and his image in the Law, are so straitly united, as one cannot wrong the one, and not the other" (*Regula Vitae, The Rule of the Law under the Gospel,* 1631). If God turned back His law, said Anthony Burgess, He would "deny his own justice and goodnesse" (*Vindiciae Legis,* 1646). Thus the Puritans did not, like many modern believers, tamper with or annul any part of God's law. "To find fault with the

Law, were to find fault with God" (Ralph Venning, *Sin, the Plague of Plagues,* 1669). Therefore, in Puritan theology the law of God, like its author, was eternal (cf. Edward Elton, *God's Holy Minde Touching Matters Morall,* 1625), and as such "Christ has expunged no part of it" (John Crandon, *Mr. Baxters Aphorisms Exorcized and Anthorized,* 1654).

Unlike modern theologians who evaluate God's requirements according to their cultural traditions and who follow the Satanic temptation to define holiness according to their own estimate of moral purity, the Puritans did not seek schemes by which to shrink the entire duty of man in God's law to their preconceived notions. Venning concluded, "Every believer is answerable to the obedience of the whole Law."[2]

As usual, the Puritans were here eminently scriptural. God's holiness is the standard of morality in Old and New Testaments, and that holiness is reflected in our lives by obeying His every commandment. "Sanctify yourselves, therefore, and be ye holy, for I am the Lord your God. And ye shall keep my statutes and do them" (Lev. 20:7-8). And a life that is truly consecrated to God, one which is genuinely holy, respects every dictate from God. He says that the way to "be holy to your God" is to "remember to do all My commandments" (Num. 15:40). To lay aside any of God's law or view its details as inapplicable today is to oppose God's standard of holiness; it is to define good and evil in

---

2. For these quotations see Ernest F. Kevan, *The Grace of Law* (Grand Rapids, Michigan: Baker Book House, [1965] 1983).

that area of life by one's own wisdom and law, to become a rival to God as a law-giver.

Of course this suppression of God's own standard of moral perfection — the law's transcript of His holiness — is a blow at the very heart of biblical ethics. It is to be "God-like" in exactly the wrong way. It is to seek moral perfection for some aspect of life which was originally covered by God's law but is now defined according to one's own determination of good and evil. This was the untoward character of Adam's rebellion against God's holy word: His own law replaced God's.

Conclusion

The law reflects the holiness of God, and God's holiness is our permanent standard of morality. Moreover, God's character is eternal and unchanging. "I am the Lord, I change not" (Mal. 3:6). There is no variableness in Him (James 1:17). From everlasting to everlasting He is God (Ps. 90:2). Therefore, because His holiness is unchanging, the law which reflects that holiness cannot be changed. Whether we read in the Old or New Testaments, we find that a man's attitude toward God's law is an index of his relationship to God himself (Ps. 1; Rom. 8:1-8). As John so plainly says, "The one who says 'I have come to know Him,' and does not keep His commandments is a liar, and the truth is not in him" (1 John 2:4). God's unchanging holiness and thereby His unchanging law is an abiding standard of knowing Him and being like Him.

7

THE SON'S MODEL RIGHTEOUSNESS

"Christ perfectly obeyed the law of God, and this has unavoidable implications for Christian ethics — for imitating the Christ portrayed in the Bible."

The Bible was written over many years, by many people, and about many things. Yet central to the Bible is the person of Jesus Christ. He is of paramount importance throughout. We know that He was, as the Word of God, active at the creation of the world (John 13), and that He providentially upholds all things by the word of His power (Hebrews 1:3). After Adam's fall into sin through disobedience to God's command, relief from the wrath and curse of God was promised in terms of one who, as the seed of the woman, would crush Satan (Genesis 3:15). The entire Old Testament prepares for the coming of this promised Messiah — the prophet (Deut. 18:15-19), priest (Ps. 110:4), and king (Isa. 9:6-7), of God's own choosing.

The New Testament gospels tell us of His life and saving ministry, and Acts tells us of the work He continued to do through His church. The epistles are letters written from Him through His chosen servants (for example, Galatians 1:1) to his elect people, who constitute His kingdom. The final prophetic book of the Bible is "The Revelation of Jesus Christ." His church now labors to make all nations His disciples (Matt. 28:18-20), and at the consummation of history Christ will return again to judge all mankind (Acts 17:31). From beginning to end, the Bible speaks of Jesus Christ who is "the Alpha and the Omega" (Rev. 22:13). He is the key to God's special revelation and the one who should have pre-eminence in our lives (Col. 1:18).

It is easy to understand why. Because of our sinful disobedience to God's commandments, Christ came to atone for our offenses and become our eternal Savior. As such, He deserves our undying devotion and gratitude. As the resurrected and ascended Son of God, Christ is Lord over all and deserves our obedience and service. Thus the lifestyle and ethic of those who have been redeemed by Christ as Savior and Lord will naturally center or focus on Him.

At many times in the history of the church, Christian living has been understood most generally as "the imitation of Christ." Because Christ is the central personage of the Bible, there is a sense in which Biblical ethics can likewise be summarized as imitating Christ—striving to be like Him, taking His behavior as the model of Christian ethics. Indeed, to take upon oneself the name of "Christian" is to be a disciple or follower of Christ (cf. Acts 11:26). Believers take their direction from the example and teaching of Christ. Accordingly, *Biblical* ethics is the same as *Christ-ian* ethics.

Jesus and God's Law

What specifically can be said about a Christ-like ethic of morality? If we wish to imitate *the moral perfection of Christ,* what will this entail? A short survey of Biblical teaching discloses that God does not save His chosen people by lowering His moral standards; the very reason why those people need His saving mercy is because they have violated His moral standards. If such standards were expendable or arbitrary, then God could choose to ignore their transgression and save people by sheer fiat or decree of pardon. However, the law could not be thus ignored. To save His people, God sent His only-begotten Son to die sacrificially in their place. In order to qualify as the Savior, Christ lived a life of perfect obedience to the commandments of God. In order to atone for sins, Christ died in alienation from the Father to satisfy the law's demand for punishment. Consequently in His life and death Christ perfectly obeyed the law of God, and this has unavoidable implications for Christian ethics — for imitating the Christ portrayed throughout the Bible.

The Scriptures regard the *work* of Christ as that of obedience. In defining the purpose of His Messianic advent, Christ said "I have come down from heaven to do the will of Him who sent Me" (John 6:38). The pivotal event in the accomplishment or redemption was Christ's laying down His life and taking it up again — His death and resurrection; in these things Christ was obeying His Father's commandment (John 10:17-18). His work of atonement was performed in the capacity of a suffering servant (cf. Isa. 52:13 — 53:12). As such He was subjected to the law (Gal. 4:5) and justified us by His obedience (Rom. 5:19). Obedience to the will and commandment of God was therefore crucial to the life and ministry of our Savior. As our great High Priest He was sacrificed to discharge the curse of the law against our sin (Gal. 3:13; Heb. 2:17 — 3:1; 4:14 — 5:10). As the prophet of the law, Christ rendered its proper interpretation and peeled away the distorting traditions of men (Matt. 5:17-48; 15:1-20). And because He obeyed the law perfectly and hated all lawlessness, Christ has been exalted as the annointed King (Heb. 1:8, 9). Therefore we see that Christ's saving work and His three-fold office are determined by *His positive relation to the law of God,* the permanent expression of His holy will.

As one could readily expect, since Christ is the exact representation of God's nature (Heb. 1:3) and since the law is a transcript of the holiness of God, Christ embodied the law perfectly in His own person and behavior. Christ challenged His opponents with the stunning — virtually rhetorical — question, "Which of you convicts me of sin?" (John 8:46). Of course, no one could, for Christ alone was in a position to declare, "I have kept my Father's commandments and abide in His love" (John 15:10).

Christ was tempted at every point with respect to obeying the commands of God, yet He remained sinless throughout (Heb. 4:15). Because He kept the law perfectly, Christ had no need to offer up sacrifice for His own sins (Heb. 7:26-28). Instead He offered Himself up without spot to God, a lamb without blemish as the law required, in order to cleanse us of our sins (Heb. 9:14). As the Old Testament had foretold, "righteousness will be the belt about His loins" (Isa. 11:5), and the Messiah could declare, "Thy law is within my heart" (Ps. 40:7-8; Heb. 10:4-10).

We read in Galatians 4:4 that "when the fulness of the time came, God sent forth His Son, born of a woman, born under the law, that he might redeem them that were under the law." Christ was neither lawless nor above the law; He submitted to its every requirement, saying "it becomes us to fulfill all righteousness" (Matt. 3:15). He directed the healed to offer the gift commanded by Moses (Matt. 8:4), kept the borders of his garments (9:20; 14:36), paid the temple tax (17:24-27), attended to the purity of the temple (21:12-17), etc. He directed His followers to do those things which conformed to the law's demand (Matt. 7:12), told the rich young ruler to keep the commandments (19:17), reinforced the Old Testament law by summarizing it into two love commandments (22:40), indicted the Pharisees for making God's commandments void through traditions of men (Mark 7:6-13), and insisted that even the most trite or insignificant matters of the law ought not to be left undone (Luke 11:12).

Speaking of the moral teaching of Christ, Herman Ridderbos says,

> It is the 'ethics' of *obedience* in the full sense of the word. . . . If, therefore, the question is asked by what Jesus' commandments are regulated, the ultimate answer is only this: *by God's will as it is revealed in his law.* . . . Jesus' ethical preaching does not have a deeper ground than the law as the revelation of God's will to Israel, the people of the covenant. Again and again it is the law, and only the law, the meaning and purpose of which is also the meaning and purpose of Jesus' commandments.[1]

In the light of these things, we recall how Jesus severely warned His followers not even to begin to think that His coming had the effect of abrogating even the slightest letter of the law; teaching that even the least commandment had been annulled would eventuate in one's demotion in the kingdom of God (Matt. 5:17-19). Throughout His life and teaching, as we have seen, Jesus upheld the law's demands in the most exacting degree.

Moreover, Christ submitted to the law of God even to the very point of suffering its prescribed penalty for sin. He died the death of a criminal (Phil. 2:8), taking upon Himself the curse of the law (Gal. 3:13) and cancelling thereby the handwriting which was against us because of the law (Col. 2:14). "He

---

1. *The Coming of the Kingdom* (Philadelphia: Presbyterian and Reformed, 1962), pp. 290-91.

was wounded for our transgressions, he was bruised for our iniquities. . . . Jehovah has laid on him the iniquity of us all" (Isa. 53:4-6). Sin cannot avoid the dreadful judgment of God (Nahum 1:2-3; Habakkuk 1:13), and therefore God does not save sinners without righteousness and peace kissing each other (Ps. 85:9-10); He remains just, while becoming the justifier of His people (Rom. 3:26). Accordingly the law's demands could not be arbitrarily pushed aside. Christ had to come and undergo the curse of the law in the place of His chosen people; He had to satisfy the justice of God. That is why it can be said that the death of Christ is the outstanding evidence that God's law cannot be ignored or abrogated. According to the law there is no remission of sin apart from the shedding of blood (Heb. 9:22; Lev. 17:11). *"Therefore* it was *necessary* that Christ offer up himself in sacrifice for sin" (Heb. 9:23-26). The necessity of the law's continuing validity is substantiated by the saving death of Christ on our behalf.

Imitating Christ

Christians should therefore be the last people to think or maintain that they are free from the righteous requirements of God's commandments. Those who have been saved were in need of that salvation precisely because God's law could not be ignored as they transgressed it. For them to be saved, it was necessary for Christ to live and die by all of the law's stipulations. Although our own obedience to the law is flawed and thus cannot be used as a way of justification before God, we are saved by the imputed obedience of the Savior (1 Cor. 1:30; Phil. 3:9). Our justification is rooted in His obedience (Rom. 5:17-19). By a righteousness which is alien to ourselves—the perfect righteousness of Christ according to the law—we are made just in the sight of God. "He made the one who did not know sin to be sin on our behalf in order that we might become the righteousness of God in Him" (2 Cor. 5:21).

It turns out, then, that Christ's advent and atoning work do not relax the validity of the law of God and its demand for righteousness; rather they accentuate it. Salvation does not cancel the law's demand but simply the law's curse: "Christ redeemed us from the curse of the law, having become a curse for us" (Gal. 3:13). He removed our guilt and the condemning aspect of the law toward us, but Christ did not revoke the law's original righteous demand and obligation. Salvation in the Biblical sense presupposes the permanent validity of the law. Furthermore, the Holy Spirit indwelling all true believers in Jesus Christ makes them grow in likeness to Christ—"to the measure of the stature which belongs to the fulness of Christ" (Eph. 4:13, 15; cf. Gal. 4:19).

Christian ethics is a matter of imitating Christ, and for that reason it does not call us to flee from the law but to honor its requirements. We are to have in ourselves the attitude which was in Christ Jesus, who humbled himself and became obedient (Phil. 2:5, 8). We are to follow in His steps of righteous behavior (1 Pet. 2:21), showing forth righteousness because the Holy Spirit unites us to Him (1 Cor.

6:15-20). Therefore the Biblical ethic is the Christian ethic of following after the example of Christ's obedience to God's law. John expresses this point clearly: "Hereby we know that we are in Him: he that saith he abideth in him ought himself also to walk even as he walked" (1 John 2:5-6). And as we have abundantly seen above, Christ walked according to the commandments of God. We cannot escape the conclusion that the Christian ethic is one of obedience to God's law, for Christ's perfect righteousness according to that law is our model for Christian living.

From beginning to end the Bible centers on Jesus Christ. From beginning to end His life was lived in conformity to the law of God. And from beginning to end the Biblical ethic of imitating Christ calls us likewise to obey every command of God's word.

8

THE SPIRIT'S DYNAMIC
FOR LIVING

**"The Holy Spirit does not replace the law of
God in the Christian's life, nor does He oppose
the law of God in our behavior."**

We have seen previously that God's holy
character, of which the law is the transcript, is unchanging and beyond challenge; accordingly God's
holy law cannot be altered today or brought into
criticism by men's traditions. We have also observed
that Christ's perfect obedience, which is the model
for the Christian's behavior, was rendered to every
detail and facet of God's commandments; accordingly, every believer who makes it his aim to imitate
the Savior must be submissive to the law of God as
honored by Christ. The character of God the Father
and the life of God the Son both point to the law of
God as morally binding for Christians today. In addition, the work of God the Spirit cannot be viewed

as in any way detracting from our obedience to God's law; otherwise the unity of the Triune Godhead would be dissolved and we would have three gods (with separate wills and intentions, diverse attitudes and standards) rather than one.

The truth is, as presented by Scripture, that the Holy Spirit is the Spirit "of God" (1 Cor. 2:12) and is given by the Father (John 14:16; 15:26; Acts 2:33). He is likewise designated the Spirit "of the son" (Gal. 4:6; cf. Phil. 1:19; Rom. 8:9) and is sent by Christ (John 15:26; 16:7; 20:22; Acts 2:33). The Holy Spirit does not work contrary to the plans and purposes of the Father and Son but rather completes them or brings them to realization. The harmony of His workings with the Father and Son is illustrated in John 16:15, where we read that everything possessed by the Father is shared with the Son, and in turn whatever is possessed by the Son is disclosed by the Spirit. The Father, Son, and Holy Spirit work as one. They are not in tension with each other. Consequently, we should not expect that the work of the Holy Spirit in our lives would run counter to the character of the Father and the example of the Son. We should not expect that this Spirit, who inspired the writing of God's holy law, would work contrary to that law by undermining its validity, replacing its function, or leading us away from obedience to it.

When we think of Biblical ethics or Christian behavior we should think of a Spirit-filled and Spirit-led life. The Holy Spirit gives new life to us (John 3:3-8), renews us (Titus 3:5-6), and enables us to make profession of faith in Christ (1 Cor. 12:3); indeed, without the work of the Spirit, a person cannot be a Christian at all (Rom. 8:9; Gal. 3:2). The Holy Spirit illumines the believer (Eph. 1:17), leads him (Rom. 8:14), and writes God's word upon his heart (2 Cor. 3:3); by the Spirit we can understand the things freely given to us by God (1 Cor. 2:12-16). The Spirit seals the believer (Eph. 1:13; 4:30), indwells him with inner refreshment as an ever-flowing river of living water (John 14:17; Rom. 8:9; 1 Cor. 3:16; John 7:38-39), and constitutes the down payment from God on our eternal inheritance (Eph. 1:14).

The "Spiritual" man—the believer as subject to such influences of God's Spirit—will show the dramatic effects or results of the Spirit's ministry in his life. By the Spirit he will put to death the sinful deeds of his body (Rom. 8:13), for the Spirit produces holiness in the lives of God's people (2 Thess. 2:13; 1 Peter 1:2). Being filled with the Spirit (Eph. 5:18), the believer's life will manifest worship, joyful praise, thanksgiving, and submission to others (vv. 19-21). Christians are to walk by the Spirit (Gal. 5:16), thereby evidencing the harvest of love, joy, peace, patience, kindness, goodness, faithfulness, gentleness, and self-control (vv. 22-24). Christian living and behavior can therefore be summarized as "living by the Spirit."

Sanctification

This has far-reaching consequences for believers. In the first place it indicates that salvation necessitates sanctification in one's life. The believer in Christ is not only saved from his moral guilt before God, but he is also saved from the moral pollution in which he formerly lived. Christianity is not merely a matter of believing certain things and anticipating eternal comfort; it does not start and end with forgiveness for our sins because we have come to Christ as Savior. Christianity likewise requires living continually under the Lordship of Christ, eliminating indwelling sin, and walking righteously before God.

The Christian is one who has been freed not only from the curse of sin but from the bondage of sin as well. Christian experience extends beyond the moment of belief and pardon into the daily exercise of pursuing sanctification without which no one will see God (Heb. 12:14). It entails life in the Holy Spirit, which can only mean progressive holiness in one's behavior. We are saved by grace through faith (Eph. 2:8-9)—unto a life of obedience: "we are His workmanship created in Christ Jesus unto good works" (v. 10).

If living by the Spirit indicates that salvation must bring sanctification, then it means that salvation produces a life of glad obedience to God's law. Salvation frees one from sin's bondage so that he can walk lawfully (James 1:25; Gal. 5:13-14), which is to say lovingly (cf. 1 John 5:1-3), for the leading evidence of the Spirit's work in one's life is love (Gal. 5:22). Those who have been saved by faith must be diligent to exercise the good works of love (Titus 3:5-8; James 2:26; Gal. 5:6), and the standard of good behavior and loving conduct is found in God's revealed law (Ps. 119:68; Rom. 7:12, 16; 1 Tim. 1:8; John 14:15; 2 John 6).

The *Holy Spirit* works in the believer to bring about conformity to the inspired *law of God* as the pattern of *holiness*. The "requirement of the law" is "fulfilled in us who do not walk according to the flesh, but according to the Spirit" (Rom. 8:4). When God puts His Spirit within a person it causes that person to walk in the Lord's statutes and keep His ordinances (Ezk. 11:19-20). Therefore, since salvation requires sanctification, and since sanctification calls for obedience to the commandments of God, the New Testament teaches us that Christ "became the author of eternal salvation unto all those who *obey Him*" (Heb. 5:9). This does not contradict salvation by grace; it is its inevitable outworking.

The Church and God's Law

Sadly, the church today often tones down the demands of God's law out of a misconceived desire to exalt God's grace and avoid any legalism wherein salvation is grounded in one's own law-works. Rather than finding the *proper* place for God's law within the plan of salvation and pursuing its function within the kingdom of Christ, the church frequently promotes an "easy believism" which does not proclaim the need for heart-felt repentance, clearly manifest the sinner's utter guilt and need of the Savior, or follow up conversion with exhortation and discipline in righteous living.

Of course without the law of God which displays the unchanging will of God for man's attitudes and actions in all areas of life, there is a corresponding de-emphasis on concrete sin for which men must repent, genuine guilt which drives men to Christ, and specific guidelines for righteous behavior in the believer. Taking Paul out of context, some churches and teachers would make their message "we are not under law but grace." They would present evangelism and Christian nurture as though mutually exclusive of concern for God's righteous standards as found in his commandments. They would focus on the extraordinary work of the Spirit in a supposed second blessing and the charismatic gifts. The whole of the Biblical message and Christian life would be cast into a distorted, truncated, or modified form in the interests of a religion of pure grace.

However, God's word warns us against turning the grace of God into an occasion or cause of licentious living (Jude 4); it insists that faith does not nullify God's law (Romans 3:31). One has to be *deceived,* Paul says, to think that the unrighteous could possibly inherit the kingdom of God (1 Cor. 6:9-10). Those who demote even the slightest requirement of God's law will themselves be demoted in the Lord's kingdom (Matt. 5:19).

The answer to legalism is not easy believism, evangelism without the need for repentance, the pursuit of a mystical second blessing in the Spirit, or a Christian life devoid of righteous instruction and guidance. Legalism is countered by the Biblical understanding of true "life in the Spirit." In such living, God's Spirit is the gracious author of new life, who convicts us of our sin and misery over against the violated law of God, who unites us to Christ in salvation that we might share His holy life, who enables us to understand the guidance given by God's word, and who makes us to grow by God's grace into people who better obey the Lord's commands.

The precise reason that Paul asserts that we are *under grace* and therefore *not under the condemnation or curse of the law* is to explain how it is that sin does not have dominion over us — to explain, that is, why we have become slaves to obedience and now have lives characterized by conformity to God's law (Rom. 6:13-18). It is God's grace that makes us Spiritual men who honor the commandments of our Lord.

Spiritual Powers

The answer to legalism is not to portray the law of God as contrary to His promise (Gal. 3:21) but to realize that, just as the Christian life began by the Spirit, this life must be nurtured and perfected in the power of the Spirit as well (Gal. 3:3). The dynamic for righteous living is found, not in the believer's own strength, but in the enabling might of the Spirit of God. We are naturally the slaves of sin who live under its power (Rom. 6:16-20; 7:23); indeed, Paul declares that we are *dead in sin* (Eph. 2:1). However, if we are united to Christ in virtue of His death and resurrection we have become *dead to sin* (Rom. 6:3-4) and thus no longer live in it (v. 2).

Just as Christ was raised to newness of life by the Spirit (1 Tim. 3:16; 1 Pet. 3:18; Rom. 1:4; 6:4, 9), so also we who have His resurrected power indwelling us by the life-giving Spirit (Eph. 1:19-20; Phil. 3:10; Rom. 8:11) have the power to live new lives which are freed from sin (Rom. 6:4-11). The result of the

Spirit freeing us from sin is sanctification (v. 22). The gracious power of the new and righteous life of the Christian is the resurrection power of the Holy Spirit. Here is the antidote to legalism.

We must observe in this regard that the Holy Spirit does not replace the law of God in the Christian's life, nor does He oppose the law of God in our behavior. The gracious Spirit who empowers our sanctification does not speak for Himself, giving a new pattern for Christian behavior (John 16:13). Rather He witnesses to the word of the Son (John 14:23-26; 15:26; 16:14). The Spirit is not an independent source of direction or guidance in the Christian life, for His ministry is carried out in conjunction with the already given word of God (cf. 1 Cor. 2:12-16).

In terms of our sanctification this means that *the Spirit enables us to understand and obey the objective standard of God's revealed law.* It does not mean that Christians who are indwelt by the Spirit become a law unto themselves, spinning out from within themselves the standards by which they live. *What the Spirit does is to supply what was lacking in the law itself—the power to enforce compliance.* "What the law could not do, weak as it was through the flesh, God did: sending His own Son in the likeness of sinful flesh and as an offering for sin, He condemned sin in the flesh *in order that* the requirement of the law might be fulfilled in us, who do not walk according to the flesh, but according to the Spirit" (Rom. 8:3-4).

Conclusion

God's law is still the blueprint for sanctified behavior. This is completely unaffected by the Spirit's ethical ministry in the believer. The Holy Spirit does not oppose that law in the slightest degree but, instead, empowers obedience to it. "I will put My Spirit within you and cause you to walk in My statutes, and you will be careful to observe My ordinances" (Ezk. 36:27). Whereas the letter of the law brought death to man because he was unable of himself to comply with it, the Spirit of God enlivens men so that they can conform to God's standards (2 Cor. 3:6). Therefore the sure test of whether someone has the Spirit abiding in him or not is found in asking if he *keeps the commandments of God* (1 John 3:24). A Biblical view of the work of the Holy Spirit reinforces the validity of God's law for the Christian, showing how the law (as pattern) and the Spirit (as power) are both indispensable to sanctification.

.

9

A MOTIVATIONAL ETHIC
ENDORSES THE LAW

"All of God's people, throughout both testaments, have a heart which longs to obey the commandments of the Lord, for the law is established against the background of God's mercy toward His people."

Those who are genuine believers in Christ know very well that their salvation cannot be grounded in their own works of the law: ". . . not by works of righteousness which we did ourselves, but according to His mercy He saved us, . . . that being justified by His grace we might be made heirs according to the hope of eternal life" (Titus 3:5-7). The believer's justification before God is grounded instead in the perfect obedience of Jesus Christ (Gal. 3:11; Rom. 5:19); it is His *imputed righteousness* that makes us right before the judgment seat of God (2 Cor. 5:21). "A man is justified by faith without the deeds of the law" (Rom. 3:28).

Consequently, a truth that is dear to the heart of every Christian is the summary provided by Paul in Ephesians 2:8, "by grace have you been saved through faith, and that not of yourselves, it is the gift of God—not of works, lest any man should boast." Salvation is grounded in the grace of God, and the instrumental means by which we gain it is saving faith. The law does not save us but rather strikes us dead (Rom. 7:9; 2 Cor. 3:6-7).

It is true, therefore, that the Christian life and ethic should be characterized by the grace of God and saving faith; the believer's behavior should be a reflection of his faith in the mercy of God. The Christian ethic ought not to stand in opposition to salvation by grace through faith. As Paul said, "by the grace of God we have had our behavior in the world" (2 Cor. 1:12), and the Christian life can be designated "the good fight of faith" (1 Tim. 6:12). However, this does not mean that the Christian life is one of antagonism to the law of God, as many people seem to infer. It is too often thought that, since the law condemns us and cannot save us, grace and faith release us from any obligation to God's law. A gracious ethic of faith, we are told, cannot tolerate rules, regulations, or commands from God—that would be "legalism," it is said. But such thinking and reasoning is not biblical. Such antinomian implications must be corrected by God's word.

Law and Grace Are Correlative

God's law defines my sin and thereby my need for the Savior. Christ has saved me from the guilt and power of sin just because the law of God is so important; it displays the kind of life required by God, and the *consequences of disobedience* to it must not be ignored. In being saved from the wrath of God upon law-breakers, I will naturally (supernaturally) desire now to keep the formerly transgressed standard of God's law. In that light we can observe that Scripture portrays law and grace as correlative to each other. God's grace operates within the parameters of His law—in justifying His people, God does not violate His own justice (Rom. 3:26). And God's law is gracious (Ps. 119:29). The two support each other: the law promotes the fulfillment of God's promise (Rom. 5:20-21), and God's grace works to fulfill the law (Rom. 8:3-4).

When Paul says that we are saved by grace through faith, he immediately adds that as God's workmanship *we are expected to walk in good works* (Eph. 2:10). Although it is popular today to look upon the law as an intolerable burden for modern man, the beloved apostle wrote that for the believer God's law is not burdensome (1 John 5:3). When the Psalmist reflected upon the lovingkindness of the Lord, he longed to be taught His statutes and rose at midnight to render thanks for His righteous ordinances (Ps. 119:62-64). Moses viewed the giving of God's law as a sure sign of his love for the people (Deut. 33:2-4).

All of God's people, throughout both testaments, have a heart which longs to obey the commandments of the Lord, for the law is established against the background of God's mercy toward His people (for example, Ex. 20:2). *The first-hand experience of God's redemption is a strong motive for keeping the law* (Deut. 7:10-11). The grace of God, that is, brings men to exclaim: "I long for Thy salvation, O Lord, and Thy law is my delight" (Ps. 119:174). Paul, for example, wrote, "I delight in the law of God after the inward man" (Rom. 7:22). God's law, you see, had been graciously written upon his heart (Heb. 10:16).

In Romans 6, Paul discusses the implications of being under God's grace. He begins by asking whether we should continue in sin (law-breaking) so that grace might abound; his answer is a dramatic "God forbid!" (vv. 1-2). Those who have had their old man crucified with Christ, those who are united with Christ in his death and resurrection, those who have risen with Him must walk in newness of life, no longer in bondage to sinful living (vv. 3-11). So Paul exhorts us, "let not sin reign in your mortal body so that you should obey its lusts; neither present your members unto sin as instruments of unrighteousness." Those who are saved by grace from the power of sin should be finished with violating God's law. Instead they must, having been made alive from the dead, present their members as instruments of righteousness (vv. 12-13).

Why is this? How can it be that we are obliged to obey the righteous requirements of God's law if we are saved by grace? Paul answers: "Because sin shall not have dominion over you: you are not under law, but under grace" (v. 14). Ironically, although many groups have used this declaration out of context to support release from the law's demand, the verse is one of the strongest biblical proofs that *believers must strive to obey the law of God!*

Because we are no longer under the *curse* of the law and shut in to its inherent impotence in enabling obedience—because we are under *God's enabling grace,* not under law—we must not allow violations of the law (i.e., sin: 1 John 3:4) to dominate our lives. It is in order that the righteous ordinance of the law may be fulfilled in us that God has graciously put His Spirit within our hearts (Rom. 8:4). "So then, shall we sin because we are not under law but under grace? God forbid!" (Rom. 6:15). "The grace of God has appeared unto all men, bringing salvation, instructing us to deny ungodliness and worldly desires and to live sensibly, righteously and godly in the present age," for Christ has "redeemed us from every lawless deed" (Titus 1:11-14). God's grace upholds His law.

It is to be expected, therefore, that Paul would ask the following question and supply the obvious answer: "Do we then nullify the law through faith? May it never be! On the contrary we establish the law" (Rom. 3:31). Faith which does not bring obedient works—that is, faith which is divorced from God's law—is in fact insincere and dead (James 2:14-26). This kind of faith cannot justify a man at all.

The Westminster Confession of Faith (1646) is true to Scripture when it teaches that "good works, done in obedience to God's commandments, are the fruits and evidences of a true and lively faith" (XVI:2). By saving faith, the Confession says, a man will yield obedience to the commands of Scripture (XIV:2). Genuine saving faith always is accompanied by heart-felt repentance from sin and turning unto God, "purposing and endeavoring to walk with Him in all the ways of His commandments" (XV:2). We conclude, then, that the Christian's life of grace and faith is not one which is indifferent or antagonistic to the law of God. God's grace and saving faith establish the validity of the law.

Christian Love and God's Law

The same can be said for the basic Christian ethic of love. Because God has shown His love toward us, we are now to live in love to Him and our neighbor (Eph. 5:1-2; 1 John 4:7-12, 16-21). On these two love commandments — toward God and toward our neighbor (as taught in the Old Testament [Deut. 6:5, Lev. 19:18]) — hang all the law and the prophets, said Jesus (Matt. 22:37-40). Indeed, "love is the fulfillment of the law" (Rom. 13:10). But in the thinking of Jesus and the apostles, does this mean that Christians can dispense with the law of God or repudiate its details? Not at all. Moses had taught that loving God meant keeping His commandments (Deut. 30:16), and as usual Jesus did not depart from Moses: "If you love me, you will keep my commandments" (John 14:15).

The love which summarizes and epitomizes Christian ethics is not a vague generality or feeling that tolerates, for instance, everything from adultery to chastity. John wrote: "Hereby we know that we love the children of God, when we love God and do

His commandments. For this is the love of God, that we keep His commandments" (1 John 5:2-3). Love *summarizes* the law of God, but it does not abrogate or replace it. As John Murray once wrote, "the summary does not obliterate or abrogate the expansion of which it is a summary."[1] God's commandments give the specific character and direction to love as exercised by the believer. Rather than being a law unto itself (autonomous), love is a reflection of the character of God (1 John 4:8) and must therefore coincide with the dictates of God's law, for they are the transcript of God's moral perfection on a creaturely level.

God has loved us in that He saved us by grace through faith. Accordingly the Christian life ought to reflect the principles of grace, faith, and love; without them it is vain and insignificant. However, far from eliminating the law of God, a gracious ethic of faith and love establishes the permanent validity of—and our need for—the Lord's commandments.

---

1. John Murray, *Principles of Conduct* (Grand Rapids, Michigan: Eerdmans, 1957), p. 192.

10

A CONSEQUENTIAL ETHIC ENDORSES THE LAW

"It will be for our good, our neighbor's good, and our society's good, if all our actions and attitudes are governed by an interest in the kingdom of Jesus Christ."

We have said earlier that all of life is ethical: people are constantly making moral decisions, forming attitudes, and setting goals. We have also noted that there are many competing views of ethics. Let us delineate *three basic approaches* to ethical decision-making and ethical evaluating of ourselves, our actions, and our attitudes. First, some people weigh all moral issues and make their choices according to a *norm* or standard of good and evil. Second, others will determine how actions and attitudes are to be morally graded on the basis of one's *character* — his traits, intentions, or motives. Third, there will be others who see the *consequences* which follow from a person's behavior as counting the most in ethical planning and evaluating; if the effects which come from some action (or the anticipated results) are beneficial (or more beneficial than alternatives), then the action is deemed morally good and acceptable. In summary we can call these the normative, motivational, and consequential approaches to ethics. (Sometimes the technical designations are rendered as the deontological, existential, and teleological approaches to ethics.)

Now then, *the Bible has a focus on ethics from beginning to end,* this interest is expressed along the lines of all three of the ethical perspectives we have just outlined. That is, the Bible looks to the standard which we are to follow, encourages a certain kind of character and motivation in us, and sets before us goals or consequences we should pursue.

The *normative* and *motivational* perspectives have been somewhat explored already. We have seen that God has lovingly and graciously set down in His inspired word a code of moral behavior for His creatures to follow; the commandments or law of God constitute the norm of ethics for all men, whether they accept it or not. God's law is found throughout the Bible and is fully valid as a standard of morality today. This is a uniform standard, binding all men in all ages, for it reflects the unchanging holiness of God. It was this law which Christ perfectly obeyed as our Savior, thereby leaving us an example to follow, and it is this law which the Holy Spirit fulfills in us by sanctifying us daily. Thus the Bible gives us the law of God as our normative approach to morality; when God the Lawgiver speaks, His voice is one of authority and must be obeyed. His standard is absolute — unqualified, all-embracing, and beyond challenge.

We have also seen the kind of *character* which God requires in those who meet His favor. The moral man is one characterized by a holiness which reflects the nature of God — as expressed in His revealed law. The follower of Christ will attempt to emulate the Savior's virtues — as corresponding to God's law. The genuinely Spiritual man will follow the leading of God's Spirit, thereby walking in the paths of God's commandments. What we have seen is that the motivational approach to ethics is not to be divorced from, or set in contrast to, the normative approach to ethics.

Christians will want the *grace of God* that saved them to be *manifest in their actions and attitudes;* they will want to live out every moment of life in a faithful and loving way so as to be a witness to what God's faithful love has done for them. And again, when we look at Scripture to find the implications of a·gracious lifestyle which is characterized by faith and love, we learn that God's law shows us our way. The motivational and normative approaches to ethics go hand in hand in the word of God.

The Benefits of Righteousness

Let us now turn to the consequential approach to ethics according to the Bible. Consequences are important when we evaluate our past actions or contemplate future decisions. Paul communicates this well in saying that we would have to be deceived to think God could be mocked. Evil living will not bring about happiness and blessing, for then the justice and holiness of our God would be a mockery. Rather, says Paul, "whatsoever a man soweth, that shall he also reap" (Gal. 6:7). Those who live according to their rebellious nature will suffer corruption, while those who live by God's Spirit will gain eternal life (v. 8). And on that basis Paul exhorts believers, "let us not be weary in well-doing." Why? Because "in due season we will reap, if we faint not" (v. 9).

It is noteworthy here that Paul focuses on the benefits which will accrue to us if we engage in well-doing. It is not — contrary to modern-day versions of Christian asceticism — somehow ignoble or sub-ethical for a Christian to be motivated by the thought of reward for righteous living. God often sets before us the prospect of divinely granted benefits as an incentive for moral living.

For instance, Jesus said, "Seek ye first the kingdom of God and its righteousness, and all these things (daily provisions of life) shall be added unto you" (Matt. 6:33). Paul taught that "Godliness is profitable for all things, since it holds promise for the present life and also for the life to come" (1 Tim. 4:8). The Old Testament prophet Malachi exhorted God's people that if they would obey Him (here, by bringing in their tithes), God would open the windows of heaven and pour out a blessing for which there would not be enough room to take in (Mal. 3:10). Even earlier, the great leader of the Israelites, Moses, had written that obedience to the Lord would result in blessings on the society's children, crops, rain, herds, cities, and fields; it would bring peace to the people from without and prosperous economy and health from within (Deut. 7:12-15; 11:13-15; 28:1-14; 30:15, 19; Lev. 26:3-12). In ethical decision-making, we should properly consider the end, aim, or consequences of our behavior. Doing the right thing or having a proper attitude will result in benefits. But benefits for whom? Should our aim be to benefit ourselves, the other person, or the society as a whole? The Bible indicates that each of these is a subordinate, but vital, interest that we should have. For example, when Christ commands, "Thou shalt love thy neighbor as thyself" (Matt. 22:39), He tells us to seek the benefit of the other *just as* we seek our own benefit. Hence Paul tells husbands to love their wives (the other) as their own bodies (the self) precisely because nobody hates himself (Eph. 5:28-29).

Egoism (note: *not* egotism) and altruism both have a place in Christian ethics, as does a concern for the wider collection of people in one's society. Thus, the Bible often exhorts the interest of the one to be relinquished for the benefit of the many (for example, 2 Cor. 8:9; Phil. 1:24). However, all of these interests are subordinate to the one *supreme goal* for all of our actions: the kingdom of God. Within that kingdom the varying interests of one's self, the other, and the many are all harmonized.

Our Lord plainly declared that we were to "Seek *first* the kingdom of God and His righteousness." The kingdom of Christ is to have top priority when we contemplate the consequences of our actions, for

Christ has *pre-eminence* over all (Col. 1:18). It will be for our good, our neighbor's good, and our society's good if all of our actions and attitudes are governed by an interest in the kingdom of Jesus Christ.

How do we pursue that kingdom? How do we gain the *benefits* which God promises to those who will live according to His righteousness? Obviously, by obeying the King and manifesting His righteousness in our lives. God's word shows us how to do just that by setting down the law of the Lord for us. Biblical law is a pathway to divine benefits—not an ugly, dour, painful course for believers. It is not only a demand, it is something to desire! As John said, "His commandments are not burdensome" (1 John 5:3). They are the *delight* of the righteous man who receives God's blessing (Ps. 1). If we wish to have a morality which promises blessed consequences, then our morality must be patterned after the law of God.

Consider what God's word says about following the commandments of God. It brings to us life and well-being (Deut. 30:15-16), blessing and a strong heart that does not fear (Ps. 119:1-2; 112:5-7). Obedience produces peace and security (Ps. 119:28, 165, 175; Prov. 13:6; Luke 6:46-48). The Lord's loving-kindness is upon those who obey His precepts (Ps. 103:17-18), and they walk in liberty (Ps. 119:45; Jas. 2:25). As indicated already above, keeping God's word results in prosperity with respect to all of our daily needs and interests (cf. Joshua 1:7). Moreover, collective obedience will bring blessing upon a society as well. "Righteousness exalts a nation" (Prov. 14:34), giving it health, food, financial well-being, peace, and joyous children.

In short, we see that a *consequential* approach to ethics cannot be functional without the *normative* approach as well; the two work together because the way of blessing is diligent obedience to the law of God. Seeking first the righteousness of Christ's kingdom requires heart-felt obedience to the dictates of the King, and in response to that He grants us every blessing for this life and the next. We see again why the validity or authority of God's law cannot be dismissed today. Without that law we would be lost when it comes to pursuing the beneficial consequences for ourselves, others, and our society in all of our moral actions and attitudes. As God clearly says, He has revealed His law to us *for our good* (Deut. 10:13). Opponents of God's law, therefore, cannot have our good genuinely in mind; they wittingly and unwittingly mislead us into personal and social frustration, distress, and judgment (Prov. 14:12).

11

THE NEW TESTAMENT EXPLICITLY SUPPORTS THE LAW

> "The New Testament message and morality are squarely founded on the validity of God's law. Without that foundation the gospel would be expendable, and the Christian walk would be aimless and self-serving."

In previous chapters we have traced numerous lines of biblical thought which teach and require the validity of God's commandments—all of them throughout Old and New Testaments—and their continuing authority in our lives. Because we live in an age which is so antagonistic to God-given directives, and because such vast portions of the current church are likewise disinclined toward God's revealed stipulations, it is crucial that we pay close attention to the precise teaching of God's inspired, unerring, and authoritative word. Biblical ethics is not opposed to the law of God; rather, that law is essential to Christian morality. The wise man will establish his moral perspective on the rock-foundation words of Christ in Scripture. Therein we are instructed that God is unchanging in His standards for righteousness, not altering them from age to age or from person to person. Since God's law defined righteousness in the Old Testament, it continues to define righteousness for us today. God has no double-standard. Whether the Christian strives to imitate the holiness of God, to model his behavior after the life of Christ, or to be led by the Spirit, he will invariably be directed by Scripture to heed the law of God; the law is a *transcript of God's unchanging holiness*, the standard of righteousness followed by the Savior, and the *pattern of sanctification* empowered by the Spirit.

The continuing authority of God's law today is inherent to a biblically based theology. Time does not change or wear out the validity of God's commands, and a change of geography or locality does not render them ethically irrelevant. With the coming of the New Covenant and the spreading of the church throughout the world, we still read in Scripture that the law of God is to be *written on our hearts,* and we are to disciple all nations and teach them to observe whatsoever the Lord has commanded. The Biblical doctrines of God, Christ, the Holy Spirit, and the Covenant of Grace all harmonize in pointing to the abiding validity of God's inspired law.

The Three Approaches
If one takes a normative approach to ethics, a motivational approach to ethics, or a consequential

approach to ethics, he is always brought to the same conclusion: *God's law is authoritative for contemporary ethics*.

The norm which God has given to direct our lives and to define our sin is revealed in His law, a law from which we are to subtract nothing; since the Lawgiver has not altered His law — indeed, the Son of God has confirmed that law for His followers — it must remain valid for us today.

If we turn to the motivational approach to ethics, our concern will be to live in a way appropriate to our gracious salvation; we will want to be the kind of people who are characterized by faith and love. Scripture shows us that those who are grateful for God's grace will strive to live in obedience to His commandments; rather than cancelling the commandments of God in ethics, faith establishes the law, and love is a summary of the law's requirements. So then, a motivational approach to ethics — like the normative approach — declares the current validity of God's law.

Finally, the consequential approach to ethics evaluates actions and attitudes according to their beneficial results or comparative lack thereof. Christ teaches us in his word that the primary goal of our moral behavior is the kingdom of God; when we make it that, every temporal and eternal blessing will be ours. The righteousness of this kingdom is defined by the law of the King, and thus Scripture promises that obedience to the law of God will eventuate in outstanding blessing for ourselves, our neighbors, and our society. In short, the law of God was revealed for our good.

Therefore, the validity of God's law has been substantiated in previous chapters by the cardinal doctrines of the Christian faith and by all of the major perspectives on ethics. The present authority of the Lord's commandments is inescapable on any honest reading of God's word.

Moreover the validity of God's law extends to *all* of His righteous commandments. None can be subtracted from the stipulations which bind us without His authority, and such subtraction has no biblical warrant. Both Old and New Testaments teach God's people to live by *every word* from God's mouth, for God does not alter the words of His covenant. Every one of His ordinances, we are taught, is everlasting. Accordingly, Christ emphatically taught that His advent did not in the least abrogate one jot or tittle of the Old Testament law; according to His teaching, even the minor specifics of the law were to be observed—as a measure of our standing in the kingdom of God.

Paul maintained that every Old Testament scripture has moral authority for the New Testament believer, and James pointed out that not one point of the law was to be violated. Reflecting the unchanging righteousness of God, every commandment has abiding validity for us. To subtract even the least commandment is to transgress God's explicit prohibition and to be least in the kingdom of God. Hence the morality of the Old Testament is identical with that of the New.

New Testament Affirmations

There are many ways in which the New Testament undergirds the summary statements that have been rehearsed above. Attention to the teaching of the New Testament will disclose the emphatic endorsement it gives to the Old Testament law of God. For instance, the New Testament is concerned that men who are guilty of sin be redeemed by Christ and learn to live without sinning by the power of the Holy Spirit. Because sin is defined as transgression of God's law (1 John 3:4; Rom. 7:7), the thrust of the New Testament message presupposes the validity of God's law for today. Throughout the New Testament, the believer's perpetual moral duty is that of *love,* and yet love is defined by the New Testament in terms of God's law (Matt. 22:40; Rom. 13:10; 1 John 5:2-3). Consequently the New Testament message and morality are squarely founded on the validity of God's law. Without that foundation, the gospel would be expendable, and the Christian walk would be aimless and self-serving.

We can briefly summarize a number of other ways in which the New Testament indirectly but forcibly indicates the authority of all of God's law for this age.

The Teachings of Jesus

Oftentimes the people who are introduced in the New Testament as blessed or favored by God are characterized as obedient to God's law in particular —for instance, Elisabeth, Zacharias, Joseph, and Mary (Luke 1:6; 2:21-24, 27, 39). During his ministry on earth Christ often appealed to the law of God to bolster his teaching (John 8:17), vindicate his behavior (Matt. 12:5), answer his questioners (Luke 10:26), indict his opponents (John 7:19), and give concrete identity to the will of God for men (Matt. 19:17). He taught his disciples to pray that God's will would be done on earth (Matt 6:10), and after his resurrection He directed them to teach all nations to observe whatsoever He had commanded (Matt. 28:18-20). In all of these ways — without elaborate introductions or explanations for departing from a general principle or perspective — the New Testament simply *assumes* the standing authority of every command of the Lord found in the Old Testament. If the Old Testament law were invalidated by the advent or work of Christ, the preceding examples would be incredibly out of character and call for some convincing explanation. Yet none was needed.

Jesus affirmed with solemn authority that not even the least commandment of the entire Old Testament was to be taught as without binding validity today (Matt. 5:19), for according to his perspective "Scripture cannot be broken" (John 10:35). Accordingly Christ reaffirmed elements of the decalogue, for example "Thou shalt not kill" (Matt. 19:18). He also cited as morally obligatory, aspects of the Old Testament case law: for instance, "Do not defraud" (Mark 10:19), and "Thou shalt not test the Lord thy God" (Matt. 4:7). He even cited with approval the penal code of the Old Testament with respect to incorrigible delinquents (Matt. 15:4).

Jesus expected the weightier matters of the law to

be observed without leaving the minor details undone (Luke 11:42). He was concerned that His own
behavior be correctly seen as in accord with God's
law (Mark 2:25-28), and He directed others to live
by the law's regulations (Mark 1:44; 10:17-19). None
of this could make sense except on the obvious
assumption that all of the Old Testament law continues to be an authoritative standard of morality in
the New Testament era. Because that law is indeed
our standard of ethics, Christ the Lord will one day
judge all men who commit lawless deeds (Matt.
7:23; 13:41).

The Teaching of the Apostles

The apostolic attitude toward the law of the Old
Testament parallels that of Christ. The keeping of
the law is greatly significant (1 Cor. 7:19), for the
believer is not without the law of God (1 Cor.
9:20-27). Law-breaking is not to have dominion
over the believer (Rom. 6:12-13; 1 John 3:3-5), for
the Holy Spirit fulfills the ordinance of the law
within him (Rom. 8:4). The law is written on the
New Covenant believer's heart (Heb. 8:10), so that
those who loyally follow Christ are designated by
John as those "who keep the commandments of God
and hold the testimony of Jesus" (Rev. 12:17; 14:12).

The apostles often supported their teaching by
appealing to the law (for example, 1 Cor. 14:34; Jas.
2:9)—its general precepts found in the decalogue
(for example, "Thou shalt not steal," Rom. 13:9), the
case law applications of those details (for example,
"Thou shalt not muzzle the ox when he treads,"

1 Tim. 5:18), the penal code (for example, "if I am an evildoer and have committed anything worthy of death, I refuse not to die," Acts 25:11; cf. Deut. 21:22; Rom. 13:4), and even "holiness" requirements in the ceremonial law (for example, 2 Cor. 6:14-18).

Conclusion

We must conclude that anyone whose attitude toward the Old Testament law is informed by the teaching and practice of the New Testament must maintain the law's full and continuing validity today. Those who, in the name of a distinctive "New Testament ethic," downgrade or ignore the Old Testament law are sternly warned by the Apostle John: "He that saith, I know him, and keepeth not his commandments, is a liar, and the truth is not in him" (1 John 2:4). In genuinely Biblical ethics, the Old Testament will not be pitted against the New Testament at any point.

12

NEW TESTAMENT ETHICAL THEMES ENDORSE THE LAW

"The presupposition of the New Testament authors is continually and consistently that the Old Testament law is valid today."

The New Testament utilizes a large number of expressions and concepts in communicating moral instruction to God's people — so large that one short study cannot mention them all. The *variety* of themes found in New Testament ethics helps to drive home to our hearts God's message and demand. It covers our moral obligation from many perspectives, offers us numerous models and motivations for a proper manner of life, and facilitates the production and maintenance of ethical maturity in us.

Yet the large variety of New Testament ethical themes does not imply a correspondingly large diversity of ethical systems of *conflicting* expectations. God is consistent and changes not (Mal. 3:6); with

Him there is no variableness or turning (Jas. 1:17). His word does not equivocate, saying "yes" from one perspective but "no" from another (2 Cor. 1:18; cf. Matt. 5:37). Therefore His standards of conduct do not contradict each other, approving and disapproving of the same things depending upon which theme in New Testament ethics we are considering. The Lord prohibits us from following conflicting authorities (Matt. 6:24) and requires our behavior in the world to reflect "godly sincerity"—that is, unmixed attitude and singleness of mind or judgment (2 Cor. 1:12).

New Testament ethical instruction thus shows a diversity of expression but a unity of expectation. This is simply to say that all of the various moral themes in the New Testament are harmonious with each other. As we survey a few of these New Testament themes, it will be significant to note how they consistently assume or explicitly propogate the standard of God's Old Testament law—which, given the unchanging character of God and the consistency of His ethical standards, is not at all surprising. God's law is woven throughout the ethical themes of the New Testament.

Kingdom Righteousness

The central demand of Jesus in the Sermon on the Mount is that of a righteousness befitting the kingdom of God. Righteousness and God's kingdom are intimately related: persecution for the sake of righteousness is rewarded in the kingdom (Matt. 5:10), and the Lord requires a righteousness exceeding that of the scribes and Pharisees in order to enter the kingdom at all (Matt. 5:20). Just as Moses delivered a divine pronouncement from the Mount, asserting God's standard of righteousness, so also Jesus speaks from the mount with God's requirement of righteousness, confirming every detail of even the least commandment in the Old Testament (Matt. 5:19). He proclaimed, "Seek first the kingdom of God and His righteousness!" (Matt. 6:33). How is such kingdom righteousness to be accomplished? Jesus explained in the Lord's prayer: when we ask "Thy kingdom come," we are praying "Thy will be done on earth as it is in heaven" (Matt. 6:10). The doing of God's will, which Jesus found in the Old Testament law, is crucial to the New Testament theme of kingdom righteousness.

God is portrayed in the New Testament as a God of righteousness (John 17:25), and the fruit that He brings forth in people is that of righteousness (Eph. 5:9). "If you know that He is righteous, you also know that everyone who practices righteousness has been begotten of Him" (1 John 2:29), and "whosoever does not practice righteousness is not of God" (1 John 3:10). As Paul says, we are not to be deceived: "the unrighteous shall not inherit the kingdom of God," and as examples of the unrighteous he lists violators of God's law (1 Cor. 6:9-10). Kingdom righteousness, then, is demanded of all believers. "Follow after righteousness" can serve for Paul as a short summary of Timothy's moral duty (1 Tim. 6:11).

But where is the character of this kingdom righteousness to be found for New Testament writers? What does righteousness entail in behavior and attitude? Paul tells Timothy that an all-sufficient "instruction in righteousness" is found in *every* scripture of the Old Testament (2 Tim. 3:16-17), thereby encompassing the law of God found therein. In fact, speaking of the Old Testament law, Paul categorically declares that "the commandment is . . . righteous" (Rom. 7:12). Kingdom righteousness, therefore, cannot be understood as contrary to the righteous commandments of the King. In Paul's perspective, it is "the doers of the law" who shall be accounted righteous (Rom. 2:13).

Righteousness in the New Testament is portrayed as having absolutely no fellowship with *lawlessness* (the Greek word for "iniquity," 2 Cor. 6:14). To love righteousness is precisely to hate all lawlessness (Heb. 1:9). God's law cannot be discarded or despised by those who would practice the righteousness of God's kingdom according to the New Testament understanding of ethics. That entails, as we have seen, every last commandment in every scripture of the Old Testament — "uprightness" allows no deviation from perfect conformity to God's rule (cf. Deut. 6:25).

The Way of Righteousness

In his second epistle Peter describes New Testament Christianity as "the way of righteousness" (2:21). "The Way" was an early designation for the Christian faith (for example, Acts 9:2; 19:9, 23; 22:4; 24:22), probably stemming from Christ's own self-declaration that He was "the way" (John 14:6). The expression is adapted throughout the New Testament, where we read of "the way of salvation" (Acts 16:17), "the way of God" (Matt. 22:16; Acts 18:26), "the way of the Lord" (Acts 13:10), "the way of peace" (Luke 1:79; Rom. 3:17), "the way of truth" (2 Peter 2:2), and "the right way" (2 Peter 2:15). However, the distinctive terminology of 2 Peter 2:21 is "the way of righteousness," and Peter treats the phrase "the holy commandment" as interchangeable with it in this verse. Professing Christians who know the way of righteousness and then turn back from the holy commandment are the apostates. Michael Green says in his commentary here that it is "a fair inference from the text that the first stage in their apostasy was the rejection of the category of law. . . . Rejection of God's law is the first step to the rejection of God, for God is a moral being."[1] The "way of righteousness" describes the true kingdom of God in the New Testament. Thus New Testament Christianity cannot be set over against the law of God, opposing its standard, for such opposition would amount to turning away from the holy commandment delivered by our Lord and Savior (cf. 2 Peter 3:2).

Christ himself spoke of "the way of righteousness" in connection with the ministry and message of John the Baptist: "John came unto you in the way of righteousness" (Matt. 21:32). Of course John was preem-

---

1. Michael Green, *The Second Epistle of Peter and the Epistle of Jude*, Tyndale New Testament Commentaries, ed. R. V. G. Tasker (Grand Rapids, Michigan: Eerdmans, 1968), p. 120.

inently a righteous preacher belonging to the era of the law and prophets (Matt. 11:11, 13). He proclaimed that the coming of God's kingdom demanded repentance (Matt. 3:2), the confession of sin (3:6), and bringing about the good fruit worthy of repentance (3:8, 10). As the last preacher in the era of the law and prophets (and forerunner of the Lord), it must be obvious what the *standard* of sin, repentance, and good fruit would have been for John and his hearers — *the law of God*. Confirmation of that is found in the details of his preaching where the requirements of God's law were expounded (Luke 3:10-14, 19; Mark 6:18).

John came in "the way of righteousness," applying God's law. This was only to be expected of the one who fulfilled the awaited coming of Elijah to restore all things (Matt. 11:14; 17:10-13). The angelic message of John's coming birth makes it clear that the ministry of Elijah which John would perform was according to the pattern of Malachi's prophecy: "Remember the law of Moses my servant, which I commanded unto him in Horeb for all Israel, even statutes and ordinances. Behold, I will send you Elijah the prophet before the great and terrible day of Jehovah comes" (Mal. 4:4-5; cf. v. 6 with Luke 1:17). John's preaching in "the way of righteousness" was anything *but* antagonistic to the law of the Lord found in the Old Testament. Likewise, those who belong to "the way of righteousness" today must recognize the important place which the law of God has in Christian ethics.

Of course, whether we consider the righteousness of God's kingdom or the way of righteousness, our attention must be focused on God Himself as the model of all righteousness. The faithful described in Revelation 15 who have been victorious over the Beast are portrayed as singing to the Lord, "righteous and true are Thy ways, Thou King of the ages" (v. 3). Those who extol the righteousness of God here are believers who resisted the Beast's attempt to replace God's law with his own (cf. Rev. 13:16 and Deut. 6:8), and the song which they sing is designated "the song of Moses, the servant of God" — a phrase reflecting Joshua 22:5, "Only take diligent heed to do the commandment and the law which Moses the servant of Jehovah commanded you, to love Jehovah your God, and to walk in all his ways, and to keep His commandments, and to cleave unto Him, and to serve Him with all your heart and with all your soul."

The righteousness of God is expressed in His law. Accordingly, the kingdom righteousness demanded by Christ and the apostles and the "way of righteousness" encompassing the Christian faith both assume and apply the law of God. Whenever these themes appear in New Testament ethics, they are expressive of the standard of God's commandments as found throughout the Old Testament. Such was the understanding of the New Testament writers themselves.

Holiness and Sainthood

A Biblical concept closely related to that of righteousness is the concept of holiness. While the former emphasizes a just and upright conformity with a standard of moral perfection, the latter lays stress on utter separation from all moral impurity. However, the norm for both is the same in Scripture. An unrighteous man cannot be deemed holy, and an unholy person will not be seen as righteous.

Above all God is "the Holy One" (1 John 2:20; as applied to Christ, Mark 1:24; John 6:69; Acts 3:14; Rev. 3:7). When He saves us and draws us to Himself, He *makes us holy*—that is, "sanctifies" us—as well. We were chosen in Christ before the foundation of the world "in order that we should be holy and without blemish" (Eph. 1:4); from the beginning God chose us to be saved in believing the truth and in holiness (sanctification) produced by the Holy Spirit (2 Thes. 2:13). By His own sacrifice and the work of reconciliation accomplished by his death (Heb. 10:14; Col. 1:22), Christ sanctifies the church, aiming to present it as holy and without blemish before God (Eph. 5:26-27). It is God who makes us holy (1 Thes. 5:23), especially through the ministry of the Holy Spirit in us (1 Peter 1:2).

Holiness is thus an important ethical theme in the New Testament. Believers are called by God precisely to be holy ones—that is "saints" (Rom. 1:7; 1 Cor. 1:2). Christians in a particular locality or church are customarily designated as God's "saints" (Acts 9:13, 32; Rom. 15:25; 2 Cor. 1:1; Phil. 4:22); these holy ones are those for whom the Holy Spirit makes intercession (Rom. 8:27), to whom God makes known His mysteries (Col. 1:26), and for whom we are to show acts of love (Col. 1:4; Rom. 12:13; Heb. 6:10; 1 Tim. 5:10). They have been chosen, redeemed, and called to be "sanctified," which is to say *set apart,* consecrated to God's service, or holy before Him.

The inclusion of the Gentiles in God's redemptive kingdom means that they have become "fellow-citizens with the saints" (Eph. 2:19) in the "commonwealth of Israel" (2:12). Accordingly, the church is made up of those *sanctified* in Christ Jesus and called to be *holy ones* or "saints" (1 Cor. 1:2). Christians are the "holy brothers" (Heb. 3:1), a "holy temple of God" (1 Cor. 3:17; Eph. 2:21), purged vessels of honor "made holy for the Master's use" and ready for every good work (2 Tim. 2:12).

Any conception of New Testament ethics which skirts holiness or encourages anything contrary to it is in diametric opposition to the text of God's word. Holiness of life is an *inescapable requirement* for God's people. They must present their bodies as holy sacrifices (Rom. 12:1) and their members as servants of righteousness unto sanctification or holiness (Rom. 6:19). God has called them to holiness rather than uncleanness (1 Thes. 4:7) and freed them from sin so that they might produce the fruit of holiness (Rom. 6:22).

As believers we must establish our hearts unblameable in holiness before God (1 Thes. 3:13) and see to it that our behavior in the world is in holiness (2 Cor. 1:12). Everywhere we turn in the New Testament, the ethical theme of holiness keeps reappearing; its demand is constant. Paul's stirring exhortation summarizes this demand well: "let us cleanse ourselves from all defilement of flesh and spirit, perfecting holiness in the fear of God" (2 Cor. 7:1).

What is the character of this holiness which the New Testament takes as a pervasive moral theme? By what standard is holiness measured and where is concrete guidance in holiness found? The fact that Christians are to be holy is so often stated in the New Testament that we must certainly assume that *the norm or criterion of holiness was already well known;* little needs to be said to explain to New Testament readers what this holiness requires. The suggestion is unavoidable that the Old Testament standards of morality already sufficiently defined the holiness which God sought in His people. Hebrews 12:10 indicates that God chastens us so that we may become "partakers of His holiness," and thus New Testament holiness is nothing less than a reflection of God's character on a creaturely level.

How does one who is a sinner in thought, word, and deed come to know what God's holiness requires of him? Peter makes it clear what is implicit in the pervasive New Testament theme of holiness when he writes, "even as he who called you is holy, be yourselves also holy in all manner of living; because it stands written, 'You shall be holy, for I am holy' " (1 Peter 1:15-16). Here Peter quotes the Old Testament law from such places as Leviticus 11:44-45; 19:2, and 20:7, where it is evident that God's people would be sanctified and be holy by following all the statutes of God's revealed law. Christ was surely including the Old Testament in His reference, when he prayed that His people would be *sanctified* by His word of truth (John 17:17). Indeed, Paul explicitly says that the Old Testament law is our standard of holiness today even as it was for the saints of Israel: "So then the law is *holy*, and the commandment holy, and righteous, and good" (Rom. 7:12). In the book of Revelation, John leaves no doubt about the place of God's law in the holiness of God's people. He defines the "saints" (holy ones) precisely as "the ones keeping the commandments of God and the faith of Jesus" (14:12; cf. 12:17).

In the moral theology of Jesus, Peter, Paul, and John, the concept of holiness explicitly conforms to the law of God found in the Old Testament word of truth. We therefore see again that New Testament ethics cannot be pitted against God's law without doing damage to a central theme of the New Testament scriptures.

Separation from the World

Another ethical theme in the New Testament, one which is closely allied with that of holiness (i.e., "separation" unto God and away from defilement), is the theme of separation from the world. Of course, this does not denote a desire to withdraw from the affairs of life or the community of men. Christ made this abundantly clear in praying for us in this fashion: "I do not pray that you should take them out of the world, but that you should keep them from evil (or the evil one)" (John 17:15).

When the New Testament speaks of separation from the world, *the term "world" is used for the ethical condition of sinful rebellion against God.* The "course of this world" is Satanic and makes one a disobedient child of wrath (Eph. 2:2-3). "Friendship with the world is enmity with God," says James (4:4), and therefore true religion is "to keep oneself unspotted from the world" (1:27). The "world" is understood as the locus of corruption and defilement (2 Peter 1:4; 2:20). John puts it dramatically and clearly when he says, "the whole world lies in the evil one" (1 John 5:19) — even as his gospel continually shows that "the world" is understood as the domain of disobedience, disbelief, and ethical darkness (John 1:29; 3:17, 19; 4:42; 6:33, 51; 8:12; 9:5; 12:46, 47; 16:8). John says elsewhere that "all that is in the world" is "the lust of the flesh and the lust of the eye and the vainglory of life" (1 John 2:15-17).

Hebrews 12:14 exhorts us to "follow after . . . the sanctification without which no man shall see the Lord," indicating that those who are acceptable to God must be "set apart" (sanctified) unto Him and "separated" from the sinful pollution of the world. This entails cleansing from defilement (2 Cor. 7:1), leading a spotless life (2 Peter 3:14) — language reminiscent of the purity and sacrificial laws of the Old Testament. Second Timothy 2:19 summarizes the New Testament theme of separation from the world: "Let every one that names the name of the Lord depart from unrighteousness."

How is this to be done? What is the nature of such separation from unrighteousness and defilement? By what standard does the New Testament Christian separate himself from "the world"? James instructs us that the word of God — which for James surely included the Old Testament scriptures of his day — is the key to this ethical separation: ". . . putting away all filthiness and overflowing of wickedness, receive with meekness the implanted word, and not hearers only, deluding your own selves" (1:21-22). *We can put away worldly vice and corruption by doing what is stipulated in the word of God,* including the stipulations of the Old Testament and its law: ". . . he that looks into the perfect law of liberty and continues, not being a hearer who forgets it but a doer that practices it, this man shall be blessed in his doing" (1:25).

Paul's theology agrees with this. "For the grace of God has appeared to all men, bringing salvation, instructing us to deny ungodliness and worldly desires and to live sensibly, righteously, and godly in the present age"—looking for the appearance of Christ who "redeemed us from every lawless deed" (Titus 2:11-14). Salvation provided by Christ enables us, by avoiding *lawless* behavior, to deny the unethical direction of worldliness. In his commentary on this passage, Calvin wrote, "The revelation of God's grace necessarily brings with it exhortations to a godly life. . . . In God's Law there is complete perfection to which nothing else can ever be added."

Paul exhorts us to "have no *fellowship* with the unfruitful works of darkness" (Eph. 5:11), and it is evident that for Paul the Old Testament law directed God's people as to how they could avoid such evil fellowship. Citing the law at Deuteronomy 22:10, Paul said "Be not unequally yoked with unbelievers, for what fellowship has righteousness with lawlessness?" (2 Cor. 6:14). Further citing the Old Testament regarding the laws of holiness by which Israel was "separated from" the Gentile nations, Paul goes on to write: "Come out from among them and be separate, says the Lord, and touch no unclean thing; and I will receive you" (v. 17).

An example of these Old Testament laws which separated Israel from the world is found in Leviticus 20:22-26, where we see that the observation of such laws (for example, distinguishing unclean from clean meats) was but *symbolic of* separation from worldy customs. All meats are now deemed clean (Mark 7:9; Acts 10:14-15), yet God's people are still obligated to separate themselves from worldliness (Rom. 12:1-2) and union with unbelievers (2 Cor. 6:14-17). How was holy separation accomplished, according to Leviticus 20? "You shall therefore keep my statutes and all mine ordinances and do them" (v. 22).

The Good, Well-pleasing, and Perfect Will of God

A passage expressing the ethical themes of holiness and separation from the world is Romans 12:1-2. Paul there says, "Therefore I beseech you, brothers, by the mercies of God to present your bodies a living sacrifice, holy, well-pleasing to God, which is your reasonable service; and do not be conformed to this world (age), but rather be transformed by the renewing of your mind, so that you may prove what is the will of God, the good and well-pleasing, and perfect." Going beyond the themes of holiness and separation, Paul speaks of the good, well-pleasing, and perfect will of God. These same concepts are combined in the benediction at the end of the book of Hebrews: "Now the God of peace . . .

make you *perfect* in every *good thing* to do *His will,*
working in us that which is *well-pleasing* in His sight,
through Jesus Christ, to whom be the glory for ever
and ever. Amen" (13:20-21).

Perhaps the most fundamental ethical concept in
either the Old or New Testament is that of the will of
God. All ethical decisions and moral attitudes of
God's people must be in accord with the will of the
Lord by which He prescribes what is good, or well-
pleasing, or perfect in His sight. Anything conflicting with that will is immoral and displeasing to God,
quite naturally. Jesus said that His "meat" was to do
the will of the Father who sent Him (John 4:34), and
that those who did the will of the heavenly Father
were His "brother and sister and mother" (Matt.
12:50); we manifest whose children we are by our
righteous behavior or lack of the same (1 John 3:1).
Christ taught His disciples to pray, "Thy will be
done on earth as it is in heaven" (Matt. 6:10). Doing
God's will is not merely a matter of words but of *concrete acts of obedience* (Matt. 21:28-31); the will of God
must be done from the heart (cf. Eph. 6:6). Therefore, not those who cry "Lord, Lord," but only those
who do the will of the Father in heaven will enter
into the kingdom (Matt. 7:21); those who know the
Lord's will and fail to do it will be beaten with many
stripes (Luke 12:47). On the other hand, if a man
does the will of God, he will be able to *discern* the doctrine which comes from God (John 7:17), and his
prayers will be heard (John 9:31; cf. 1 John 5:14).
While the world and its lusts pass away, he who does
the will of God abides forever (1 John 2:17). Conse-

quently, Paul can encapsulate New Testament ethics in one stroke, saying "be not foolish, but understand what the will of the Lord is" (Eph. 5:17). Indeed, we are to aim to stand perfect, fully assured in all the will of God (Col. 4:12).

The Source of Man's Standards

Where do we learn, understand, and become assured of God's will? The New Testament offers little by way of an explicit answer to such a question. We learn that the will of God stands over against the lusts of men (1 Peter 4:2), and in a very few cases we are told what the will of God specifically requires (for example, abstaining from fornication and giving thanks in all things, 1 Thes. 4:3; 5:18). However, there is no detailed discussion of the requirements of God's will, and concrete guidance in God's will as such is not systematically explored. Why not? Especially since the will of God is such a crucial ethical theme, we might have expected differently.

The answer lies in recognizing that the common conviction of the inspired New Testament writers is that the will of God has already been given a specific and sufficient explication in the Old Testament. It is simply assumed that one can speak of "the will of God" without explanation because it is obvious that God's will traces back to the revelation of His will in the law previously committed to Scripture. Accordingly, 1 Samuel 13:14 can be quoted about David, "a man after My heart who will do all My will" (Acts 13:22), and it is expected that the reader will recall that in the Old Testament setting of this statement

David is contrasted with **Saul** precisely with respect to the keeping of God's commands.

Paul convicts those who glory in God and claim to know His will, and yet transgress the law, thereby dishonoring God (Rom. 2:17-18, 23). And John would add, "And hereby we know that we know Him, if we keep His commandments. He that says, 'I know Him,' and keeps not His commandments, is a liar and the truth is not in him" (1 John 2:3-4). In the New Testament, God's will is assumed to be found in His law and commandments.

The Good

The good, goodness, or "good works" is also a key theme in New Testament ethics. John says, "beloved, imitate not that which is evil but that which is good. He that does good is of God; he that does evil has not seen God" (3 John 11). Paul declares, "Faithful is the saying, and concerning these things I desire that you affirm confidently, to the end that they who have believed God may be careful to maintain good works" (Titus 3:8). Although guarding diligently the truth that salvation is by grace through faith, Paul nevertheless taught that "we are His workmanship, created in Christ Jesus unto good works, which God before prepared that we should walk in them" (Eph. 2:10).

By what standard, then, do we judge what is ethically good? Again, the New Testament is here resting on the revelation of God's law for its understanding of the ethical theme of the good. When asked what good thing should be done to inherit eternal life, Jesus responded: "If you would enter into life, keep the commandments" (Matt. 19:16-17)—and He makes it crystal clear that He is referring to the Old Testament law (vv. 18-19). Likewise Paul could state without qualification that "the commandment is holy, and righteous, and good. . . . I consent unto the law that it is good" (Rom. 7:12, 16). Elsewhere he expresses the common outlook of the Christian faith, "we know that the law is good" (1 Tim. 1:8).

Pleasing God

Another concern of New Testament ethics is to realize what is "well-pleasing" unto God. Paul says, "we make it our aim . . . to be well-pleasing unto Him" because all will appear before His judgment seat to receive the things done in the body, whether good or bad (2 Cor. 5:9-10). Elsewhere Paul identifies the kingdom of God with righteousness, peace, and joy in the Holy Spirit, "for he that herein serves Christ is well-pleasing to God" (Rom. 14:17-18). Those who have no fellowship with the unfruitful works of darkness but who walk rather as children of light, the fruit of which is all goodness, righteousness, and truth, are actually "proving what is well-pleasing unto the Lord" (Eph. 5:9-11).

Thus it is basic to New Testament morality that our actions and attitudes should be well-pleasing in the sight of God, but how can we make them so? How does anyone *know* what pleases God or not? It is unusual for Paul to give a specific or concrete instance (for example, Phil. 4:18) for this broad concept. However, at one point when he does so, it is not difficult to see what his ethical standard was. In

Colossians 3:20 Paul instructs children to obey their parents, "for this is well-pleasing in the Lord." The commandments of the law, therefore, can serve and did serve as detailing what is well-pleasing to God, even in New Testament morality.

Perfection

Perfection is another moral theme of the New Testament which deserves our attention. Paul would have believers "stand perfect and fully assured in all the will of God" (Col. 4:12). John discourses against fear because it is inconsistent with being made perfect in love (1 John 4:18), and for John love is tested by adherence to God's commandments (cf. 5:2-3). James teaches that steadfastness through trials will have "its perfect work," so that we are lacking in nothing (1:2-4), and he sees every perfect gift — in contrast to sin — as coming from God above (1:17). With an insight into the special power of sins of the tongue, James tells us that if any man does not stumble in word he is a perfect man (3:2).

Studying perfection as a moral concept in the New Testament, we once again are taken back to the standard of God's law. Christ taught that our perfection must be modelled after the heavenly Father: "Therefore you shall be perfect, as your heavenly Father is perfect" (Matt. 5:48). Significantly, this exhortation follows and summarizes a discourse on the full measure of the Old Testament law's demands (vv. 21-48). When Christ was later approached by one who presumed to be obedient to the law, Christ taught him that to be perfect he would need to renounce every sin against God's commandments and every hindrance to complete obedience to them (Matt. 19:21). Accordingly, we learn that God's law is our standard of moral perfection today. James instructs believers that the man who is blessed of God is the one who is a doer of the word, having "looked into the perfect law" (Jas. 1:25).

Summary

We may return now to Romans 12:2, where Paul's ethical guidance to the New Testament believer is to follow the will of God, that which is good, well-pleasing, and perfect. We have seen that the New Testament consistently *assumes* as common knowledge (and explicitly applies the truth) that *the commandments of God's law in the Old Testament are a sufficient and valid standard of God's will, of the good, of the well-pleasing to the Lord, and of perfection.* Whenever these themes appear in the New Testament scriptures the authority of God's law is repeatedly being applied. Our obligation to that law is reinforced many times over when Paul summarizes the ethical standard for New Testament morality as "the good, well-pleasing, and perfect will of God." God himself is to receive the glory for bringing our lives into conformity with this unchallengeable norm for Christian conduct. He is the One who, through the ministry of His Son, makes us "perfect in every good thing to do His will, working in us that which is well-pleasing in His sight" (Heb. 13:20-21).

Every attempt to reject the law of God in the New Testament era meets with embarrassment before the text of the New Testament itself. The righteousness of God's kingdom, the way of righteousness, holiness and sainthood, our separation from the world, and the good, well-pleasing, perfect will of God, all require that our behavior conform to the standard of God's commandments as revealed once and for all in the Old Testament. This standard is woven implicitly throughout New Testament ethical teaching.

Spiritual Freedom

Further important ethical themes in the New Testament would include freedom in the Holy Spirit, love, the fruit of the Spirit, and the golden rule. Jesus declared, "Everyone who commits sin is the slave of sin" (John 8:34), and only the Son of God can truly set us free from that bondage (8:36). He does this by applying the redemption which He has accomplished for us in His death and resurrection — applying redemption through the Holy Spirit, who frees us from the bondage of sin and death (Rom. 8:1-2). This Spiritual freedom does not give us the prerogative to live or behave in just any way we please; Spiritual freedom is not the occasion of moral arbitrariness. Paul says, "Being made free from sin now, and become servants to God, you have your fruit unto sanctification" (Rom. 6:22). The Holy Spirit does not give us the freedom to sin — that is, the freedom to transgress God's law; rather, the Spirit gives us the freedom to be the *slaves of Christ* and produce holy behavior. The regenerate man is happy and willing to "serve the law of God" (Rom.

7:25). The very bondage from which the Spirit releases us is described by Paul as precisely the sinful nature's *inability* to be *subject* to the *law of God* (Rom. 8:7). Obviously, freedom from this inability must now mean *being subject* to the law of God! This freedom does not turn the grace of God into licentiousness (cf. Jude 4) but inclines the heart of those once enslaved to sin to the Spirit-given law (Rom. 7:14).

The "ordinance of the law" is to be "fulfilled in us who walk not after the flesh but after the Spirit" (Rom. 8:4). Therefore the Bible makes it quite clear that our Spiritual freedom is not liberty *from* God's law, but liberty *in* God's law. James calls the commandments of God "the perfect law of liberty" (2:25), thereby combining two descriptions of the law given by the Psalmist: "The law of the Lord is perfect" (Ps. 19:7) and "I will walk at liberty, for I seek Thy precepts" (Ps. 119:45). Genuine freedom is not found in flight from God's commands but in the power to keep them. God's Spirit frees us from the condemnation and death which the law brings to sinners, and the Spirit breaks the hold of sin in our lives.

However, the freedom produced by the Spirit never leads us away from fulfilling God's law: "For you, brethren, were called for freedom; only use not your freedom for an occasion to the flesh, but through love be servants one to another. For the whole law is fulfilled in one word, even in this, You shall love your neighbor as yourself" (Gal. 5:13-14). When Paul teaches that "where the Spirit of the Lord is, there is liberty" (2 Cor. 3:17), it is taught in the context of the Spirit's New Covenant ministry of writing God's law upon the believer's heart and thereby enabling obedience to that law (2 Cor. 3:3-11; cf. Jer. 31:33; Ezk. 11:20). Consequently, the ethical concept of Spiritual freedom in the New Testament is anything but indifferent to the law of God. The Spirit frees us from law-breaking for the purpose of law-keeping.

Love

One of the most conspicuous ethical themes in the New Testament is that of love. Indeed, the New Testament is a story about love — God's love for sinners (John 3:16) and their subsequent love for Him and others (1 John 4:19). One of the most sustained ethical essays in New Testament literature is in fact a discourse on the necessity, supremacy, and characteristics of love (1 Cor. 13). Love is at the heart both of the gospel and of Christian behavior (1 John 4:10-11). Few who are knowledgeable of the New Testament writings will deny that love summarizes in one word the Christian ethic.

It is noteworthy that the New Testament writers demonstrate the ethical authority of love by reference to the Old Testament law. Why is love so important? What gives love its ethical preeminence? Why must the dictates of love be respected? What makes love such an authoritative standard? Precisely that *it communicates the substance of the law's demands!* In summarizing our moral duty in love, Christ actually quoted the love commands from the Old Testament case law (Matt. 22:37-39). He said that love to God and neighbor were crucial because "On these two commands hang the whole law and prophets" (v. 40).

Love is a moral necessity for Paul precisely because it fulfills the law (Rom. 13:8-10; Gal. 5:14). *Love* for your neighbor means that you do not commit adultery with his wife, steal his car, or slander him behind his back — just as the law requires. Likewise, James considers love the fulfillment of the royal law (2:8), and John specifically writes, "This is the love of God, that we keep His commandments" (1 John 5:3). The *assumption* of the New Testament writers and the development of their thought is that *God's law is morally authoritative;* because love expresses and follows that law, love too is a fitting standard of moral guidance. The foundational authority of love cannot be isolated from the law of God.

The Fruit of the Spirit and the Golden Rule

The same can be said for other New Testament summaries of our moral duty. A prominent pattern of godly living is set forth by Paul in the list of "the fruit of the Spirit," which Paul sets over against the fruit of the sinful nature (or flesh) in Galatians 5:16-24. The attitudes or character traits mentioned by Paul as the outcome of the Spirit's work in a believer's life ("love, joy, peace . . .") are a model for Christian morality. Yet Paul makes it clear that the ethical authority of these traits rests on the underlying authority of God's law. Having listed the Spirit's fruit, Paul explains why these traits are so important in Christian ethics: ". . . against such there is no law" (v. 23). In the same way we can observe that the popular and pervasive summary of New Testament living known as the "golden rule" — or whatever you would have men do to you, do even so unto them — is presented as morally authoritative by Christ just *because* "this is the law and the prophets" (Matt. 7:12). The golden rule communicates the essential demand of the law of the Old Testament, and as such it is a standard of ethics which we must respect. Thus we observe that the most common summaries of New Testament morality — whether love, the fruit of the Spirit, or the golden rule — derive their importance and binding character from the law of God which they express. The presupposition of the New Testament authors is continually and consistently that the Old Testament law is valid today.

Conclusion

Any attempt to speak of New Testament ethics *apart from* kingdom righteousness, or the holiness of Christ's saints and their separation from the world, or the good, well-pleasing, perfect will of God, or the stature of Christ, or resurrection life, or Spiritual freedom, or love, or the fruit of the Spirit, or the golden rule, is bound to be inadequate. And any attempt to understand these concepts *apart from* the Old Testament law is bound to be inaccurate.

13

NEW TESTAMENT MORAL JUDGMENTS ENDORSE THE LAW

"The attempt made by some Christian teachers today to reject or circumscribe the authority of the Old Testament law will over and over again meet with embarrassment before the text of the New Testament."

The Old Testament law of God gives definitive substance to many of the central themes of New Testament ethics — as we have illustrated before. When we ask what it means to follow the will of God or to be holy, as the New Testament requires, we find that the law of God defines these ethical themes. Likewise, the law of God is assumed in notions like kingdom righteousness or the golden rule. The law functions as a standard and a guide when we heed New Testament exhortations to attain the stature of Christ or demonstrate the fruit of the Spirit. New Testament ethical themes quite often take for granted the validity of God's Old Testament commandments.

The complete, continuous, and thus contemporary validity of the Old Testament law which is assumed without challenge in many *themes* of New Testament ethics is brought out explicitly in moral *judgments* which fill the pages of the New Testament. In particular circumstances, when some kind of moral evaluation, direction, or exhortation is called for, New Testament preachers and writers often show that they stand firmly on the Old Testament law in making their judgments. They treat and utilize the standing rules of ethics as found in the Old Testament as though these rules were meant for them to keep—even though these rules were given a great many years earlier, before the advent of Christ our Savior. Particular instances of ethical decision-making in the New Testament illustrate once again that the commandments of God found in the Old Testament have not been discarded, repudiated, or ignored as somehow no longer authoritative and valid.

Use and Validity

Imagine that you wake up some morning to an exasperating problem: the plumbing under the kitchen sink needs repair, and a pool of water sits on the floor. After you mop up the mess, you stop and take thought as to what should be done to solve your plumbing problem. You think about calling a plumber, but reject that plan as too expensive and perhaps unnecessary. Upon reflection, you come to believe that you might very well be able to repair the plumbing yourself—if only you had some good direction. Therefore, you conclude that you will go down to the public library this morning and check out a self-help book on kitchen plumbing. Add one more feature to this scenario, namely, that you are reasonably informed as to the operating procedures of a public library. That is, you realize that the library is not open all of the time and that only those with library cards may have the privilege of checking out books.

So then, let us go back to your decision to check out a self-help book on plumbing this morning. What does such a decision tell us about your current beliefs? Among other things it tells us that you believe (rightly or wrongly) that the public library is open this morning, that you have a library card there, and that the library card is still valid. If you decided to use the library's self-help plumbing book this morning but knew either that the library was closed, that you had no card, or that your card was expired, you would most likely be irrational or a crook. People do not normally plan to use things which are closed down (for example, the library), non-existent, or expired (for example, your library card).

Likewise when you wait in line at the Mobil Oil gasoline station, fill your car's tank with gas, and then hand the attendant your credit card, you are expecting that the card is still valid. Whether you scrupulously check the expiration date on the credit card before submitting it for payment to the attendant or not, the very fact that you use the card reveals the assumed validity of that card. And the attendant's acceptance of that card shows that he too believes it to be a valid one. When something has expired or is no longer valid, we do not have the authority to use it. Dishonesty aside, an expired library card or invalid credit card is useless. On the other hand, the use of something indicates its validity.

Rules

Much of the same can be said regarding rules. Invalid or expired rules have lost their authority and as such are useless (except for purposes of historical illustration). A professor may draw laughs from his class by reading some of the city ordinances which were on the books a century ago, but a policeman would be out of place in trying to enforce them. A rule which has been repealed, amended, or replaced is no longer authoritative and cannot be used as a rule any longer. Thus if a rule is put to use, the assumption must be that it is (or is thought to be) a valid rule. When a football referee allows a touchdown to count which was accomplished by means of a forward pass, it is futile for the other team to complain against the pass on the grounds that the forward pass was once illegitimate in football. The old prohibition against the forward pass has been repealed, and football is now played by slightly different rules. When a baseball umpire does not allow a designated hitter to bat for the pitcher, it is evident that the umpire is taking National League rules to be valid instead of American League rules. The *use* of the particular rule instead of alternative rules demonstrates *the current authority and validity of the particular rule*. For this reason a driver who is stopped by a highway patrolman for travelling sixty-five miles per hour will not avoid a ticket by appealing to the former law which set the maximum speed at sixty-five. The use of the fifty-five mile per hour speed law by the courts and the police establishes the validity of this law over against the older one. We do not use expired rules if we are informed and honest. Looking at library cards and credit cards, and reflecting on civil rules and sports rules, we have seen that the use of them assumes their validity. Invalid cards and rules are unauthoritative.

We can now apply this reasonable insight to the practice of the New Testament speakers and writers. Like policemen and umpires, the inspired speakers and writers of the New Testament were called upon to make decisions on the basis of rules; they needed to draw moral judgments in particular situations. When that time came, which rules did they utilize? Did they—being infallibly informed in their utterances—ignore the moral rules (commandments) of the Old Testament as though they were expired, inapplicable, or invalid? What does New Testament usage of the Old Testament law tell us about that law's authority today?

Antinomian Doctrines

The current validity of the standing rules of Old Testament morality is either challenged or drastically reduced by many within the Christian church today. We find some who teach that the New Testament

Christian has nothing whatsoever to do with the law of the Old Testament; the believer, it is said, is not bound to the law at all. We find others who would put stiff limits on the extent of the Old Testament law's validity; the believer, they say, is bound to follow only a portion of the Old Testament moral code (usually the ten commandments).

But what does the inductively ascertained practice of the New Testament speakers and writers reveal about this? Do they ignore the law in moral judgments? In ethical decision-making do they restrict themselves to the Decalogue? Simply put, the answer is "No." The New Testament speakers and writers themselves are more than willing to put the Old Testament law — Decalogue and extra-Decalogue — into service in critical moral judgments. They do not treat the Old Testament commandments like an expired library card or a repealed speed limit. Just the opposite is the case! They make free and unexplained use of the Old Testament law, thereby assuming its moral authority for the New Testament age (extending from Christ to the consummation).

Moreover the use of the Old Testament law in New Testament moral judgments is quite thorough. It is not limited to a single New Testament writer (although that would be enough to establish the law's authority), to a single New Testament book (although, again, the authority of one infallible document is sufficient), or to one restricted Old Testament source. In contexts of moral application, New Testament citations and allusions are taken from portions of Genesis, Proverbs, Psalms, Isaiah, Jere-

miah, Habakkuk, and Zechariah; however, even
more frequently and consistently does the New Testament make moral judgments on the basis of the
Law portion of the Old Testament, citing Exodus
20, 21, 22, 23, Leviticus 11, 18, 19, 20, 21, 24, 25,
Numbers 18, 30, and Deuteronomy 1, 4, 5, 6, 8, 13,
15, 17, 19, 21, 22, 23, 24, 25, 27. The moral use of
these Old Testament passages will be found scat-
tered throughout Matthew, Mark, Luke, John,
Romans, 1 and 2 Corinthians, Galatians, Ephesians,
1 Timothy, Hebrews, James, 1 Peter, 1 John, and
Revelation. Therefore, the attempt made by some
Christian teachers today to reject or reduce the authority of the Old Testament law will over and over
again meet with embarrassment before the text of
the New Testament.

New Testament Moral Judgments

Let us examine some New Testament texts
where moral judgments can be found; they illustrate
how the Old Testament law was regarded as a valid
ethical standard. Specifically, we can see how the
current authority of the law was not viewed by them
as restricted to the Decalogue (ten commandments).

Jesus vs. His Opponents

We can begin for convenience with the discussions of Jesus with His opponents and inquirers. Of
course His greatest opponent was Satan, the temptor
who had led Adam astray from obedience to God.
Christ, the second Adam, directly encountered
Satan in a forty day period of temptation in the

wilderness. Satan repeatedly tempted Jesus to depart from the course of redemption laid down by the Father, and each time Jesus overcame the temptation by citing the authoritative word of God. For instance, Satan tried to entice Jesus into a test of God's care and fidelity, challenging Him to leap from the pinnacle of the temple. Many years earlier, Israel — also in the wilderness — had been lured into testing the care and fidelity of God (Ex. 17:1-7). As a result, the law of God recorded: "You shall not put Jehovah your God to the test, as you tested Him at Massah" (Deut. 6:16). Such a law would surely seem conditioned by its historical setting and restricted to its Jewish recipients. Yet in the face of the Satanic temptation Jesus cited this very commandment to thwart His adversary: "Jesus said unto him, 'Again it stands written, You shall not make a test of the Lord your God' " (Matt. 4:7). Clearly the law of God was deemed valid and was not restricted to the ten commandments.

Of course Jesus also deemed the ten commandments to be authoritative — but not uniquely so. When He was asked to judge which commandments should be kept in order to enter eternal life, He made use of a portion of the Decalogue (Matt. 19:16-19; Mark 10:17-19). However at the same time He included the relevant case law, "Do not defraud" (Mark 10:19, from Deut. 24:14), and the summary command, "Love your neighbor as yourself" (Matt. 19:19, from Lev. 19:18). He used the extra-Decalogical commands just as authoritatively as the Decalogue's own requirements. Indeed, when asked to judge which was the greatest commandment in the entire Old Testament, Jesus did not go to the ten commandments at all, but chose rather two laws outside of the Decalogue: love God with all of your heart, and love your neighbor as yourself (Mark 12:28-31, from Deut. 6:4-5 and Lev. 19:18).

Distilling the Old Testament's moral demand into these two particular extra-Decalogical laws was apparently already known and discussed in Jesus' day (Luke 10:25-28). It was a commonplace among the rabbis to distinguish between "heavy" and "light" commands in the Old Testament, the heavier laws being those from which moral commands could be deduced from others. Such rabbinic efforts can be traced to the Old Testament itself, where its precepts are summarized in a different number of principles by various writers: eleven by David (Ps. 15), six by Isaiah (Isa. 33:15), three by Micah (Micah 6:8), and one by Amos (Amos 5:4) and by Habakkuk (Hab. 2:4).

According to Jesus the "greatest" commandments—the "first of all"—on which "the whole law hangs" were the extra-Decalogical love commandments (Matt. 22:33, 36; Mark 12:28, 31). The problem with the Pharisees, said the Lord, was precisely that they attended to the minor details of the law (tithing) and "have left undone the *weightier* matters of the law—justice, and mercy, and faith" (Matt. 23:23), that is, "the love of God" (Luke 11:42). It is important at just this point that we pay attention to Jesus' words, for He does not encourage *exclusive* attention to the weightier love commandments of the

Old Testament law. He says quite precisely, "these you ought to have done and not to have left the other undone." Our obligation to the weightier matters of the law does not cancel our obligation to the minor details.

Consequently, the practice of Jesus does not encourage a disregard for the details of God's law, as though New Testament moral duty is bound to a small sub-section of the Old Testament law. Jesus was often challenged by the traditionalists (who took their authority from outside of the Scriptures) about His activities on the Sabbath. In His defense He would respond, "Have you not read in the law . . . ?" (Matt. 12:5; John 7:23), citing the Sabbath activity of the priests. Had the law been outmoded by His coming, of course, such a vindication of His behavior would have been baseless. Over and over again Jesus could show that the traditionalists — whose boast was in the details of the law — were actually violating and twisting the law's demands (for example, Matthew 5:21-48). On an occasion when Christ's disciples were accused by the Pharisees of violating their traditions, Christ replied that the traditionalists actually transgressed the commandments of God in order to preserve their traditions instead (Matt. 15:3, 6-9).

It is striking to note the specific illustration which Jesus chooses to use (among many available ones) in this particular moral judgment. He says that while the law of God requires honor for one's parents and death for those who dishonor them, the Pharisees allow a subterfuge by which one can withhold financial aid to his parents (Matt. 15:4-5). The Mosaic law which Christ holds up as valid — the standard by which to judge the Pharisaical performance — is the detail of the law (commonly ridiculed today) which requires the death penalty for cursing one's parents!

Jesus' Instructions to the Church

Another illustration of Jesus' use of the Old Testament's moral standards (outside the Decalogue) can be found when He lays down instructions for the new organization of the people of God. As the church replaced national Israel in the plan of redemption, it needed its own operating instructions, for instance regarding discipline. In the moral judgment delivered by Christ regarding this matter He asserted the demand of the Old Testament law: "at the mouth of two or three witnesses every word may be established" (Matt. 18:16, cf. John 8:17, based on the law at Deut. 17:6 and 19:15) — the same Old Testament law of legal evidence promoted by Paul (1 Tim. 5:9).

Sexual Ethics

The use of the Old Testament law in matters of sexual relations, payment to workers, and revenge toward enemies further substantiates *the New Testament dependence on the law's validity*. When Paul prohibits marrying an unbeliever, he cites the Old Testament requirement that unlike animals are not to be yoked together (2 Cor. 6:14, from Deut. 22:10). "Be not unequally yoked together" is a well-known verse

used by many pastors to discourage their young people from marrying outside the faith, and yet many of
these same pastors will elsewhere insist that the believer is not under the requirements of the Old Testament law!

When Paul was confronted with the wicked situation of incest within the church, his moral judgment
on the matter was taken from the Old Testament prohibition (1 Cor. 5:1, based on Lev. 18:8 and Deut.
22:30). Ask just about any evangelical pastor today
whether incest is immoral from a biblical standpoint,
and he will surely insist that it is — thereby enlisting
the moral standards of the Old Testament, even if he
proclaims elsewhere (and inconsistently) that they
are repealed and invalid. Or ask him about homosexuality. He may refer to Paul's words in Romans.
However, when Paul delivered this apostolic judgment as to the immorality of homosexuality, he simply reiterated the standard of the Old Testament
(Rom. 1:26-27, 32, from Lev. 18:22 and 20:13).

Economic Ethics

Turning from sexual to economic ethics we again
find that the New Testament makes unhindered use
of the Old Testament commandments in Christian
moral judgments. Paul's argument that congregations should pay their pastors is especially enlightening as to the extent of the law's validity. He argues
from the case law principle of the Old Testament
that "You shall not muzzle an ox as it treads" (1 Cor.
9:9, from Deut. 25:4), thereby revealing the assumed
contemporary authority of the laws outside the Deca-

logue. An invalid rule would be useless here. But even more striking is Paul's willingness to appeal to the moral principle embodied in one of the *ceremonial* laws! Pastors should earn their livelihood from the gospel ministry because priests derived their sustenance from the altar (1 Cor. 9:13-14, based on such texts as Lev. 6:16, 26; 7:6, 31ff.; Num. 5:9-10; 19:8-20, 31; Deut. 18:1). Pastors who wish to teach consistently the invalidity of the Old Testament law might accordingly stop drawing pay from their congregations.

In a related economic matter James delivered a moral judgment regarding the rich who fraudulently withhold their workers' pay, basing his judgment on the Old Testament law requiring prompt pay for workers (James 5:4, from Lev. 19:13 and Deut. 24:14-15). In financial matters, no less than in sexual matters, the New Testament practice was to utilize the Old Testament moral standards of God's law.

Interpersonal Relationships

The same is true for interpersonal matters. Few Christians will dispute the New Testament standard that we ought not to avenge ourselves but rather go to the one who wrongs us and show him his fault (Rom. 12:19; Matt. 18:15), and yet this standard is taken over directly from the Old Testament law at Leviticus 19:17-18. Another commonly endorsed New Testament ethical judgment which is in fact based on the Old Testament law is the injunction to care for one's enemies (Matt. 5:44; Rom. 12:20, rooted in the illustration of Ex. 23:4-5). As often as

Christians condemn private vengeance and hatred of one's enemies, they reaffirm the continuing authority of God's law (even if unwittingly).

Conclusion

One cannot escape the authoritative use of the Old Testament law in New Testament moral judgments. Upon reflection, one should recognize that such use teaches the full validity of God's law today. Invalid rules might be used in fallacious moral judgments—but not in inspired ones.

14

THE CATEGORIES OF GOD'S LAW

"By recognizing the various categories of God's Old Testament law we can readily understand the continuing validity of every stroke of God's commandments for today."

The law of the Lord is fully and forever valid; as such it holds moral authority over all men today, just as it did previously during the Old Testament era. This biblical truth has been substantiated in numerous ways in past studies — from cardinal doctrines of the Christian faith, direct assertions of God's word, and all three of the major perspectives on ethics: normative, motivational, and consequential (standard, motive, and goal). Christ spoke clearly and forcefully on the subject when He said, "Do not think that I have come to abrogate the law or the prophets; I have come not to abrogate, but to fulfill. For verily I say unto you, until heaven and earth pass away, until all things have come about, not one letter or stroke shall by any means pass away from the law. Therefore, whoever breaks the least of these commandments and teaches men so shall be called least in the kingdom of heaven" (Matt. 5:17-19).

Those who oppose keeping the law or paying attention to its details today have a great deal to explain and defend in light of the teaching of God's word—for instance the strong affirmation of the Lord quoted above. If the validity of the law (or a portion thereof) has expired in the New Testament, as some claim, then what are we to make of scriptural assertions that God does not alter His covenant word, does not allow subtraction from His commandments, is unchanging in His moral character (which the law reflects), and does not have a double-standard of right and wrong? Why then is the writing of the Old Testament law on our hearts central to the New Covenant? Why does the Bible say His commandments are everlasting? Why do New Testament writers say that the entire Old Testament is our instruction in righteousness and to be obeyed? Why do they cite its stipulations with authority and use them to bolster their own teaching? Why are we expected to model our behavior on Christ's, while we are told that He obeyed the law meticulously and perfectly? Why does the sanctifying work of the Holy Spirit entail the observance of God's law? Why does love summarize the law in particular? Why does faith establish the law for us to keep, and why does God's grace teach us to walk in the law's path of righteousness? Why are we told in numerous ways that the law brings blessings to those who heed it?

Why are the law's requirements never criticized or explicitly repudiated in the New Testament? Why are those who do not keep the law but claim to know the Savior called liars? God's inspired word says all of these things and more. What reply can the detractors from God's law today make in the face of such insurmountable evidence of the law's full validity?

The reply that is commonly, albeit fallaciously, made is that we find details in the Old Testament law which are somehow too strange or harsh to obey today, or we find particular requirements in the law which we in fact do not and should not observe in our day. Of course, such replies as these do not face the issues raised above. Surely God was completely aware of the law's details when He revealed those truths in His word which, as observed above, contradict the relaxing, ignoring, or disobeying of His law. If Scripture does not make an exception for us, we do not have the moral prerogative to make exceptions for ourselves when it comes to the law's authority over us. No extra-biblical standard, reason, or feeling can be legitimately used to depart from the law of God, for God's word has supreme and unchallengeable authority. If the Lord says that His commands are to be kept, no creature may draw His word into question. So then, the attempt to belittle obedience to God's law today by pointing to allegedly odd or harsh requirements in that law is doomed to theological failure. It also borders on disrespect for the Lawgiver whose holiness is transcribed for the creature in God's law. "O man, who are you who replies against God?" (Rom. 9:20). It is never our place to become judges of the law, for our calling is to be doers of the law (Jas. 4:11).

Nevertheless, there do seem to be Old Testament requirements which are not kept by New Testament Christians, and there are some legal provisions which seem culturally outdated or at least inapplicable to our modern world. How are we to accomodate that fact—without becoming judges of the law and without disregarding Christ's declaration that every minor detail of the law has enduring validity? The answer lies in recognizing the nature of the various Old Testament laws, seeing the kind of categories into which they fall. That is, it is necessary to understand the laws of God according to their own character, purpose, and function. Only in that way will the law be "lawfully used" (cf. 1 Tim. 1:8).

Moral and Ceremonial Laws

The most fundamental distinction to be drawn between Old Testament laws is between *moral* laws and *ceremonial* laws. (Two subdivisions within each category will be mentioned subsequently.) This is not an arbitrary or ad hoc division, for it manifests an underlying rationale or principle. Moral laws reflect the absolute righteousness and judgment of God, guiding man's life into the paths of righteousness; such laws define holiness and sin, restrain evil through punishment of infractions, and drive the sinner to Christ for salvation. On the other hand, ceremonial laws—or redemptive provisions—reflect the mercy of God in saving those who have violated His moral standards; such laws define the way of redemption, typify Christ's saving economy, and maintain the holiness (or "separation") of the redeemed community.

To illustrate the difference between these two kinds of law, the Old Testament prohibited stealing as a moral precept, but it also made the provision of the sacrificial system so that thieves could have their sins forgiven. When Christ came He obeyed perfectly every moral precept of God's law, thereby qualifying as our sinless Savior; in order to save us, He laid down His life as a sacrificial lamb in atonement for our transgressions, and thereby giving substance to the Old Testament foreshadows of redemption. While the moral law sets forth the perpetual obligation of all men if they are to be perfect as their Father in heaven is perfect, the ceremonial law is "the gospel in figures," proclaiming God's way of redemption for imperfect sinners.

The *ceremonial law* can be seen to have sub-divisions: (1) laws directing the redemptive process and therefore *typifying Christ*—for instance, regulations for sacrifice, the temple, the priesthood, etc., and (2) laws which taught the redemptive community its *separation from the unbelieving nations*—for instance, prohibitions on unclean meats (Lev. 20:22-26), on unequal yoking of animals (Deut. 22:10), and on certain kinds of mixing of seed or cloth (Deut. 22:9, 11).

None of these laws is observed today in the manner of the Old Testament shadows, and yet they are confirmed for us. The *principle* they taught is still valid. For instance, the ceremonial law prescribed the necessity of shed blood for atonement (Lev.

17:11), and accordingly when Christ made atonement for our sins once for all, "it was therefore *necessary*" that He shed His blood for us (Heb. 9:22-24); the Old Testament redemptive system called for a Passover lamb to be sacrificed, and Christ is that lamb for us (1 Cor. 5:7; 1 Peter 1:19). The ceremonial law separated Israel from the nations by requiring a separation to be drawn between clean and unclean meats and by prohibiting the unequal yoking of animals; in the New Testament the outward form of such laws has been surpassed—the spreading of the redeemed community to the Gentiles renders all meats clean (Acts 10), and the sacrifice of Christ has put the system of ordinances which separated the Jews and Gentiles out of gear (Eph. 2:11-20)—but their basic requirement of holy separation from the unclean world of unbelief is still confirmed and in force (2 Cor. 6:14—7:1). The ceremonial law is therefore confirmed forever by Christ, even though not kept in its shadow-form by New Testament believers.

The *moral law* of God can likewise be seen in two subdivisions, the divisions having simply a literary difference: (1) general or summary precepts of morality—for instance, the unspecified requirements of sexual purity and honesty, "thou shalt not commit adultery" and "thou shalt not steal," and (2) commands that specify the general precepts by way of illustrative application—for instance, prohibiting incest, homosexuality, defrauding one's workers, or muzzling the ox as he treads.

The Puritans termed these case-law applications of the Decalogue "judicial laws," and they correctly held that we are not bound today to keep these judicial laws as they are worded (being couched in the language of an ancient culture that has passed away) but only required to heed their underlying principles (or "general equity," as they called it). The Old Testament required that a railing be placed around one's roof as a safety precaution, since guests were entertained on the flat roofs of houses in that ancient society; with our sloped roofs today we do not need to have the same literal railing, but the general underlying principle might very well require us to have the fence around our backyard swimming pool—again, to protect human life.

There is abundant evidence that the New Testament authoritatively cited and applied these case-law illustrations to current situations. To use examples mentioned above, the New Testament echoes the Old Testament law in prohibiting incest (1 Cor. 5:1), homosexuality (Rom. 1:26-27, 32), defrauding employees (Mark 10:19), and muzzling the ox as he treads (1 Tim. 5:18). Many more examples of ethical injunctions outside of the Decalogue being enforced in the New Testament are available. Therefore, we conclude that Jesus has forever confirmed the moral laws of God, their summary expressions as well as their case-law applications.

By recognizing the various categories of God's Old Testament law we can readily understand the continuing validity of every stroke of God's commandments for today. It is simply a matter of properly reading the law itself.

15

CONTINUITY BETWEEN THE COVENANTS ON THE LAW

"God's eternal and righteous law is unalterable, according to the joint teaching of the Old and New Testaments."

The purpose of the next two chapters will simply be to compare and contrast the outlook on the law of God which we find in the Old and New Testaments. Granted, there are many ways to summarize the theology of law in either testament; the present is only one among many. However it hopefully serves a useful purpose: that of stressing the continuity between Old and New Testaments regarding God's law — over against contrary misconceptions fostered by some teachers — and of indicating salient points of discontinuity — over against the baseless fears of some that those who acknowledge the continuing validity of God's law today suppress or ignore important differences.

Continuity Between the Testaments

I. *God's law is perpetual in its principles.*

(A) The commandments of God are not deemed a uniquely Mosaic administration but as obliging man from the beginning.

(1) *Before man's fall into sin,* God delivered to him commandments which were his moral obligation, for instance the creation ordinances of marriage (Gen. 2:24), labor (Gen. 2:15), and the Sabbath (Gen. 2:1-3), as well as the cultural mandate of dominion over creation (Gen. 1:28). Paul too would view the standards of morality as in force from the very beginning, being constantly communicated through general revelation (Rom. 1:18-21). In particular, the creation ordinances (for example, Matt. 19:5) and cultural mandate (for example, 1 Cor. 10:31) are applied in the New Testament.

(2) The Old Testament shows that, as the New Testament teaches (Rom. 5:13-14), *between Adam and Moses,* law was in the world. The Adamic covenant establishes a marital order (Gen. 3:16) and the requirement of labor (Gen. 3:19) which are both authoritative in the New Testament (1 Tim. 2:12-14; 2 Thes. 3:10). The Noahic covenant reaffirmed the cultural mandate (Gen. 9:1) and revealed God's standard of retribution against murderers (Gen. 9:6), which are again valid in the New Testament (for example, Rom. 13:4). In the Abrahamic covenant we see that Abraham had commandments, statutes, and laws to keep (Gen. 18:19; 26:5), and the New Testament commends to us Abraham's obedient faith (Jas. 2:21-23; Heb. 11:8-19).

Moreover, prior to the special revelation of the Mosaic law we can see the perpetual validity of its moral standards in the example of God's judgment on Sodom (Gen. 19), which was punished for violating the case law against homosexuality (Lev. 18:23) — for their "lawless deeds" according to the New Testament (2 Peter 2:6-8). Indeed, according to Paul, all men know God's moral standards through general revelation — showing "the work of the law written in their hearts" (Rom. 2:14-15). This universal communication of God's law is as broad as His ethical demands, not being restricted narrowly to the Ten Commandments (for example, Rom. 1:32, where condemned homosexuals are said to know "the ordinance of God").

(B) The principles of God's law are perpetual because they reflect the character of God, who is unchanging.

Leviticus 20:7-8 declares, "Be holy, for I am Jehovah your God, and you shall keep My statutes and do them"; this is how God's people sanctify themselves — becoming holy as God is holy (1 Peter 1:15-16) or imitating His perfection (Matt. 5:48, in the context of the law's demands). The Old Testament teaches that the law of God is perfect (Ps. 19:7), being holy, just, and good like God (Deut. 12:28; Neh. 9:13), and the New Testament viewpoint is the same: the law is perfect (Jas. 1:25), holy, just, and good (Rom. 7:12).

II. *God's law is thorough in its extent.*

(A) His commandments apply to matters of the

heart, and not simply to external affairs.

In the Old Testament God required His people to seek Him with all their hearts (Deut. 4:29) and to circumcise their hearts (Deut. 10:16), even as the New Testament continues to show that we are to love Him with all of our hearts (Matt. 22:37) and submit to His law in our thoughts, attitudes, and intentions (for example, Matt. 5:21-48).

(B) God's law applies to every area of life.

The commandments of God called His people to love Him with everything they had (Deut. 6:4-6), throughout the day (v. 7), at home and away from home (v. 9), whether in thought or deed (v. 8). Indeed, man was to live by every word from God's mouth (Deut. 8:3, 6). Likewise the New Testament requires that every aspect of man's life and being be given over to the love of God (Matt. 22:37) and that God's people demonstrate their holiness "in all manner of living" (1 Peter 1:15-16).

(C) God's law is a standard for all nations (not simply Israel).

Deuteronomy 4:6, 8 clearly taught that the commandments delivered by Moses to Israel were to be her *wisdom in the sight of the nations,* who would exclaim "what great nation is there that has statutes and ordinances so righteous as all this law?" Similarly Paul indicates that the standards of God's law are declared through natural revelation and are binding upon *all* men (Rom. 1:32; 2:14-15). Because the nations once occupying Canaan violated the standards of God's law, God would punish them by expelling them from the land (Lev. 18:24-27) — even as He would expel Israel if she violated His laws (Deut. 30:17-18). The moral standard and the judgment on disobedience were the same between Israel and the nations.

Accordingly, Paul teaches that all men, Jews and Gentiles, have sinned by violating God's law (Rom. 2:9; 19-20), and Jude declares that God will judge all ungodly men for all of their ungodly deeds (Jude 14-15). Where the Old Testament taught that "Righteousness exalts a nation, but sin is a reproach to any people" (Prov. 14:34), the New Testament teaches that whatever Christ has commanded is to be propagated to the nations (Matt. 28:20). *God's law binds all men at all times in all places.* To this point we have seen that the Old and New Testament agree perfectly that the law of God is perpetual in its principles — not being uniquely Mosaic, but reflecting the eternal character of God — and thorough in its extent — touching matters of the heart, applying to all areas of life, and binding all mankind to obedience. At this juncture it will be important to add that:

III. *God's law is complementary to salvation by grace.*

(A) The law was not to be used as a way of justification.

The Old Testament teaches that in God's sight "no man living is righteous (or justified)," for if God marks iniquities no man can stand (Ps. 143:2; 130:3). Instead, "the just shall live by faith" (Hab. 2:4). The Psalmist saw that "Blessed is the man unto whom

Jehovah imputes not iniquity," and "He that trusts in Jehovah, lovingkindness will compass him about" (Ps. 32:2, 10). Old Testament saints were not saved by law-obedience but by faith in the coming Savior, typified in the sacrifices of the Old Testament system. Likewise the New Testament declares in no uncertain terms that "by the works of the law shall no flesh be justified in His sight" (Rom. 3:20). Indeed, "if righteousness is through the law, then Christ died for nothing" (Gal. 2:21). God's law is the standard of righteousness, but because sinners cannot conform to that standard their salvation must come by God's grace through faith (Eph. 2:8-9). This was true in both Old and New Testaments.

(B) Obedience to God's law is harmonious with grace and saving faith.

The Old Testament indicates that God's law was specially revealed to Israel in the context of His redeeming and delivering His people from bondage (Ex. 19:4; 20:2); those who were willing to keep His law had already been shown His grace. In this vein David could sing, "Grant me thy law graciously" (Ps. 119:29)—feeling no tension between a proper use of God's grace and law. Those who were justified by faith in the Old Testament, such as Abraham and Rahab, were those who were so *renewed by God's grace* that they were *willing to obey His demands* (cf. James 2:21-25). Those who were justified and living by faith, due to the grace of God, desired to obey the commandments of God out of respect for His authority, love of His purity, and gratitude for His salvation.

The same holds true for saints in the New Testament. Paul says that we have not been saved *by* good works, but we have been saved *for* good works — that is, in order to live obediently before God (Eph. 2:10). God's grace teaches us to renounce lawless deeds (Titus 2:11-14), and by faith we actually establish — rather than nullify — what was taught in the law of God (Rom. 3:31).

IV. *God's law is central to His one covenant of grace.*

(A) The law can epitomize or stand for the covenant itself. We read in Genesis 17:10, 14 that circumcision could represent the very covenant itself that God made with Abraham. In like manner, the stipulations of the Mosaic law could be used to stand for the covenant itself, as in Exodus 24:3-8 (cf. Heb. 9:19-20). Just as circumcision is the covenant, so also is the law God's covenant. This is why the tables of *law* and commandments which God gave to Moses on Mount Sinai (Ex. 24:12) can actually be called "the tables of the *covenant*" (Deut. 9:9, 11, 15). Accordingly, when Jeremiah speaks of the New Covenant which is to come, he indicates that the law of God is central to its provisions: "I will put my laws into their mind, and on their heart will I write them" (Jer. 31:33). This is quoted when the New Testament reflects upon the character of the New Covenant (Heb. 8:10), using these words as a summary for the whole (Heb. 10:16). Concern for the covenant, then, entails concern for the law of God in both Old and New Testaments.

(B) The law given through Moses served the Abrahamic covenant of promise, rather than being antithetical to it.

According to the Old Testament, it is precisely as the God of Abraham, and it is just because of the covenant made with Abraham, that God dealt with Moses in a covenantal fashion (Ex. 2:24; 3:6). The exodus or deliverance granted to the Israelites through Moses was a realization of the promise made to Abraham (Ex. 6:1-8). God had promised in the Abrahamic covenant to be a God to Abraham and his seed, who would become God's people (Gen. 17:7-8). This same blessing was held forth in God's deliverance through Moses (Ex. 6:7). In particular, this Abrahamic promise would be the reward for conformity to the Mosaic law: "If you walk in my statutes, and keep my commandments, and do them, . . . I will be your God, and you shall be my people" (Lev. 26:3, 12). The Old Testament did not recognize an antagonism between the Abrahamic covenant of promise and the Mosaic covenant of law. Neither does the New Testament.

Paul reflects with inspired accuracy on the relationship between the Abrahamic promise and the Mosaic law (cf. Gal. 3:17) and asks, "Is the law then against the promises of God?" His answer is decisive: "May it never be!" (Gal. 3:21). The law rather served to bring about the fulfillment of the promise made with Abraham (Gal. 3:19, 22, 29). The Mosaic law which established the commonwealth of Israel at Sinai is deemed by Paul as one of "the covenants of *the promise*" (Eph. 2:12). Throughout Scripture the law is congruent with the promise.

(C) Likewise, the Abrahamic promise which is realized in Christ serves the purposes of the Mosaic law.

The Old Testament perspective was that *the people who enjoyed the promise ought to obey the law of God.* It was expected that when Israel received what "the God of your fathers has promised unto you," the people would "keep all his statutes and his commandments" as revealed by Moses (Deut. 6:1-3). Likewise the New Testament sees those who belong to Christ —the one to whom Abraham's promise was given (Gal. 3:16)—as the seed of Abraham and heirs according to promise (Gal. 3:7, 29). They receive the promise by faith and thus should not desire to be under the law as a way of justification lest they fall from grace (Gal. 3:2, 6-14, 24-26; 4:21; 5:4).

However, those who enjoy the Abrahamic promise in Christ do so by a faith working through love (Gal. 5:6), which is to say *a faith that obeys the law* (Gal. 5:13-14)—a faith that walks by the Spirit and thereby does not violate the law (Gal. 5:16-23). God's Son of promise makes us to walk after the Spirit so that we keep the ordinance of the law (Rom. 8:3-4). Therefore, we observe that *the promise serves the law,* even as *the law serves the promise,* and this reciprocal relation is revealed in both the Old and New Testaments alike. The law plays an integral role throughout God's one covenant of grace.

V. *God's law is taken by His people as a redemptive token*

and delight.

The preceding discussion of the law of God has focused on its objective character and function. It is important that we also take note of the subjective attitude which is expressed toward the law of God in both Old and New Testaments. The negative polemic against the law which is often heard today cannot be squared with the feeling and evaluation of the inspired biblical writers. According to them:

(A) Obedience to the law is their token of redemption, proof of their love, and sign of their dedication to the Lord.

The Old Testament taught that the very meaning of God's law and obedience to it was that God had delivered His people (Deut. 6:20-25; for example, 5:15). Indeed, not keeping the commandments of God was identified as forgetting one's redemption (Deut. 8:11-17), and it was clear that salvation was far from those who did not desire God's statutes (Ps. 119:155). Similarly in the New Testament, where life eternal is to "know Christ" (John 17:3), we indicate that "we know him if we keep his commandments," and it is a lie to say that one knows Christ who does not keep his commandments (1 John 2:3-4).

The Old Testament said that those who love the Lord will obey His commandments (Deut. 10:12-13), and New Testament love for the Lord is proved in the same way (John 14:15; 1 John 5:3). Dedication to God and His purposes was signaled in the Old Testament by adherence to God's law (Deut. 26:17; Joshua 22:5). Things are not different in the New

Testament, where those who choose to follow Christ rather than the beast are identified as "those who keep the commandments of God and the faith of Jesus" (Rev. 12:17; 14:12). In either Old or New Testament it would be unthinkable for a redeemed saint, who loved the Lord and was dedicated to Him, to spurn, criticize, or disobey the law of God.

(B) God's law was to be loved as a delight and blessing.

Although men may scoff, the delight of the godly man is found in the law of the Lord (Ps. 1:2; 119:16); that man is happy, said the Old Testament, who greatly delighted in God's law (Ps. 112:1). Paul's New Testament viewpoint was identical: "I delight in the law of God after the inward man" (Rom. 7:22). To John the law of God was such a joy that he could declare, "His commandments are not burdensome" (1 John 5:3b). It is sin—that is, according to both testaments, violation of God's covenants (Joshua 7:11; Isa. 24:5; 1 John 3:4)—that is detested by God's people, for it brings death (Rom. 6:23). Apart from man's sinful inability, the law itself is graciously ordained rather unto life (Lev. 18:5; Neh. 9:29; Ezk. 20:11, 13, 21; cf. Prov. 3:7-8).

It is not the Old Testament only that recognizes this fact. Paul discerns the connection between obedience to the law and life in the Spirit (Rom. 8:2-4, 6-7, 12-14) and confesses that, apart from his sinful corruption, *the law is meant to communicate life* (Rom. 7:10). Anything that is against the law's demands, then, is also against health-giving (sound) doctrine, according to 1 Timothy 1:8-10 (cf. 6:3). God gave us His law for our good, and for that reason Old and New Testament writers rejoice in it. It is to our shame if we do not emulate their attitude.

VI. *God's law is eternal and is not to be altered.*

In a day when many view the law of the Lord as arbitrary, expendable, or temporary in its authority for the life of man, it is highly valuable to observe the outlook of the inspired writers. Moses wrote that *forever* it would go well with God's people to observe the commandments which He revealed (Deut. 12:28). David exclaimed that "All his precepts are sure; they are established forever and ever" (Ps. 111:7-8; cf. 119:152). Indeed, the eternal authority of God's commands characterizes each and every one of them: "Every one of thy righteous ordinances endureth forever" (Ps. 119:160). Looking unto the fearful day of the Lord when the wicked will be consumed with fire (Mal. 4:1), the prophet Malachi pronounces as one of the final words of the Old Testament, "Remember the law of Moses my servant" (4:4).

However, in the pages of the New Testament we hear the words of one who is far greater than Moses, David, or any prophet of old. Their testimony to the eternal authority of God's law is pale in comparison to the absolutely clear and utterly unchallengeable declaration of Jesus Christ that God's commandments—each and every one—is everlastingly valid: "Truly I say unto you, until heaven and earth pass away, until everything has come about, one letter or one stroke shall by no means pass away from the law" (Matt. 5:18). The Old and New Testaments unite in this doctrine.

The voice of the two Testaments is further united in saying that God's law is not to be altered. David recognized that God commands only what is just and right, and thus to depart from His commands is to deviate from moral integrity. "I esteem all thy precepts concerning all things to be right, and I hate every false way. . . . All thy commandments are righteousness" (Ps. 119:128, 172). To change or ignore any of God's commands is necessarily to create an unrighteous or unjust pattern for behavior. Therefore the law itself guards against alterations within itself: "You shall not add unto the word which I command you, neither shall you diminish from it, in order that you may keep the commandments of Jehovah your God" (Deut. 4:2; cf. 12:32). No man has the prerogative to tamper with the requirements laid down by God. Only God himself, the Law-giver, has the authority to abrogate or alter His commandments. Yet the testimony of God incarnate in the New Testament is that the law is not to be changed, even with the momentous event of His coming: "Do not think that I came to abrogate the law or the prophets. . . . Therefore whoever shall break one of the least of these commandments and shall teach men so shall be called least in the kingdom of heaven" (Matt. 5:17, 19). God's eternal and righteous law is unalterable, according to the joint teaching of the Old and New Testaments.

VII. *Therefore, we are obligated to keep the whole law today.*

Anyone who suggests, without authorization from the word of God, that some law of the Old Testament is not binding upon our behavior today would fall under the double censure of both the Old Testament and New Testament writers. Such a suggestion would contradict the perpetuity and extent of God's law as taught in both testaments; it would evidence forgetfulness of God's mercies, violate the covenant, and deprive God's people of one of their delights. Such a suggestion would stand diametrically opposed to the eternality and immutability of the law as set forth in the Old and New Testaments. To challenge the law without Biblically revealed direction from the Lord is to grieve and challenge Him, so that those who do so will be demoted within God's kingdom.

Unless Scripture itself shows us some change with respect to God's law or our obedience to it, the principle which governs our attitude and behavior should be the same as the Bible's categorical assumption—namely, that our instruction in righteous behavior is found in every Old Testament Scripture (1 Tim. 3:16-17), every point of the law (Jas. 2:10), even the least commandment (Matt. 5:19; 23:23), every word (Matt. 4:4), and every letter (Matt. 5:18). This is clear from the major points—to which both Old Testament and New Testament give assent—that have been reviewed about the law above. Given these agreed-upon points, we have no reason to expect that the New Testament would categorically or silently release the believer from his moral duty to God's law.

Conclusion

To summarize: we must assume continuity of moral duty between the Old Testament and New Testament. Accordingly, by operating upon this biblical assumption, *the burden of Scriptural proof lies directly and heavily upon anyone who would deny the validity or the relevant authority of some particular Old Testament stipulation for our day.* The next time you hear someone say, "we need not follow that commandment because it is the *Old* Testament law," you should say to yourself (if not also to him). "That kind of assertion will require some explanation and clear biblical proof before any faithful Christian can accept it." Faithful and inspired authors of Scripture—both Old and New Testaments—wrote to just the opposite effect.

16

DISCONTINUITY BETWEEN THE COVENANTS ON THE LAW

"The New Covenant surpasses the Old in glory, power, realization, and finality."

What has been said above does not in the least deny that there are some forms of discontinuity between the Old Testament and the New Testament — that is, between the *Old Covenant* and the *New Covenant* — regarding the law of God. What it does indicate is that any such discontinuity must be taught *by God's word* and not be brought as a categorical, theological assumption *to* God's word. We can turn now to such Biblically grounded discontinuities between the Old and New Covenants. Because the law of God plays a central role in His covenantal dealings with His people, it is altogether appropriate that the contrast between these two covenants should have a bearing on our relationship to that law.

I. *The New Covenant surpasses the Old Covenant in glory.*

(A) While the Old Covenant was fundamentally a ministration of condemnation and death, the New Covenant is a ministration of righteousness and life.

Paul reflects upon the distinctives of the New Covenant in 2 Corinthians 3, proving that anyone who exalts the law over the gospel (as did the legalistic Judaizers)—anyone who is so absorbed in the commandments that he obscures or overlooks the good news of redemption—has made a grave mistake. The New Covenant, teaches Paul, far outshines in glory the law of the Old Covenant. The law certainly has its glory (2 Cor. 3:9, 11), but despite that glory, what stands out in the Old Covenant is the feature of condemnation which brings death (3:6, 7, 9).

The law is good—indeed, ordained unto life. However, the sinfulness of man works through the good law to produce death (Rom. 7:12-16). The outstanding feature of the Old Covenant to Paul's mind was the external tables of the law which, although they *commanded* good things, *could not confer* good things. These external ordinances necessarily condemn all unrighteous men and demand their death: as Paul said, "the letter kills" (2 Cor. 3:6). There is no way that sinful men can be justified by doing the law (Gal. 2:16; 3:11).

When Moses returned from receiving the law his face shone with the glory of God, and after reading the law to the people, he needed to put up a veil over his face for the sake of the people (2 Cor. 3:7, 13). Paul sees in this fact the double character of the Old

Covenant: (1) it was glorious, but (2) it continually accused and condemned those who, due to sin, could not endure to behold the glory of Moses' face.

Nevertheless, when Moses appeared with Christ on the Mount of Transfiguration, it was only the face of the Savior which shone with God's glory. Christ, the mediator of the New Covenant, "has been counted worthy of more glory than Moses" (Heb. 3:3). The Old Covenant law condemned and killed, but by contrast Christ takes away the curse of the law by enduring its penalty and gives His life-producing Spirit to create an obedient heart in us. Accordingly, the New Covenant is distinctively "a ministration of the Spirit" or "a ministration of righteousness" (2 Cor. 3:8, 9) which "imparts life" (3:6). Christ "has done what the law, weakened by the flesh, could not do" (Rom. 8:3). Accordingly, Paul says that, in contrast to the covenant epitomized by tables of stone, the New Covenant "exceeds in glory" (2 Cor. 3:9).

The Old Covenant law commanded good things, but only the gospel could fully confer them; the righteousness demanded by the law was only supplied with the redemptive work of Christ. Thus, the New Covenant has a greater glory than the Old. The old declared the law and thereby condemned. The new satisfies the law and makes us right with God. The leading and far greater glory of the New Covenant is that it secures the righteousness of God's people through God's Son and Spirit, rather than serving primarily to condemn sinfulness. The latter function required only the glory, genuine though it be, of stone tablets; the former required God to manifest the glory of His only-begotten Son, full of grace and truth (John 1:14). Hence Calvin said, "the law, however glorious in itself, has no glory in the face of the gospel's grandeur" (Commentary at 2 Cor. 3:10). As such the approach of the New Covenant believer to God's law is significantly different from that of the Old Covenant believer. Since the *threat* of the law has now been decisively removed through Christ's expiation and the Holy Spirit's indwelling, the law can be more fully a delight to the believer today.

(B) The New Covenant provides the believer with a greater confidence in approaching God.

The Old Covenant law promised forgiveness to the sinner on the basis of animal sacrifices, but the tentativeness of this arrangement was evident from the fact that mere animals were offered up and from the fact that sacrifices were repeated over and over again (Heb. 10:4ff.). There was still some distance between the believer and God, for only the High Priest could come before the very presence of God in the Holy of Holies once a year. A veil separated the people from their God. But with the sacrificial work of Christ which cleanses New Covenant believers the veil has been torn in two (Mark 15:58; cf. Heb. 10:20). Through Christ, the mediator of the New Covenant, we can have bold access to the throne of grace. The way into the holy place was not manifest under the Old Covenant (Heb. 9:8), but under the New Covenant we have "boldness to enter into the holy place by the blood of Jesus" (Heb. 10:19; cf. 4:15-16; 6:18-20). The assurance of forgiveness, the purity of the believer, and the nearness of God are far greater in the New Covenant than anything the Old Covenant law could secure. So Calvin rightly remarks: "The person who still holds to or wishes to restore the shadows of the law not only obscures the glory of Christ but also deprives us of a tremendous blessing, in that he puts a distance between us and God, to approach whom freedom has been granted us by the gospel" (Commentary at Heb. 7:19).

(C) Unlike the Old Covenant, the New Covenant has a permanent and unfading glory.

In 2 Corinthians 3, Paul likens the glory of the Old Covenant with its law to the glory which shone in Moses' face after receiving that law (vv. 7, 13). What Paul repeats over and over again is that this glory was "passing away" (vv. 7, 11, 13) and had to be veiled (vv. 7, 13-16). But the New Covenant has a transforming glory seen in the face of Christ (3:18; 4:4, 6); this glory is beheld with unveiled face, permanently and progressively making us over into the same image "from glory to glory." Moses mirrored the glory of God only intermittently with a fading glory—such was the excellence of the Old Covenant law. We constantly mirror the unfading glory of Christ who is the very image of God. Indeed, "we rejoice in our hope of sharing the glory of God" (Rom. 5:2). Distinctive to the New Covenant is a glory surpassing the law, a glory which can be gazed upon, as well as mirrored, without interruption.

What we have found is that the New Testament writers can set the New Covenant over against the Old Covenant by taking the law as their point of departure. Believers today have greater benefits than Old Covenant believers could have in their relationship to the law. The law stood for the threat of death, God at some distance, and a fading glory. In the New Covenant the threat is removed, God draws nearer, and the glory is permanent. This provides us with a different context within which to use the law of God and determines the attitude with which we must approach the law. To be content with the law itself or to emphasize it over and above the gospel would evidence a terribly perverted sense of judgment. The New Covenant puts the law into proper perspective by showing us a far greater glory than the law possessed.

II. *The New Covenant surpasses the Old Covenant in power.*

(A) The New Covenant provides us with further and stronger motivations to obey the law.

Everything found in the Scripture is for our instruction in righteousness and our spiritual discipline (cf. 2 Tim. 3:16-17), and thus we cannot be perfectly furnished unto all good works without paying attention to all aspects of scriptural revelation — its history (for example, 1 Cor. 10:6, 11), its promises (for example, John 14:16-18), its wisdom (for example, Jas. 3:13-18), its prayers (for example, Acts 4:24-31), its praise (for example, Rev. 5:9-14), etc. Each of these aspects functions to equip us better for righteous living.

The New Covenant provides us with further Scripture that tells us of God's redemptive work with its accomplishment and application. It should serve to make us ever more grateful for what God has done. Redemption, new creation, indwelling of the Spirit, unity of the body—these and many more themes in the New Covenant's revelation are motivations for godliness which go *beyond* the motivations available to Old Covenant saints. Ethical exhortations in the New Testament are commonly founded on consideration of these New Covenant benefits.

(B) Unlike the Old Covenant law, the New Covenant empowers obedience to the revealed pattern of righteousness.

Looking again at 2 Corinthians 3, where Paul contrasts the Old Covenant with the New, we read that Paul's New Covenant ministry had the effect of changing the hearts of his hearers—as though Christ himself had written upon their hearts (v. 3). God had written the law with His own finger upon two tables of stone at Mount Sinai, but Jeremiah looked forward to the day of the New Covenant when God's law would be written upon men's hearts (Jer. 31:33) —hearts made of responsive flesh rather than stone (Ezk. 11:19-20; 36:26). Proverbs teaches that "out of the heart are the issues of life." With the law written upon man's heart he would finally be able to walk in God's commandments and do them.

Although the Spirit worked in the lives of Old Covenant believers to help them obey the law of

God, He did so in a way which was both limited and provisional — looking ahead to the great day of Pentecostal power. Paul in 2 Corinthians 3 notes that the Spirit is the agent of the writing done upon the New Covenant believer's heart (v. 3). The letter of the Old Covenant brought death, but the Spirit of the New Covenant communicates life and righteousness (vv. 6:8-9, 18). What was once external and accusing (the law written on tables of stone) is now internal and activating (the law written on tables of the heart). We are told that "the law made nothing perfect" (Heb. 7:19), but the new and "better covenant" has "better promises" — in particular the *internalization of the law* by means of Christ's sacrificial and priestly work so that the law is kept (Heb. 8:6-10). The "eternal covenant" makes us perfect in every good work to do God's will (Heb. 13:20-21).

We find here one of the most dramatic differences between the Old Covenant law and the New Covenant gospel. The New Covenant accomplishes what the law required but gave no ability to perform. P. E. Hughes expresses the point well: "The 'fault' of the Old Covenant lay, not in its essence, which, as we have said, presented God's standard of righteousness and was propounded as an instrument of life to those who should keep it, but in its inability to justify and renew those who failed to keep it, namely, the totality of fallen mankind. The New Covenant went literally to the heart of the matter, promising man, as it did, a new and obedient heart and the grace truly to love God and his fellow man (Ezk. 11:19f.)."[1] In the

---

1. Philip E. Hughes, *A Commentary on the Epistle to the Hebrews* (Grand Rapids, Michigan: Eerdmans, 1977), pp. 297-98.

preceding outline we already find highly significant discontinuities between the Old and New Covenants regarding the law of God. The New Covenant surpasses the Old Covenant law, according to the New Testament scriptures, both in glory and power. The New Covenant puts the law into perspective and puts it into practice—overcoming its basic threatening character, insecurity, and fading glory by providing further motivations to obedience as well as the power to comply with the law's demands.

III. *The New Covenant Reality Supersedes the Old Covenant Shadows.*

(A) The New Covenant secures the redemption foreshadowed in the Old Covenant.

One of the greatest points of dissimilarity between the Old Covenant and the New Covenant is found in the area of redemptive rituals, for example the Old Testament sacrifices, priesthood, temple, covenant signs, etc. The way in which the laws pertaining to such redemptive ritual were observed prior to the coming of Christ is much different than the way in which they are observed today. By bringing in the substance foreshadowed in the Old Covenant and realizing the hope anticipated in the Old Covenant, the New Covenant gives us a new perspective on the laws which regulated expiation, priestly service, and the like.

Whereas the Old Covenant believer looked ahead to the work of the Savior and showed faith by observing the redemptive ritual of the Old Covenant, the New Covenant believer looks back upon the finished work of the Savior and shows faith by clinging to Him for salvation totally apart from the old ceremonies. From Scripture it is evident that the New Covenant arrangement is better than the Old Covenant pertaining to redemption, and accordingly those redemptive laws have been made *outwardly inoperative.* Here is a discontinuity between the Covenants which can be supressed only at the cost of totally misunderstanding the teaching of the New Testament.

The logic of the writer of Hebrews is that, if a *New* Covenant has been given, then it must be a *better* covenant which as such makes the Old Covenant *outmoded.* Moses himself witnessed to the provisionary glory of the administration of God's grace found in the Pentateuch by looking beyond the shadow and promise to the realization to come (Heb. 3:5b). Likewise, Jeremiah spoke for God of a "New" covenant to come, and that very fact (according to the author of Hebrews) indicated that already the Mosaic administration was deemed obsolete and passing away, ready to vanish (Heb. 8:13).

Saying this leads the author of Hebrews right into a discussion of the first covenant's ritual ordinances (9:1ff.). The work of Christ is in every way superior to these. He is "the surety of a better covenant," "a better hope" (7:22, 19) because His priesthood is everlasting (7:21, 24-25), and His sacrifice of Himself is totally efficacious (7:26-28). The very repetition of the Old Covenant sacrifices demonstrated that they were temporary and imperfect (Heb. 10:4ff.). The superiority of Christ's ministry over the Old Covenant's Levitical ministry is found in the fact that Christ's priestly work is exercised in the true, heavenly tabernacle rather than in the earthly, shadowy one (Heb. 8:2-5). The priestly work carried on in the earthly tabernacle was figurative or anticipatory (Heb. 9:19), whereas Christ's ministry is the realization carried on in a greater tabernacle in heaven (9:11-12, 23-24). The Levitical ritual of the Old Covenant revealed by Moses was *parabolic* of the *present* order in the New Covenant (9:9a). In themselves the priestly rituals of the Old Covenant could not perfect the conscience as Christ does (9:9b); thus they were necessarily temporary, used until the time that everything is made right (9:10). The Old Covenant saints greeted the promises of God from afar (Heb. 11:13). By contrast, Christ fulfills the promises and *secures* redemption, the promised inheritance, and transforming power by His saving work (9:15; cf. 8:6-10). The redemptive rituals of the Old Testament law, then, could not perfect the believer; they were but a *shadow* of the good things *to come* (Heb. 10:1).

With the accomplished work of the Redeemer now in the past, we no longer use or apply the Old Testament laws regulating sacrifices, the priesthood, etc. in the same way. Discontinuity is definitely to be observed. And it is precisely the word of God which instructs us to see an *altered application* of those laws; indeed, we are warned against reverting back to the imperfection of the outmoded administration of God's grace in the Old Testament Levitical system. It is not surprising that the earliest Christians were accused of opposing the temple and the Mosaic law's rituals (for example, Acts 6:14; 21:28). The New Covenant word teaches that *some* of God's Old Covenant ordinances were not intended to be continuously observed in the same manner throughout redemptive history. With the coming of the Savior and His perfect priestly work, necessarily the Levitical priesthood has been changed (Heb. 7:12). Hence the sacrifices, feasts, etc. of the old order are not binding upon the believer today in their shadow forms (cf. Col. 2:13-17). They are *observed today* by *faith in Christ*.

(B) The New Covenant Redefines the Covenant People of God.

Under the Old Covenant order, Israel was constituted as a nation and adopted as the people of God, but under the New Covenant the people of God is an international body comprised of those who have faith in Christ. The kingdom has been taken from the Jews (Matt. 8:11-12; 21:41-43; 23:37-38; 1 Cor. 14:21-22), and the church is now "the Israel of God" (Gal. 6:16), "the commonwealth of Israel" (Eph. 2:12), the "kingdom of priests" (1 Peter 2:9), the "twelve tribes" of the Dispersion (Jas. 1:1; 1 Peter 1:1), and the seed of Abraham (Gal. 3:7, 29). Faithful Israel of old is included within one household of God comprising the church (Heb. 3:1-6); Israelites and Gentiles are separate branches, part of one olive tree of faith (Rom. 11:17-18). Thus, *the New Testament church is the restoration of Israel* (Acts 15:15-20), and the New Covenant to be made with Israel and Judah is actually made with the apostles who are foundational to the church (Luke 22:20; cf. Eph. 2:20). This biblically grounded redefinition of the people of God brings with it some corresponding alterations in the application of the Old Testament law.

(1) Because the New Covenant does not define God's people as an earthly nation among others, it does not require political loyalty to national Israel as did the Old Covenant (Phil. 3:20). Christ's kingdom, unlike Old Testament Israel, is not to be defended with the sword (John 18:36; cf. 2 Cor. 10:4).

(2) Because the significance of Canaan as the promised land of inheritance has passed away with the establishment of the kingdom which it foreshadowed (cf. Gal. 3:16; cf. Gen. 13:15; Heb. 11:8-10; Eph. 1:14; 1 Peter 1:4), Old Covenant laws which are directly concerned with this land (for example, division of the land into family portions, locations of the cities of refuge, the Levirate institution) will find a changed application in our day.

(3) The separation from unholy peoples required by God through the dietary laws, which symbolized this separation by a separation made between clean and unclean meats (cf. Lev. 20:22-26), will no longer be observed by avoidance of the Gentiles (Acts 10) or typified by abstaining from certain foods (Mark 7:19; Acts 10:15; Rom. 14:17). For the Christian, this now requires separation from any ungodliness or compromising unbelief anywhere they may be found (2 Cor. 6:14-18).

IV. *The New Covenant surpasses the Old Covenant in finality.*

(A) It surpasses the Old Covenant law in *clarity.* With the giving of further relevant information in the scriptures of the New Covenant, God's moral requirements are made even clearer to us. For instance, Christ corrects misinterpretations and narrowing of the law's demand (Matt. 5:21-48). Moreover, His own life is an illustration of what the law would have us do and thus is a new example of what love requires. The radical character of love is so dramatically displayed in the atonement that the old commandment of loving one another can be considered a "new command"; Christ's explanation of love surpasses that of the Old Covenant when he says that His people are to love one another "even as I have loved you" (John 13:34-35; cf. 15:12-13; 1 John 2:7-11; 3:11-18, 22-24; 4:7-11).

(B) The New Covenant surpasses the Old in its *efficiency.*

Through the Old Testament God's moral demand was progressively revealed and explained; a revelation of His requirements would be followed by later revelations which amplified the first. However, with the coming of the New Covenant, the law of God would never receive further additions. The canon is complete and closed. Once and for all God has set down the moral standards which we are to faithfully apply to our lives. Everything needed for complete equipping in righteous living has now been given (2 Tim. 3:16-17).

(C) The New Covenant brings greater responsibility for *obedience*.

With the giving of new light and new power in the New Covenant, the responsibility of men to obey the voice of God is increased. To whom much is given much is required (Luke 12:48). God no longer overlooks any people's disobedience but requires all people everywhere to repent because of His appointed Judge and Day (Acts 17:30-31). The revelation of the New Covenant is even more inescapable than that of the Old Covenant (Heb. 12:25), and to it we should give "the more earnest heed" (Heb. 2:1-4).

Conclusion

Our study of the New Covenant scriptures has shown us, in summary, that there are definite discontinuities between the New Covenant relation to the law and that of the Old Covenant. The New Covenant surpasses the Old in glory, power, realization, and finality. There is *no textual* indication, however, that the New Covenant brings a new *standard* of moral conduct, and there is *no textual* indication that the Old Covenant standard has been categorically laid aside. The Covenantal *administrations* are dramatically different—in glory, power, realization, and finality—but *not* as codes *defining* right and wrong behavior or attitudes.

17

GOD'S COMMANDMENTS ARE A NON-LEGALISTIC RULE OF OBEDIENCE

"The law sends us to the Gospel that we may be justified; and the Gospel sends us to the law again to inquire what is our duty as people who are justified."

The Law Valid from Every Angle

Previous chapters have explored the subject of God's law in Christian ethics from a variety of perspectives. We have learned that there is every *theological* reason to affirm that believers continue to have an obligation to obey the law of God today. When we ask what the whole Bible has to say about the standard, motive, and goal of Christian morality, the Scripture's answer consistently points to the validity of God's law in our lives.

From the *normative* perspective the Bible teaches that the entire written word of God is our standard of conduct, that God's covenantal dealings with men (inclusive of His stipulations for His people) are essentially one, that God's unchanging holiness is transcribed for us in His law, that God's Son set an example for us of keeping the law, and that God's Spirit conforms believers to the pattern of righteousness found in the law.

From the *personal* or motivational perspective the Bible shows us that grace, faith, and love all operate to produce compliance with the holy standard of God's commandments.

From the *teleological* or consequential perspective the Bible explains that the law of the Lord was revealed for the good of His people, and thus a promised blessing rests upon individuals and societies which submit to God's stipulations for their attitudes and actions.

The theological conclusion that God's law continues to be a valid rule of life today enjoys the specific support of *New Testament texts* which bear on the subject as well. We have explored the way in which New Testament authors treat the legal requirements of the Old Testament, only to find that further endorsement is given to the law's validity today. This has been observed in the *use* of the law found in the teaching of Jesus and the apostles, the assumed authority of the law in key New Testament ethical *themes,* and the application of the law incorporated into New Testament moral *judgments.*

Finally, an extensive *comparison* of what the Old Testament had to say about the law of God with corresponding concerns in the New Testament revealed that there was *a common attitude toward the law* and *a presupposed continuity between the covenants* as to God's moral standards in the law — despite the fact that the New Covenant introduced important elements of discontinuity regarding the believer's relationship to the law. In the age of the New Covenant the Old Covenant law of the Lord retains its binding authority.

So then, both theological insight and specific New Testament teaching agree in supporting the law of God as a standard of conduct. If a person wishes to please the Lord, then he must seek to bring his thoughts, words, and deeds into conformity with the norms laid down in the law of God. Christian ethics is surely concerned with more than the law of God (for instance, it considers issues like ethical enablement, motivation, maturation, discernment, insight, application), but it cannot be concerned with less than the law of God — for the law supplies a pattern and criterion of godly living.

The Law Is Natural, Universal

Because that pattern and criterion is an unchanging one, the law continues to be a major concern of Christian ethics today. The standard of holiness revealed by the law is not peculiar to Old Testament Jews, nor is it somehow uniquely for those redeemed by God. That standard is universally binding on all created men, being "natural" in the sense that it is appropriate to the Creator-creature relation, and in the sense that it is revealed as binding to all mankind (either through the created realm and conscience, or through special written revelation).

The standard of the law remains unmitigated in its demand on our behavior as God's creatures. Failure to comply with it makes us sinners. Christ came, not to remove the standard which constitutes us as sinners, but to atone for the sin which we commit. The Spirit which He supplies to believers works to bring obedience to the previously spurned standard of righteousness in the law. At the final judgment, all men will be judged in the light of that same unchanging standard. *In whatever age, state, or circumstance man is found, his norm of godliness remains the revealed law of God.*

Accordingly, in 1774 John Newton, the theologian, hymn writer, and former slave ship owner turned abolitionist, wrote: "It is an unlawful use of the law, that is, an abuse of it, an abuse of both law and Gospel, to pretend, that its accomplishment by Christ releases believers from any obligation to it as a rule. Such an assertion is not only wicked, but absurd and impossible in the highest degree: for the law is founded in the relation between the Creator and the creature, and must unavoidably remain in force so long as that relation subsists. While he is God, and we are creatures, in every possible or supposable change of state or circumstances, he must have an unrivalled claim to our reverence, love, trust, service, and submission."[1]

---

1. *Letters of John Newton* (London: Banner of Truth Trust, 1960, p. 46).

The Law Upheld in the Westminster Tradition

One of the commissioners to the Westminster Assembly was Samuel Bolton, a reverent Reformed scholar who was disturbed by the claims being made in his day by those called "antinomians" (those who were against the law of God as a rule of obedience, on the alleged ground of God's free grace in the New Testament). In 1645, while the Westminster Assembly was still at work, Bolton published a treatise entitled, *The True Bounds of Christian Freedom.* [2] In it he laid out argument upon argument from Scripture to prove that we are not free today from the moral obligations of the law of God and that the law was compatible with God's grace. The thrust of Bolton's treatise is summarized in these words from it: "We cry down the law in respect of justification, but we set it up as a rule of sanctification. The law sends us to the Gospel that we may be justified; and the Gospel sends us to the law again to inquire what is our duty as those who are justified."[3]

Speaking of Matthew 5:17-18, Bolton said, "this seems to be very full and very plain for the continuance of and obligation to the law," and he went on to buttress his observation by appeal to Romans 3:31; 7:12, 22, 25; James 28; and 1 John 2:4; 3:4. "Therefore, since Christ, who is the best expounder of the law, so largely strengthens and confirms the law (witness the Sermon on the Mount, and also Mark 10:19); since faith does not supplant, but strengthens

2. Reprinted, London: Banner of Truth Trust, 1964.
3. *Ibid.*, p. 71.

the law; since the apostle so often presses and urges the duties commanded in the law of God in his mind, and that he was under the law of Christ (1 Cor. 9:21); I may rightly conclude that the law, for the substance of it, still remains a rule of life to the people of God. . . . If Christ and His apostles commanded the same things which the law required, and forbade and condemned the same things which the law forbade and condemned, then they did not abrogate it but strengthened and confirmed it. And this is what they did: see Matt. 5:19. . . . But he that breaks the law does sin, as says the apostle: 'Sin is the transgression of the law' (1 John 3:4), and 'Where no law is there is no transgression' (Rom. 4:15). Therefore Christians are bound, if they would avoid sin, to obey the law."[4]

Bolton recognized, of course, that the Old Testament corpus of law was easily categorized into moral, judicial, and ceremonial laws—that is, general principles, illustrative applications, and the way of atonement. Bolton saw the ceremonial law as providing the Jews with a way of worship which both anticipated the saving work of Christ and established a separation between God's people and the world (the Gentiles). The judicial law provided "a rule of common and public equity" in civil matters.[5]

It is evident from chapter 19 of the Westminster Confession of Faith—especially in light of the Larger Catechism's exposition of God's law—that the au-

---

4. *Ibid.*, pp. 61, 62, 66.
5. *Ibid.*, p. 56.

thors of the Confession saw eye to eye with Bolton in these matters. The law of God as delivered to Moses expresses the same perfect rule of righteousness which was binding upon man as created, even prior to the fall (19:1-2).

The corpus of law contained ceremonial laws typifying the saving work of Christ and certain moral instructions pertaining to the holy separation of God's people from the unbelieving world (19:3). It also contained judicial laws particularly worded for the ancient Jewish civil state, the general equity of which continues to bind men (19:4). Although the law is not a way of personal justification, it continues to be a rule of life both for the saved and the unsaved; Christ in the Gospel does not dissolve but rather strengthens this obligation (19:5-7).

This is Not "Legalism"

We must agree with the Publisher's Introduction to the Banner of Truth reprint of Bolton's work against antinomianism: "The slur of 'legalism' often cast upon those who framed the Westminster Confession of Faith finds no justification in this instructive and edifying work."[6] To maintain the full authority of God's law today—a conclusion to which every line of Biblical study drives us — will be unpopular in some degree with many people today, and it will be maligned as "legalism." To that charge John Murray could simply answer: "It is strange indeed that this kind of antipathy to the notion of keeping

---

6. *Ibid.*, p. 12.

commandments should be entertained by any believer who is a serious student of the New Testament."[7]

Rather than deal with the numerous lines of textual and theological support for the law's validity today, some would rather effortlessly dismiss the idea by blindly attaching the label of "legalism" to it. The label will not stick. Nor will the substance of our moral duty before God disappear by the mere incantation of a word.

---

7. *Principles of Conduct* (Grand Rapids, Michigan: Eerdmans, 1957), p. 182.

18

NEW TESTAMENT OPPOSITION TO THE ABUSE OF GOD'S LAW

"Paul's words imply that there is an unlawful use of God's law, a use which runs counter to the law's character and intent, so that the law's good nature might be perverted into something evil."

The New Testament, as does the entire Bible, surely supports the continuing validity of God's law. To say this is simply to submit one's thoughts to the Lawgiver Himself—it is not "legalism." And yet the New Testament contains passages which certainly seem to be taking a decidedly negative attitude toward the law of God. Paul declares that he "died unto the law that I might live unto God" (Gal. 2:19). He says, "you are not under the law, but under grace" (Rom. 6:14). Again, "we have been discharged from the law" (Rom. 7:6). For those who believe, we can conclude apparently, "Christ is the end of the law"

(Rom. 10:4). In light of such passages, some believers are led to see promotion of the law of God as our standard of morality as legalistic bondage. How can Scripture's seeming ambivalence toward God's law be understood in a way which absolves it of contradiction? How can the Bible contain two completely different evaluations of the law of God?

Paul himself supplies the resolution to the apparent problem when he delivers his categorical conclusion regarding the status of God's law for the Christian today. He says, "We know that the law is good, if a man uses it lawfully" (1 Tim. 1:8). It is indisputable and well established that the law is a good thing, reflecting perfectly the righteous standards of our holy God, the Creator of all men and Redeemer of His chosen people. Paul says "we know" that the law is good. It should be common knowledge that a positive attitude and submission to the law of God are called for in us. The law is indeed *good!* To follow it and endorse obedience to its dictates cannot be disapprobated as bad. The law of which Paul speaks is clearly the Old Testament commandments, as the illustrations mentioned in verses 9-10 demonstrate. These commands are known by all to be good (cf. Rom. 2:14-15; 7:12).

Yet Paul immediately qualifies his endorsement of the good character of God's law. He says that the law is good *if it is used lawfully.* That is, when the law is used according to its own direction and purpose — when the *law* is *lawfully* applied — it is a perfectly good thing. However, Paul's words imply that there is an *unlawful* use of God's law, a use which runs counter to the law's character and intent, so that the law's good nature might be perverted into something evil. The abuse of the law is indirectly condemned by Paul.

Examples of Abuse

What might such an abuse be? Where do we find an unlawful use of the law? We need not look far in the pages of the New Testament. Throughout the ministry of Christ and persistently in the epistles of Paul we encounter the Pharisaical and Judaizing attitude that one can, by performing works of the law, find personal justification before God. Amazing pride and self-deception led the Jews to believe that they might appear righteous in the judgment of a holy God if they but strove diligently to keep the commandments (or at least their external requirements). The Pharisees liked to justify themselves before men (Luke 16:15); they trusted in themselves that they were indeed righteous (Luke 18:9)—so much so that they had no more need for a Savior than a healthy man needs a physician (Matt. 9:12-13). However, God knew their hearts all too well. Despite outward appearances of cleanliness and righteousness, they were inwardly foul, spiritually dead, and full of iniquity (Matt. 23:27-28). Because they went about trying to establish their own righteousness, the Pharisees could not submit to the righteousness of God (Rom. 10:3).

Within the early church there soon arose a party from among the Pharisees that insisted that the Gentiles could not be saved without being circumcised and keeping in some measure the law of Moses (Acts 15:1, 5). Justification may be by grace, they would teach, but not completely so; works of the law were also necessary. Because they would compel the Gentiles to live as Jews in this sense (Gal. 2:14), they were designated "Judaizers."

Paul himself could understand this mindset, for it had been his own prior to conversion. He was brought up as a Pharisee concerning the law (Phil. 3:5); at the feet of Gamaliel he was "educated according to the strict manner of the law of our fathers" (Acts 22:3). His own testimony was this: "I advanced in Judaism beyond many of my own age among my people, so extremely zealous was I for the traditions of my fathers" (Gal. 1:14). He made his boast in the law (cf. Rom. 2:17-20, 23), and from the perspective of one spiritually dead he could claim that "as to righteousness under the law" he was—in a word—"blameless" (Phil. 3:6). He was once, apart from the law, so deceived as to think he was spiritually alive and righteous, but under the influence of God's Spirit the commandment came home to his consciousness and killed his self-righteous complacency. "I was alive apart from the law once, but when the commandment came, sin revived and I died" (Rom. 7:9).

Paul's Response

What Paul discovered is that he had simply not understood the law correctly in the first place. That is why in the midst of his most earnest writing against the Judaizers he can appeal repeatedly to the

Law itself (for example, Gal. 3:6-14, alluding to Gen. 15:6; 12:3; Deut. 27:26; Hab. 2:4; Lev. 18:5; Deut. 21:23).

The Old Testament, seeing that in God's sight no man could be justified (Ps. 143:2), promised justification grounded in "the-Lord-our-righteousness" (Jer. 23:6). Righteousness had to be *imputed* even to the great father of the Jews, Abraham (Gen. 15:6). Thus, the Old Testament, abundantly testifying that God's saints were men of faith (cf. Heb. 11), taught that the just shall live by faith (Hab. 2:4). Isaiah proclaimed: "In the Lord shall all the seed of Israel be justified. . . . This is the heritage of the servants of the Lord, and their righteousness is of men, saith the Lord" (45:25; 54:17).

The ceremonial law delivered by Moses made these truths manifest over and over again during the Old Testament era. Men were not righteous in themselves but needed to be circumcised. Even in their most natural habits, their sinful pollution called for ceremonial cleansings. To be found just in the sight of God they had to abhor their sinfulness and seek forgiveness through sacrificial substitution and priestly intercession. In such things the law possessed "a shadow of the good things to come" with the saving ministry of Jesus Christ (Heb. 10:1).

By the regenerating and enlightening work of the Holy Spirit, Paul came to realize that the law never intended for men to seek personal justification by meritorious works or the law. The law itself presented salvation as a gift rather than as wages. Accordingly, those who prided themselves in the law were in truth the most extreme violators of the law! "Is the law against the promises of God?" Paul asks. Does it teach a method of justification contrary to the gracious way of salvation found in God's promises? Paul's reply is "May it never be!" (Gal. 3:21), "for if there had been a law given which could make alive, verily righteousness would have been of the law. But Scripture shut up all things under sin in order that the promise by faith in Jesus Christ might be given to them that believe." Far from distracting from justification by grace through faith, "the law became our tutor to bring us unto Christ, that we might be justified by faith" (v. 24).

So let us return to Paul's declaration in 1 Tim. 1:8, "We know that the law is good, if a man use it lawfully." By implication *there is an unlawful, distorting use of the law* — one which abuses it, even while pretending to honor the law. Paul would surely identify the abusive use of the law as the Pharisaical and Judaizing attempt to make law-works the ground of one's own justification before God. "If righteousness is through the law, then Christ died for nothing" (Gal. 2:21). But "no man is justified by the law" (Gal. 3:11). The fact that God justifies the *ungodly* (Rom. 4:5) plainly shows that justification must be grounded in the alien righteousness of Jesus Christ (by His shed blood and resurrection, Rom. 4:25; 5:9); His righteousness is imputed to those who believe upon Him (Rom. 4:3-5; 5:1-2; 2 Cor. 5:21). Indeed, the *aim* or *goal* ("end") of the law's teaching was *Christ,* who brings righteousness to all who *believe* (Rom. 10:4).

Conclusion

As we have seen, passages in Paul's writings which seem to take a *negative* attitude toward the law of God can be correctly harmonized with Paul's equally strong *endorsements* of the law by distinguishing at least two (among many) uses of the word "law" in Paul's epistles.[1] The *revelatory* use of "law" is its declaration of the righteous standards of God; in this the law is good. The *legalistic* use of "law" refers to the attempt to utilize the works of the law as a basis for saving merit; this is an unlawful use of the law and receives Paul's strongest condemnations. Paraphrasing 1 Timothy 1:8, Paul says that we know the law — as a revelation of God's unchanging will — is good, as long as one uses it "lawfully" (as it is meant to be used) instead of legalistically.

---

1. Cf. Daniel P. Fuller, "Paul and the Works of the Law," *Westminster Theological Journal,* XXXVIII (Fall 1975), pp. 28-42. For a modern statement of the covenantal position that the Old Testament did not teach justification by law-works (legalism), see Fuller's fine exegetical study, *Gospel and Law: Contrast or Continuum* (Grand Rapids, Michigan: Eerdmans, 1980).

19

WHAT THE LAW CANNOT DO

"The law could not accomplish the remission of sins, but only witness to its coming reality."

We have seen that even the good law of God can become an evil thing when abused — when put to a use which is contrary to its character and purpose. It will prove beneficial to try and summarize just what the law cannot do in itself so that we might not fall into the error of using the law unlawfully.

(1) In the first place, as discussed just previously, the law cannot contribute anything toward the personal justification of one who stands under its curse for violating its precepts. Before the standard of God's law the sinner will always stand condemned rather than being judged righteous. "By the works of the law shall no flesh be justified in His sight" (Rom. 3:20). Those who hope to find acceptance with God on the basis of their own good deeds cannot find His favor. "You have been discharged from Christ who-

soever of you are justified by the law; you have fallen away from grace" (Gal. 5:4). The very attempt to gain justification in this manner is futile, for "a man is not justified by the works of the law but through faith in Jesus Christ" (Gal. 2:16).

(2) Nor can the law break the stranglehold and power of sin in a person's life. The principle of Christ's life-giving Spirit set Paul free from the principle of sin and death. Thus he said, "For what the law could not do, in that it was weak through the flesh, God sending His own Son . . . condemned sin . . . in order that the ordinance of the law might be fulfilled by us who walk not after the flesh, but after the Spirit" (Rom. 8:3-4). By the "flesh" Paul means the sinful nature within man which is at war with God and rebellious against His righteous standards (cf. vv. 6-8). The law of God simply could never overthrow this sinful nature and bring about conformity to its pattern of righteousness. The law could not empower obedience and put a decisive end to the power of disobedience.

The law could show what was right, but the faulty character of the sinner prevented the right from being performed. In the face of this failing, the law was helpless to amend the situation. However, God did condemn sin and destroy its dreadful power by sending His own Son to save sinners. The Son supplied His Spirit to believers to give them the enabling power of obedience to the law. Where they were once impotent, they are now empowered. We must ever remember that the law is a pattern only; it cannot supply the power to follow the pattern.

Paul elsewhere expressed this truth by saying, "You are not under law, but under grace" (Rom. 6:14). *The person who is "under law" is one whose resources and powers are determined exclusively by the law.* The context of Paul's declaration is the key to understanding it correctly. Being "under law" takes a parallel position to having sin reign within oneself (v. 12), to sin having dominion over oneself (v. 14a), to being a servant of sin (v. 17). Instead of being "under law" and by its impotence enslaved to sin, Paul sees the believer as "under grace" instead — that is, under the determining power of God's merciful and mighty work of salvation. This grace makes one over into a servant of righteousness and obedience (vv. 13, 16-18).

One is now under the enabling power of God's grace *just so that* one can obey the previously transgressed law of God. This conception of Paul's meaning helps us to see his declaration's appropriate place and function in its local context. In its full form, Paul's point is this: "Sin shall not have dominion over you *because* you are not under law but under grace. What then? shall we sin since we are under grace and not under law? God forbid!" (vv. 14-15). In context it is clear that being *under law* is a *position of powerlessness* wherein the bondage to sin remains unbroken, whereas being under grace supplies the spiritual strength to break off from sinning and now to obey the righteous standards of God (found in His law).

(3) Finally, it is important to remember that the law delivered by Moses never could actually make

anything perfect (Heb. 7:19). While it beautifully foreshadowed the saving ministry of Jesus Christ in its ceremonial enactments, the law could never by its repeated sacrifices secure the eternal redemption needed by God's people (Heb. 9:11-12; 10:1-12). Only the coming of the promised Savior, His atoning death, and justifying resurrection could accomplish the hoped for salvation of believers. The law could not *accomplish* the remission of sins but only witness to its coming reality. Accordingly, the ceremonial portion of the Old Testament law was never meant to be literally followed forever in the same manner as it was by Old Testament saints. It was "imposed until a time of reformation" (Heb. 9:10).

With the coming of the Savior, the shadows are left behind. The ceremonial system is put out of gear and made inoperative. To insist on keeping these ordinances in the same way as did Old Testament believers would be to disclose in oneself a legalistic attitude toward salvation (Gal. 4:8-10; 5:1-6). It would be retrogressive and disdainful of Christ, to whom the Old Testament ceremonies pointed.

"Under Law"

In 1 Corinthians 9:20, Paul describes himself as "not being myself under the law," even though he became to the Jews as one who was under the law in order that he might win some Jews to Christ. In the next verse, he continues to describe himself, now as "not being without law to God, but under law to Christ." If nothing else, this verse refutes any idea that Romans 6:14 ("you are not under law, but under grace") can be interpreted as implying that the person under grace has been released from moral obligation to the law of God. Paul affirms his submission to the law of Christ and thereby to every detail of the Old Testament law as well (Matt. 5:17-19). Indeed, he was not at all without the law of God (cf. Rom. 3:31; 7:22; 8:4). What then does he mean when he says in 1 Corinthians 9:20 that he is *not* "under the law"?

It would appear that this expression ("under law") is not being used in the same manner in both Romans 6:14 and 1 Corinthians 9:20. In the former passage it implies *bondage to the power of sin,* and this is far from what Paul is saying about himself in the latter passage! Those enslaved to sin are *lawless,* but Paul unmistakeably asserts that he is *not* without God's law in Christ. The phrase "under law" in Romans 6:14 applies indiscriminately to all unbelievers, but in 1 Corinthians 9:20-21 it applies to only one category of unbelievers — while "without law" describes the remaining category of unbelievers.

What then does Paul mean in 1 Corinthians 9:20 by asserting that he himself is not "under the law"? Paul is showing how he became all things to all men for the sake of the gospel (vv. 22-23). "To the Jews I became as a Jew, that I might gain Jews" (v. 20). When with them he acted "as though under the law," even though with others he acted "as though without the law."

Does Scripture help us understand how Paul was not thereby acting inconsistently, immorally, and with duplicity? Yes, it does. The unbelieving Jews had not recognized as yet the dramatic change brought in by the redemptive realities of the New Testament. Although Christ had realized all that the Mosaic ceremonial law had anticipated, unbelieving Jews continued to follow these rituals. In dealing with such men, Paul accommodated himself to these customs to gain a hearing for the gospel, even though he fully knew that they were not in themselves obligatory any longer. The shadows had given way to the Savior. For instance, Paul would carry out purification rites (for example, Acts 21:20-26) and take certain vows (for example, Acts 18:18) which he knew to be morally indifferent, and he did so to preserve a hearing for the gospel among the Jews. Among the Gentiles, however, he behaved "as though without the law." There was no advantage to pursuing the ceremonies in their presence. They were not like the Jews in this respect—not "kept in ward under the law before faith came," "under a tutor" until arriving at the maturity of sons—such as New Testament believers, who enjoy freedom from that tutor of the law (Gal. 3:23-26).

The Jews lived under the ceremonial rituals handed down by Moses. In 1 Corinthians 9:20 Paul, recognizing that these rituals could not actually accomplish salvation and that they were rendered inoperative by the atoning work of Christ, says that nevertheless he acted *as though* "under the law" in order to gain the Jews for Christ. With some men he conformed to these rites, but with others he did not. He was all things to all men—without ever losing sight of the fact that he was "in-lawed to Christ" and thus *not* at all failing to submit to God's law.

20

WHAT THE LAW
CAN AND SHOULD DO

"Within the life of the believer the law receives its proper due; indeed, it is established by faith."

Our study of what the law cannot do has found that the law (1) cannot contribute anything to a man's justification, (2) cannot relieve the bondage of sin and enable obedience, and (3) cannot actually accomplish the full salvation foreshadowed by the ceremonial ritual. A thorough study of the literature of the New Testament will show that its depreciatory or negative remarks about the law of God will each and every one be associated with an oversight of the three mentioned inabilities of the law. Failing to see what the law cannot do and was never intended to do, men have tried to use works of the law for personal justification, have vainly sought to obey the law's precepts without God's gracious empowering, and have continued under the outmoded shadows of the Mosaic ritual after the advent of the Savior. It is to such unlawful uses of the law that the New Testament speaks with firm antipathy.

Yet none of the well known New Testament passages which speak against the abuse of the law go on to release believers from moral obligation to the pattern of righteous living revealed in the law. The standard of the law remains valid, showing us what is good in the sight of God. Paul's evaluation has proven very helpful in resolving the apparent conflict over the status of the law within the pages of the New Testament. Paul explained, "We know that the law is good, if a man uses it lawfully" (1 Tim. 1:8). What are the lawful uses of the law?

Proper Uses of the Law

Before Adam fell into sin, obedience to the law would bring to him life and well-being. Since the fall, however, the law became to sinners a way of condemnation and death; the law cannot bring about obedience in the sinner and cannot be used as a way of justification. The ceremonial shadows of the Old Testament — the gospel in figures — gave promise that God himself would graciously accomplish full salvation for His people, justify them from sin and break the power of rebellion in their lives. God's righteousness is effective in those who have experienced a transition from wrath to grace in their personal lives, so that grateful obedience to God's good law becomes a way of life and well-being. No longer is God's law ignored. No longer is it replaced with the commandments and wisdom of men. No longer is it misused for the purposes of self-righteousness. Within the life of the believer the law receives its proper due; indeed, it is *established* by faith (Rom. 3:31). By it we can be blessed.

According to Scripture, the law has many legitimate functions. We can try to summarize them in the following list.

(1) The law *declares the character of God* and so reveals His glory.

The kind of lifestyle and attitudes which the Lord requires of His people tells us, of course, what kind of God He is. If you wish to see the contrast between the pagan deities and the living and true God of the Bible, simply observe the difference between the things which they command. Moloch demanded child sacrifice, while Jehovah commanded the care and nurture of children — to take but one example. Psalm 119 extensively applies the attributes of God (perfection, purity, righteousness, truth) to the precepts of God. Throughout the law God reinforces the authority of His commands by following them with the declaration, "I am the Lord."

In showing the true and radical demand of the law's requirements (Matt. 5:21-47), Christ was showing us the perfection of God which is desired in us (v. 48). John Newton wrote:

When we use the law as a glass to behold the glory of God, we use it lawfully. His glory is eminently revealed in Christ; but much of it is with a special reference to the law, and cannot be otherwise discerned. We see the perfection and excellence of the law in his life. God was glorified by his obedience as a man. What a perfect character did he exhibit! yet it is no other than a transcript of the law."[1]

(2) The law *displays the demand* of God upon our lives as men. By revealing the character of God, the law quite naturally expresses what is required of men if they are going to imitate their Creator. The law's commands show how we are to be like God by propounding the will of God for us. Before delivering the summation of the law in the Decalogue, God spoke to Israel with these words: "Now therefore, if you will obey my voice indeed, and keep my covenant, then you shall be my own possession from among all peoples, for all the earth is mine; and you shall be unto me a kingdom of priests and a holy nation" (Ex. 19:5-6). Obedience to the law is obedience to the voice of the King, the Lord of the covenant, and as such it shows us what it means to be His subjects and servants. For us to pray "Thy kingdom come," is likewise to pray "Thy will be done on earth" (Matt. 6:10). And God's will is communicated by His commandments, telling us what His holiness means on a creaturely level (Lev. 20:7-8).

(3) The law *pronounces blessing* upon adherence to

---

1. *Letters of John Newton* (London: Banner of Truth Trust, 1960), p. 47.

its demands. God's commandments were laid down for our good (Deut. 10:13), and obedience to them is the pure delight of the righteous man (Ps. 1:1-2). Such obedience brings prosperity (Ps. 1:3-4) and good success (Joshua 1:7). The Lord's lovingkindness is upon those who keep His precepts (Ps. 103:17-18), blessing them and their cultures (cf. Deut. 7, 11, 28, 30). Indeed, Paul taught that "godliness is profitable for all things, since it holds promise for the present life and also for the life to come" (1 Tim. 4:8). Seeking the righteousness of God's kingdom above all will be rewarded by the supply of every need (Matt. 6:33). The law insures that when men are just and righteous, they enjoy the life and blessing which imitation of God constitutes. Thus the commandment was ordained unto life (Rom. 7:10), and the man who does the things of the law enjoys life within their sphere (Gal. 3:12).

(4) The law provides a *definition of sin*.

By showing us what God is like and what God demands, the law likewise delivers a standard for sin. Sin is lawlessness (1 John 3:4). In delineating the righteousness which pleases God, the law simultaneously provides the norm of waywardness and rebellion against God. Where there is no law, there can be no transgression (Rom. 4:15; 5:13). By the law men come to know what sin is (Rom. 3:20; 7:7).

(5) The law *exposes infractions* and convicts of sin.

The law is more than simply an objective code of right and wrong by which, if one is interested, he can judge his performance. The law, being Spiritual (Rom. 7:14), is part of that word of God which is living and active — sharper than any two-edged sword, so as to pierce deeply into the recesses of man's heart and bring to the light his darkest character. The law judges the thoughts and intents of the heart (Heb. 4:12) and produces a conviction of our sinfulness (for example, Rom. 7:9-13).

(6) Even more, the law works to *incite rebellion* in sinful men.

Not only must we recognize that the law cannot enable us to obey its demands, we must also see that the law actually works in the contrary direction — exciting within the rebel further and further expressions of disobedience. Because the mind of the flesh (sinful nature) is unable to be subject to God's law (Rom. 8:7), *God's law serves to confirm one's bondage to sin by provoking intensified rebellion.* Thus, Paul can see in the law the very power of sin (1 Cor. 15:56). To understand this one need only reflect on the sad fact that the best way for an owner of a plate glass window to get it broken is for him to post a sign prohibiting the throwing of rocks at it. The very prohibition incites rebellion in the heart. By means of the commandments, then, man's sinful nature "becomes exceedingly sinful" (Rom. 7:13), working in us all manner of sin (Rom. 7:8), causing the trespass to abound (Rom. 5:20).

(7) Consequently, the law *condemns all transgression* as deserving God's wrath and curse.

The statement of Galatians 3:10 is blunt and terrifying: ". . . cursed is every one who does not continue in all things that are written in the book of the law to do them" (cf. Deut. 27:26). James intensifies the threat, saying "Whosoever shall keep the whole law and yet stumble in one point has become guilty of all" (2:10). Every infraction of the law brings wrath upon the sinner. All men will be judged for their ungodliness (Jude 6), judged according to their deeds whether good or evil (2 Cor. 5:10), and if found guilty cast into the eternal perdition of second death (Rev. 20:12-15). The wages of sin will be death (Rom. 6:23). Therefore, the law works wrath (Rom. 4:15) upon those who are, by their sinful natures, children of wrath (Eph. 2:3).

(8) The law *drives us to Christ* for salvation.

Thus far we have noted the unmitigated, absolute, unchanging demand of the law which reflects the holiness of God and thus sets out the evil of man by glaring contrast. Those who would have hoped in their own righteousness for acceptance before God are shown the futility of this hope by looking at the high standard of the law. The law speaks, and this shuts every mouth by bringing all the world under God's judgment (Rom. 3:19). Sinners apart from Christ have no hope in this world (Eph. 2:12). The sinner's only recourse must be to the free mercy of God's promise. Enlightened as to his guilt, he cries out with Paul, "wretched man that I am! who shall deliver me from the body of this death?" (Rom. 7:24). God's gracious answer is Jesus Christ (3:25), who manifests a righteousness of God apart from our obedience to the law (v. 21) and who justifies us by the free gift of faith (Rom. 3:22-26; 5:18-21; 6:23). In this way the law serves an important function in bringing men to salvation. It demonstrates their need and leaves them no honest option but God's offer of salvation. "Before faith came we were kept in ward under the law, shut up unto the faith which should afterwards be revealed. So that the law is become our tutor to bring us unto Christ that we might be justified by faith" (Gal. 3:23-24). This passage is customarily cited for the wording which suggests that the law drives us along to Christ.

(9) The law *guides the sanctification* of the believer. Since the law sets down the pattern of God's holiness for our lives, since the law was our obligation from the beginning, and since it is precisely the violation of the law which brought about the death of Jesus Christ for sinners, it only stands to reason that those delivered from sin's guilt and bondage should now desire to follow the previously spurned law. Those who have seen the glory of God in His law and have thereby been convicted of their own sin, being driven to Christ for salvation, should strive to bring their thoughts, words, and deeds into conformity to the glorious standard of the law. God says, "You shall keep My statutes and practice them; I am the Lord who sanctifies you" (Lev. 20:8).

Christ gives His Spirit to believers "in order that the ordinance of the law might be fulfilled" (Rom. 8:4). The law offers guidance and discernment to the believer (cf. Ps. 119:24, 66, 105; Prov. 6:23) so that he can walk in the light of God's moral perfection rather than in darkness (1 John 1:5-7; 2:3-6; cf. 3:4-10; 5:2-3). Christians ought not to sin but rather to evidence love toward God and neighbor. The first epistle of John tells us that sin is violation of the law, and that love is seen in keeping God's commandments. Accordingly, Christians are properly guided in their lives by the law of God.

John Newton wrote:

> Another lawful use of the law is, to consult it as a rule and pattern by which to regulate our spirit and conversation. The grace of God, received by faith, will dispose us to obedience in general, but through remaining darkness and ignorance we are much at a loss as to particulars. We are therefore sent to the law, that we may learn how to walk worthy of God, who has called us to his kingdom and glory; and every precept has its proper place and use.[2]

Such an outlook led men like Newton to find another use of the law closely associated with its function of guiding sanctification. They often spoke of the law serving "as a test whereby to judge of the exercise of grace."[3] Such a concept, although unpopular in our day of "easy believism," was very much on the mind of the Apostle John, who wrote "Hereby we know that we know Him, if we keep His com-

---

2. *Ibid.*
3. *Ibid.*

mandments" (1 John 2:3). Obedience to the commandments was for John also a mark that one loved God and loved God's children (1 John 5:2-3).

It thus appears appropriate that believers should use the law of God as a benchmark by which to gauge and evaluate their growth by God's grace in holiness of character. Because Bolton viewed the law as "a direction of life, a rule of walking to believers," he went on to find that God's law functioned "as a glass (mirror) to reveal the imperfections in our performance of duties," "as a reprover and corrector for sin, even to the saints," and as "a spur to quicken us to duties."[4]

(10) The law also serves to *restrain the evil* of the unregenerate.

Although only believers will appreciate aright the glory of God's character revealed in the law, be convicted of their sinful pollution by comparison, and seek to be conformed to the righteous standard of the law, the law also serves a function in the life and experience of the unbeliever. Even if the unbeliever is not duly driven by the condemning finger of the law to the arms of a faithful Savior, the law should be utilized within a civil society to restrain the outward evil of ungodly men.

Indeed, in the very passage where Paul tells us that the law is good when used lawfully, the precise lawful use of the law which he has in mind is its restraining function upon rebellious men: "knowing

---

4. Samuel Bolton, *The True Bounds of Christian Freedom* (London: Banner of Truth Trust, 1964), p. 83.

this, that the law was not enacted for a righteous man, but for the lawless and unruly, for the ungodly and sinners, for the unholy and profane, for murderers of fathers and mothers, for manslayers, for fornicators, for homosexuals, or menstealers, for liars, for false swearers . . ." (1 Tim. 1:9-10). This may not be a sanctifying effect in the unbeliever's life, but it is nevertheless a preservative function within society which is honored by God. It was intended as one of the proper functions of the law when God revealed it—both through the created realm and through the medium of written legislation.

21

THE TRADITIONAL "THREE USES" OF THE LAW

"When the known ordinances of God's law are spurned by a culture, it experiences the wrath of God revealed against it in the progressive breakdown of social order and moral decency."

My preceding survey has aimed to delineate many facets of the legitimate function of the law as discussed in Scripture. However, traditional Reformed thought has tended to summarize all of these various functions under the heading of three main uses of the law. The Reformers recognized quite clearly that the law had not been abolished in the New Testament age, and yet they were keenly aware of the abuses of the law to which the medieval Roman Catholic Church was prone. Therefore, against antinomians they argued for the law's validity, and in order to prevent falling into error in the use of the law they set down the law's proper functions.

The "first use" of God's law, they believed, is "the *political* use of the law." They believed that the enforcement of God's law by the civil magistrate is necessary for the proper and legitimate restraining of ungodly behavior by ungodly men.

The "second use" of the law which they identified was called "the *pedagogic* use of the law." By providing conviction of sin and creating a sense of spiritual need in the sinner, the law was a tutor which brought him to Christ. In his well known *Commentary on the Book of Galatians* Luther wrote:

> The right use and end, therefore, of the law is to accuse and condemn as guilty such as live in security, that they may see themselves to be in danger of sin, wrath, and death eternal. . . . The law with this office helpeth by occasion to justification, in that it driveth a man to the promise of grace (at Gal. 2:17 and 3:19).

Certainly no evangelical believer can gainsay that the law properly serves such an end.

The "third use" of the law identified by the Reformers was its "*didactic* use," whereby the law supplies a rule for life to believers. Calvin wrote, "The law is the best instrument for enabling believers daily to learn what that will of God is which they are to follow."[1] Although some modern Lutherans have wished to distance themselves from this use of the law, there can be no doubt but that it is endorsed by Luther and by the Formula of Con-

---

1. *Institutes of the Christian Religion*, 2.7.12.

cord. Luther said that apart from appealing to the law for justification, "we cannot sufficiently praise and magnify those works which are commanded of God" (*Commentary* at Gal. 3:22). To remove the law from the believer, thought Luther, "is a thing impossible and against God."[2] Accordingly Luther's *Small Catechism* begins with an exposition of the Decalogue. The Formula of Concord declared, "We believe, teach, and confess that the preaching of the Law should be urged . . . also upon those who truly believe in Christ, are truly converted to God, and regenerated and are justified by faith" (Article VI.2). Although the Calvinist branch of the Reformation stresses the law as a good gift of God's grace, and the Lutheran branch stresses it as a constraint, they both agree that the law is to be used to form the life of the regenerate believer.

The Controversial "First Use"

Traditionally, Reformed thought has summarized the proper use of the law into three specific functions. It drives the convicted sinner to Christ (the second use) and provides a pattern of sanctification for the regenerated believer (the third use). Some debate has surfaced in the past over the "third" or didactic use of the law, but the Reformed faith has still persisted in the Biblical affirmation that the law retains its binding validity for the conduct of believers.

More recently disagreement has arisen with respect to what the Reformers called the "first use" of the

---

2. *Table Talk*, 286.

law, which they took to be its "political use" in restraining the ungodly behavior of the unregenerate within society. The Reformers were sure enough of this proper function for God's law that they could call it the first and most obvious use for it. In fact, the very passage where Paul suggests that there are both lawful and unlawful uses of the law of God—1 Tim. 1:8—goes on immediately to illustrate a lawful use of the law as that of curbing the outward civil behavior of unruly men (vv. 9-10).

The law provides an external standard of justice which can be applied within the civil sphere, as is evident from Paul's mentioning of transgressions that can particularly be given cognizance by human law. The law was enacted or laid down, says Paul, for the unruly—such as murderers, kidnappers, homosexuals, perjurers, and the like. The law by its very nature aims to restrain the misconduct of lawless men.

In the Publisher's Introduction to the Banner of Truth reprint of Samuel Bolton's marvellous work, *The True Bounds of Christian Freedom,* the civil importance of God's law is pinpointed nicely:

> Grievous and alarming is the present-day deterioration in the moral condition of society. For this decay the Church is partly blameworthy because, as the preserving salt of the community, she has largely lost her savour. Modern theology has defected. It has cut itself adrift from the ancient landmarks, and present-day society reaps "the evil thing and bitter" which is

the inevitable consequence. The present prevailing theology has not been able to elevate society and halt its moral decline, and unquestionably, one explanation of this is its misunderstanding of the place of the law and its usefulness in the service of the covenant of grace."[3]

When men fail to see that God's law is meant to operate as external discipline within society, when they doubt and oppose the "political use" of the law, their societies inevitably suffer the accursed consequences. Carl F. H. Henry puts the matter this way:

> Even where there is no saving faith, the Law serves to restrain sin and to preserve the order of creation by proclaiming the will of God. . . . By its judgments and its threats of condemnation and punishment, the written law along with the law of conscience hinders sin among the unregenerate. It has the role of a magistrate who is a terror to evildoers. . . . It fulfills a political function, therefore, by its constraining influence in the unregenerate world.[4]

Biblical Law and Civil Government

This political function of the law is undeniable in the Old Testament, where God delivered statutes pertaining to civil matters for His people. These

---

3. Samuel Bolton, *The True Bounds of Christian Freedom* (London: Banner of Truth Trust, 1964), pp. 10-11.

4. *Christian Personal Ethics* (Grand Rapids, Michigan: Eerdmans, 1957), p. 355.

stipulations were integral to the law and order of Old Testament society, and if Paul's New Testament declaration in 1 Timothy 1:8-10 is to be heeded, these stipulations of God's law are still valuable in modern political ethics.

> We cannot dismiss these glimpses of the means of law and order in the Old Testament without remembering that this God-given tradition is emphasized and not abrogated by the Christian gospel. . . . Though under grace we are under the Law of God and are still accountable to him and responsible to our fellow men that justice and peace prevail.[5]

The law of God continues to have an important political function within the New Testament order, as Donald Guthrie recognizes in saying:

> In the New Testament a standard of justice is assumed and there is a clear differentiation between what is right and what is wrong. There are echoes of the Old Testament view of social justice. . . . The approach to law in general in the New Testament is intricately bound up with the Mosaic Law, which makes extensive provision for social justice. . . . The importance of this evidence of the sanctity of the law is that it provides a sound basis for social action. For a stable society law is indispensable.[6]

---

5. D. J. Wiseman, "Law and Order in Old Testament Times," *Vox Evangelica,* VIII, p. 19.

6. Donald Guthrie, "The New Testament Approach to Social Responsibility," *ibid.,* VIII, pp. 53-54.

An ironic situation has arisen in our day. Evangelical Christians who might be considered to lean toward a more "liberal" position in politics, and Evangelical Christians who might be thought to favor a more "conservative" position in politics, have at least this one unwitting area of significant agreement: they both wish to make principled and authoritative use of the Old Testament law for social justice. Recent publications which have promoted an active involvement by the believer in relieving the needs of impoverished people around the world have made noteworthy appeal to the law of Jubilee, while many books and articles written to protest the tolerance of homosexuality and/or abortion in our day have made clear and unapologetic reference to the Old Testament prohibitions against them.

The law is recognized has having a continued political significance by present-day believers, even when they do not systematically work out a theological foundation for the appeals which are made to the law's authority in contemporary society, and even when they might elsewhere unwittingly contradict that assumed foundation. That foundation is the continuing validity of God's law, even in its social or political relevance. Strangely enough, it is often those who are heirs to the Reformation tradition of maintaining the political use of the law that raise objection to that notion today.

In resisting the political use of God's law, in detracting from its political relevance, and in encouraging either indifference to questions of social justice or else alternative standards for it, such men are not aligned with their Reformation forefathers. Luther and Calvin were fully in agreement that God's law was an instrument of civil government, functioning to restrain crime and to promote thereby civil order. Luther taught that

> the first use of the law is to bridle the wicked. This civil restraint is very necessary, and appointed of God, as well for public peace, as for the preservation of all things, but especially lest the cause of the Gospel should be hindered by the tumult and seditions of wicked, outrageous and proud men (*Commentary* at Gal. 3:19).

Calvin concurs:

> The first use of the law is, by means of its fearful denunciations and the consequent dread of punishment, to curb those who, unless forced, have no regard for rectitude and justice. Such persons are curbed, not because their mind is inwardly moved and affected, but because, as if a bridle were laid upon them, they refrain their hands from external acts, and internally check the depravity which would otherwise petulantly burst forth (Institutes, 2.7.10).

This continued to be the view of Reformed thinkers through the centuries. At the time of the Westminster Assembly, Samuel Bolton wrote:

> First of all, then, my work is to show the chief and principal ends for which the law was promulgated or given. There are two main ends to be observed, one was political, the other theologi-

cal or divine. The political use is hinted at by
the apostle in 1 Tim. 1:8-9 . . . ; that is, it was
made for them in such fashion that, if it were
not their rule, it should be their punishment.
Such is the political use of the law.[7]

Conclusion

The political use of the law is admittedly negative and merely *deterrent* in character. It does nothing
to regenerate the sinner or make him right with God;
it does not touch his heart or bring him any closer to
the Savior. Nevertheless, this function of the law is
crucial for man's society. When the known ordinances of God's law are spurned by a culture, it experiences the wrath of God revealed against it in the
progressive breakdown of social order and moral
decency (Romans 1). Because this important political use of the law of God is unpopular in many cir-
cles today, and because many people who are educated in the secular environment of our society carry
confused conceptions of what this political function
entails, the next few chapters will focus on the
Biblical doctrine of civil government and Biblical
law's place therein. We will see that "Righteousness
exalts a nation, but sin is a disgrace to any people"
(Prov. 14:34), in which case, we dare not dismiss the
political relevance and use of the Biblically revealed
law of God.

---

7. Bolton, p. 78.

22

THE POLITICAL IMPLICATIONS OF THE COMPREHENSIVE GOSPEL

"If we must glorify God even in our eating and drinking, then surely we must also glorify Him in the way that we vote and thereby encourage statesmen to rule our society."

It used to be the case that when a Bible-believing author wanted to write on some aspect of social morality or political policy, he had to give an introductory apologetic and defense for entering into such an area of discussion. Given the background of liberal or modernistic involvement in politics, given the threat of the social gospel, and given the evangelical withdrawal from the world encouraged by church-centered pietism and law-denying dispensationalism, anyone who wrote on subjects of political or social ethics would easily be suspected of compromise or departure from the faith. So reticence characterized evangelical and Reformed publications in these areas.

Times have obviously changed, if we pay attention to the avalanche of books which have begun to be published over the last few years on the Christian (evangelical or Reformed) approach to politics and social ethics. The pendulum has swung back so far in the other direction, in fact, that some measure of suspicion is likely to be felt toward any Bible-believing author who renounces or completely ignores such a vital concern. Trusted writers in the conservative tradition of theology have taken to penning their opinions about political morality. Men with visible political connections have written about their conversions and their Christian involvement in society's leadership. Pressing problems in the governing of the state — from tolerance toward homosexuality to legalized abortion — have forced an end to the policy of Christian silence on social issues of the day. Increased interest in the notion that Christianity pertains to the whole man (not simply his inward, "spiritual" destiny), that its principles touch on all areas of life (not merely an hour of worship on the Lord's Day), and that the coming of Christ's kingdom has implications for the renewal of the entire creation (and not only the saving of souls from hell's fire) has naturally worked itself out in an increased interest in the Christian view of science, art, economics, politics, and everything else. So, due to many factors, Christians have more and more in the last generation become politically aware and active.

None of this should legitimately suggest, of course, that Christianity is primarily or most importantly a political position. It ought not to minimize the centrality and indispensable truth of the good news that Christ came to save His people from the curse of sin and the penalty of final judgment for their rebellion; the cross and resurrection, the regenerating work of the Holy Spirit, and the necessity of justification by faith have not been forgotten or subordinated. However, the full implications of these truths are being appreciated again—even as they have been appreciated in previous days of the church's existence.

King Jesus

In 1719, Isaac Watts wrote a now famous hymn which expresses some of these implications, a hymn which Bible-believing Christians have sung (especially at "Christmas" season, and thus being joined even by many unbelievers) for over two and a half centuries:

Joy to the world! the Lord is come:
Let earth receive her King;
Let every heart prepare him room,
And heaven and nature sing.

Joy to the earth! the Saviour reigns:
Let men their songs employ;
While fields and floods, rocks, hills, and plains
Repeat the sounding joy.

No more let sins and sorrows grow,
Nor thorns infest the ground;
He comes to make his blessings flow
Far as the curse is found.

He rules the world with truth and grace,
And makes the nations prove
The glories of his righteousness
And wonders of his love.

The church has sung of the "political" implications of the gospel for years now! It has sung that earth must receive her King—a reigning Savior who rules the world, making the nations prove His righteousness. And this King is interested in more than the inward souls of men and their heavenly existence in the future. As a Savior from sin, *Christ is interested in every aspect of life infected by sin at man's fall.* "He comes to make his blessings flow, Far as the curse is found." Just because man's social existence and his political efforts have been cursed by sin, Christ the King proves His righteousness in the realm of human politics, even as he reigns over every other department of man's thoughts, life, and behavior.

The early church was well aware of the political implications of being a Christian. To be a "Christian"—a disciple or follower of Christ (Acts 11:26)—meant to confess Jesus Christ as Savior, Messiah, and Lord. Christians declared that Jesus was their Savior or *soter* (Greek), as we see in Acts 5:31 and 1 John 4:14 ("We have beheld and bear witness that the Father has sent the Son to be Savior of the world"). Despite the fact that Roman coins of the day often depicted the Emperor's face with the inscription of *soter* (or "only Savior" in some cases), the earliest Christians declared the name of *Jesus* was the one and *only* name given among men whereby we must be saved (Acts 4:12).

It was also essential for a Christian to "believe that Jesus is the Christ" (or Messiah), as it says in 1 John 5:1. Because Jesus admitted openly that He was the Christ, the Sanhedrin brought Him before Pilate for trial, where Pilate too inquired and found out that Jesus considered Himself a King (Luke 22:67 — 23:3), in which case He was deemed to be speaking out against Caesar himself (John 19:12). Finally, the New Testament shows us that it is characteristic of all Christians that they confess with their mouths that "Jesus is Lord" (Rom. 10:9; 1 Cor. 12), meaning that their allegiance in all things belongs to Him as "Lord of lords and King of kings" (1 Tim. 6:15; Rev. 17:14; 19:16) — even as he battles against the political power of the Beast and the kings of the earth. So then, like it or not, the earliest Christians comprehended that being a Christian had political ramifications. Paul and the Christians at Thessalonica were charged with political crimes because of their confession of Christ; it was alleged: "these all act contrary to the decrees of Caesar, saying that there is another King, one Jesus" (Acts 17:7).

We know that one day King Jesus will require all kings of the earth to give an account of their rule to Him as their sovereign Ruler and Judge. All thrones were created for Him, who is to have preeminence in all things (Col. 1:16-18). Kings who have been so unwise as not to serve the Lord with fear and kiss the Son will experience His wrath, perishing in the way (Ps. 2:10-12). Therefore, we can see how important and legitimate it is for Christians — Bible-believing

'Christians who want to submit to Scripture from beginning to end — to maintain God-glorifying attitudes and beliefs about politics and social ethics. If we must glorify God even in our eating and drinking (1 Cor. 10:31), then surely we must also glorify Him in the way that we vote and thereby encourage statesmen to rule our society! Indeed, we must seek first the Kingdom of God and His righteousness (Matt. 6:33) so that *His will* is done *on earth* (Matt. 6:10).

Uncertain Trumpets

But *what is* His will for political ethics? This is the critical question; yet it is the question that modern Christian writers on politics and social morality find so difficult (if not impossible) to answer clearly and specifically. With the renewed interest we are seeing in our day for Christians to rush into the political arena with a complete world-and-life-view which touches on everything of human interest, with the flood of books and articles which are now being published on "the Christian" approach to politics, what would happen if the world were all of a sudden to stop short and simply say: "All right, we see how humanism has failed so desperately. What do you Christians say we should do in matters of political ethics?" Once given the opportunity to speak out with the Christian perspective, would evangelical and Reformed writers have anything to say beyond generalizations and ambiguous platitudes? There is reason to doubt that they would. The explanation of that likely failure is not hard to find.

The reason why Christians who want to write or

take a stand on issues of political ethics have usually failed to produce distinctive and helpful answers which are clear and specific is to be found in their reluctance to endorse and publicize the law of God, precisely where the Lord has revealed definite answers to the socio-political problems of men and their civilizations.

What kind of good news or "gospel" does the Kingdom of Jesus Christ bring according to many Christian groups?

The Social Gospel

A "social gospel" is dominated by modernists and liberals, as most any Bible-believing Christian knows today. In the late nineteenth and early twentieth centuries, the higher critical movement in scholarship challenged much of the Biblical teaching and undermined the most basic theology of the Christian church. Thus the work and message of Christ were reduced, so that He performed no priestly work by His death and resurrection and secured no eternal salvation for men.

The modernistic approach to man became evolutionary and naturalistic, further denying the Christian message about man's unique dignity as God's image and special creation by His hand. As a result, modernism turned away from the verities of Biblical Christianity and concentrated almost exclusively on moralistic themes and interests, especially matters touching on the "brotherhood of all men" as seen in social relations. So liberal theologians felt no hesitation to propagate humanistic solutions to political questions, all in the name of Christianity. We must remember, however, that the fault with the "social gospel" was not that it was social, but that it was modernistic and Bible-denying.

The Fundamentalist Response

In reaction to liberalism, Fundamentalism in the twentieth century preached an "individualistic gospel" by extreme contrast. The emphasis fell upon saving men's souls from eternal damnation and changing men's hearts for church-oriented living, waiting for the imminent return of Christ to this hopelessly degenerating world. Ironically, for all the effort to distance itself from liberalism's errors, the commendable insistence on certain key fundamental doctrines of the Bible in Fundamentalism tended to create a short-sightedness to the full implications of Christianity. Once again, the work and message of Christ were reduced, for the full salvation which Christ accomplished was narrowed to the "spiritual" aspects of man and the present kingdom and rule of Christ were postponed to a later date (when sociopolitical matters would again appear on the agenda). Redemption was not seen as applying as far as sin's curse is found, and godliness was narrowly defined by abstinance from worldly abuses (like drinking, smoking, movies, dancing, etc.).

The conservatism of Fundamentalism was sorely needed in theology, of course, but the social effects were less than beneficial. Jesus said that if the salt has lost its savor, it is good for nothing but to be cast out and trodden under by the feet of men (Matt.

5:13). To the extent that this happened to Fundamentalism, it was because it did not proclaim the whole counsel of God, even for socio-political morality. Paul's ethic was not exclusively focused on the future life in heaven or the individualistic behavior of the present. He said "godliness is profitable for *all things,* having promise for the life which *now is, and* of that which is to come" (1 Tim. 4:8).

Lutheranism and Romanism

Side by side with the social gospel of modernism and the individualistic gospel of Fundamentalism we can place the "dichotomistic gospel" of Romanism and Lutheranism. The Lutheran church, to be sure, stands firmly opposed to the theological errors of the Roman Catholic Church. Luther, we recall, inaugurated the Protestant Reformation of the church by insisting on the doctrine of justification by faith, over against the Romanist notions of righteousness[1] through works of the law. Yet strangely enough, the Lutheran outlook on socio-political matters has developed into a parallel perspective to that of Rome.

The Roman Catholic church reduces the work of Christ (leaving the completion of salvation to priests and to human efforts), while the Lutheran church tends to reduce the message of Christ (drawing a strong opposition between law and gospel and laying nearly exclusive stress on the latter). The Roman Catholic outlook over the years has been that there is a distinction to be drawn between the realms of

---

1. Condign or congruent.

nature and of grace; some matters pertain to one, while different matters pertain to the other. Political questions are natural to man and his social existence, and thus the perspective of grace (special revelation) is not directly pertinent to them. In that case, man's self-sufficient and natural reason becomes the arbitrator in issues of political ethics. In parallel fashion, classic Lutheran doctrine teaches that there is a kingdom of the right hand and a kingdom of the left hand, one pertaining to salvation and the church while the other pertains to creation and society. As a result, when believers enter into political reasoning, they do so on a common platform with unbelievers.

Neither Romanism nor Lutheranism have a direct and specific word from God on political matters, but only on matters concerned with grace and salvation. As a result they both promote a neutral attitude toward politics which cannot offer distinct guidance from Scripture for society. The dichotomies which are central to these theological perspectives screen out a fully Biblical orientation to political ethics.

Neo-Orthodoxy

Rocking to yet another extreme, neo-orthodoxy and subsequent radical theologies have proclaimed the "unsure gospel" which addressed special problems in society and politics, but with no clear and specific word from God. Karl Barth was confident that the commands of the Bible were not universal truths, applicable to every age and culture, but merely time-bound witnesses to the will of God.

Emil Brunner went further to say that the Bible could not, in the nature of the case, provide us with pre-established norms of conduct, for our obligations (he thought) could only be determined by the situation in which we find ourselves—opening the door wide to the development of Joseph Fletcher's situational morality, where moral duty is relativistic. Neo-orthodoxy promoted nothing more than cheap grace which did not require men to be converted, to repent of specific sins, and to be sanctified according to an unchanging pattern of holiness. Neo-orthodoxy could not offer anything but a nebulous gospel to men, for according to it God did not communicate in infallible verbal propositions. So it was only to be expected that the neo-orthodox approach to social problems was ambiguous, unclear, and unauthoritative. It has no sure word from God by which to judge and guide the social affairs of men.

The Comprehensive Gospel

Over against the social gospel of modernism, the individualistic gospel of Fundamentalism, the dichotomistic gospel of Romanism and Lutheranism, and the unsure gospel of neo-orthodoxy and radicalism, we find the blessed and refreshing *comprehensive gospel* of Reformed theology, which is the heritage of Biblical Christianity. The good news of Christ's kingdom is that Jesus Christ graciously and powerfully saves man in the fulness of his created and sinful existence. He is a prophet, declaring God's will for ignorant men. He is a priest, interceding to God on behalf of polluted sinners. And he is a king, ruling over all men and all areas of life. The coming of the Kingdom, therefore, brings the progressive rule of Christ over the world, the flesh, and the devil (1 Cor. 15:25).

The Reformed churches have always stood for the proclamation of *sola Scriptura* and *tota Scriptura*. Scripture alone must be the standard of our theology and ethic, and we must preach all Scripture in its total relevance to the life of men. Only Scripture, but totally Scripture! Consequently we observe that the preaching of the New Testament is not apolitical. Jesus rebuked Herod as a vixen, and John the Baptist called his behavior unlawful. Paul warns against a political ruler who is "the man of lawlessness," and John calls him "the Beast." Over against these evil rulers, Christians are to stand for the law of God (cf. Revelation 12:17; 14:12) because Paul taught that the civil magistrate was obligated to be a "minister of God" who avenges His wrath against evildoers who violate God's law (Rom. 13:4). Since the New Testament is not apolitical, neither is the comprehensive preaching of the Reformed churches.

However, in recent years there has been a steady disinclination to maintain the "political use" of the law of God when it comes to declaring God's will for socio-political morality. Accordingly we take up the question of whether the civil magistrate today should obey and enforce the Old Testament law of God.

23

LAW AND POLITICS IN OLD TESTAMENT ISRAEL

"When those who rule for God depart from His laws, then they must be judged by God. The very foundation of civil order was undermined when judges did not discern between good and evil."

Many Christians want to take a distinctive stand with respect to issues of socio-political morality. However, this has become very difficult once the political use of God's law has been forgotten or rejected. Unfortunately, even writers in the general Reformed tradition of theology have repudiated that use of God's law lately. In response, we ask whether the Bible teaches that civil magistrates ought to obey and enforce the relevant portions of the Old Testament law.

In one sense, previous studies have already offered us an apparent answer to this question. We

have seen that the whole Bible is our standard of
morality today, for God does not have a double-
standard of justice. Instead, the law reflects the
Lord's unchanging holiness, being perfectly obeyed
by Christ (our example) and enforced within the believer by the Holy Spirit (our power). We have seen
that the Old and New Covenants have a uniform
view of the law of God, and that Christ Himself
declared that every stroke of the Old Testament continued to have validity after His coming to earth to
save sinners. Repeatedly the New Testament
authors assume the standard of the law in their
ethical themes and make application of the law in
their moral judgments. Every scripture, every point,
every word, and indeed every letter of the Old Testament law is upheld in the New Testament.

Therefore, it would seem obvious that the socio-
political aspects of the Old Testament law would retain their validity today — that they are authoritative
for civil magistrates of all ages and cultures. Just as
parents, farmers, merchants, and others have moral
duties laid upon them in the Old Testament law, so
also civil rulers have duties enjoined for their official
business in the law of the Lord.

Yet not everyone is willing to endorse the current
applicability of the Old Testament law in the particular domain of civil politics. The whole law may be
endorsed in the Old Testament, it it thought, but
there has come about in the New Testament a different attitude toward the civil magistrate. The view
taken seems to be that because the magistrate in Old
Testament Israel was in various ways unique — being

chosen by God in a special way, being a foreshadowing of the person of Christ, etc. — the law by which
this magistrate was to govern society must also have
been unique, meant only for Israel to follow. In
short, there was an extraordinary doctrine of the
office of civil magistrate in the Old Testament revelation for Israel, and thus what was the moral duty for
Old Testament Jewish rulers should not be taken as
the standard for political ethics today.

The fallacy embodied in this line of thought is the
assumption that if two entities are in *some* ways
different, then they are in *all* ways different. What
has been overlooked is the distinct possibility of *similarity* — not total identity and not complete difference,
but elements which are the same between two things
and elements which are distinct. A tank and a sports
car are similar with respect to their running on
wheels, but they are different in their speed, power,
and appearance. Likewise, it may very well be that
Old Testament Jewish magistrates were different
from Gentile magistrates in some respects, and yet
very much like the others in further respects.

The Civil Magistrate

The Bible appears to teach that one way in which
all civil magistrates are alike — whether they are Jewish or Gentile, Old Testament or New Testament —
is in the *standards of justice* which are laid upon them
by the Creator. God does not have a double-standard of justice. Thus, the laws which He stipulated
for Old Testament Jewish magistrates to follow are
just as applicable to pre-consummation issues of

crime and punishment today as they were in Old Testament Israel. Now as then, society needs to know how to cope with attacks upon human dignity, freedom, safety, and honor. Magistrates in all ages need guidance for dealing with murder, kidnapping, rape, perjury, and the like. And in this respect, the magistrate in Old Testament Israel would be just like any other magistrate — subject to the unchanging justice and continuing validity of God's revealed law for socio-political affairs.

We can see this if we study the biblical teaching about civil magistrates in Old Testament Israel, Gentile nations surrounding Israel, and then in the New Testament. Not only do we see, then, the continuing validity of the Old Testament law in general, but we see the basically uniform outlook on civil rule which is taught in God's word. Rulers have the same obligations and have the same standards of right and wrong in all cultures. Having surveyed this situation in Scripture, we can turn to the questions of church/state separation and penology. Our survey begins by outlining basic theses in the Biblical view of the civil magistrate in Old Testament Israel.

1. *God's appointed rulers are not to be resisted.*

God was recognized in the Old Testament as the One who ordained and removed rulers in Israel. There was no authority in Israelite society except by God, and those who ruled were ordained to such leadership by God. On the one hand the people selected and acknowledged their rulers (as in 1 Kings 12:20 or 2 Kings 9:13), and on the other hand there was a corresponding divine decree which sovereignly established the ruler (as in 1 Kings 11:31 or 2 Kings 9:1-2). God's sovereign power of appointment is made quite clear in Hosea 13:11, "I have given you a king in my anger, and have taken him away in my wrath." In Old Testament Israel, the powers that be were ordained of God.

For that reason it was strictly forbidden that people resist the authority of their political leaders. Honor had to be given to whom it was due. So the law of God prohibited any reviling of the ruler (Ex. 22:28), and Paul himself appealed to this standard in his own case (Acts 23:5). It was because Saul was the Lord's annointed that David dared not lift his hand against him (1 Sam. 24:7, 11; 26:23). The king's exalted position was such that one should obey his command, not oppose his rebuke, not defy his power, and not renounce allegiance (Ecc. 8:2-5). Old Testament citizens were accordingly taught that they were to be subject to the higher authorities, not resisting the powers ordained by God.

2. *Bearing religious titles, rulers were avengers of divine wrath.*

In the Old Testament political arrangement, the sons of the king were often political counselors at his side (cf. 1 Chron. 27:32-33). In 1 Chronicles 18:17 we read of the political office designated as "heads with respect to the power of the king," and the parallel passage in 2 Samuel 8:18 informs us that this office was filled by David's sons. What is of interest to us here is that in the latter verse, these political officers are called "priests." The same Hebrew word for the *cultic* office of priest was used of these *political* rulers —even as it was applied in similar fashion to David's officer, Ira the Jairite (1 Sam. 20:26; cf. 2 Sam. 23:38). In 1 Kings 4:2-6 we find a list of Solomon's officers, where Zabud is called a "priest," and the text immediately explains this office as "the king's friend" (his continual adviser). The head of the political "priests"—*the* priest (or prime administrator of the kingdom)—is named as Azariah in the same passage.

What we learn, then, is that the rulers of state in the Old Testament were viewed as so intimately concerned with the affairs of God's word and so strictly subject to His command, that they could be given customary religious titles. The magistrates in Israel were genuine ministers of God, authorized to rule according to His just standards as his representatives in society.

Old Testament civil rulers were ordained by God, were not to be resisted, and bore religious titles as the representatives of God in society. Their main function was that of avenging God's wrath against violators of His law for social justice.

Over and over again the Old Testament associated the sword of judgment with God, who brought historical punishment upon the rebellion of men. Even Israel was threatened with the judgment of the sword if she broke the law of the Lord (for example, Lev. 26:25, 33, 36-37)—a threat carried out in its climax when Jerusalem fell by the edge of the sword according to the word of Christ (Luke 21:24). The sword of vengeance belongs to God. And yet the sword is repeatedly associated with God's will for civil rule as well. Human government is symbolized by the sword, whether it is wielded by Pharaoh (Ex. 18:4) or by Saul (2 Sam. 1:22). The sword's proper function is that of executing criminal violators of God's law (for example, 1 Kings 1:51; 2:8; etc.). Whenever the sword is used autonomously — whenever men use political power and punishment as a law unto themselves — it is used in a sinful manner (for example, 1 Sam. 22:19). The wielding of the sword is accordingly vain if it is not used in conformity to God's law. The magistrate in Israel had no right to slay men independent of God's guidance and word.

We can observe further that *wrath and vengeance are constantly attributed to God in his purity and justice.* They are retribution expressed against those who dare to profane the covenant of the Lord (Ps. 54:20-21), to violate His laws (for example, Deut. 11:17), or to sin (for example, Num. 11:1). When the civil magistrate is said to express wrath and vengeance in the Old Testament, then, it is only natural to expect that *the ruler is expressing the wrath of God in vengeance upon evildoers* (for example, Josh. 7:25; 22:20; 2 Kings 12:5).

The Old Testament declared that vengeance belonged to God, that He would repay (Deut. 32:35, 41). It nevertheless taught that the civil magistrate was under orders to carry out vengeance against transgressions of God's law for social behavior (for example, Exodus 21:20-21; Deut. 18:19). Vengeance, you see, must be based upon the holiness of God (Ps.

98:8); it is occasioned, therefore, by sinning against His law (for example, Ezk. 7:27; 9:1; 20:4; Hosea 1:4; 2:13; Zech. 5:3). As an agent of God's wrath, the civil magistrate was seen in the Old Testament as God's vicegerent or deputy in the state.

The God of the Bible is a God of law and justice (Isa. 33:22; Deut. 32:4), not one who acts in capricious or arbitrary ways. He always judges with righteousness (Ps. 96:13), and expects others to do likewise (Lev. 19:15). To do righteousness and justice, one must keep the way of Jehovah and follow His ordinances (Gen. 18:19; Deut. 33:21). Moses confidently declared to Israel: "What great nation is there that has statutes and ordinances so righteous as all this law which I set before you this day?" (Deut. 4:8). Now, above everything else, God required that the civil rulers of Israel would demonstrate justice or righteousness in all of their decisions. "You shall do no unrighteousness in judgment . . . but in righteousness shall you judge your neighbor" (Lev. 19:15; cf. Deut. 16:18). Amos the prophet cried out so that God's people would "establish justice in the gate" (5:15) and thereby "let judgment run down as waters and righteousness as a mighty stream" (5:24).

Clearly, if the God of justice requires earthly rulers to govern with justice, then those rulers are obligated to observe the law of God in all of their judgments. Even as God does not justify the wicked (Ex. 23:7), they must not justify the wicked (Deut. 25:1). *They must judge as He judges.*

Of God it was said in the Old Testament, "Righteousness and justice are the foundation of His throne" (Ps. 89:14). The earthly king's throne was likewise to be established on justice and righteousness (Ps. 72:1-2), which it would be if the king did not turn aside from God's commandments (Deut. 17:18-20). So the Lord, we see, set kings upon their thrones "to be king for Jehovah thy God . . . to do justice and righteousness" (2 Chron. 9:8). In their decisions, "the judgment is God's" (Deut. 1:16-17), and for that reason civil judges could be designated "gods" (Ps. 82:1, 6). When they punished evildoers according to the penal sanctions of the law of God, judges made manifest that they were imaging God (Gen. 9:5-6). As God's deputies in society—representatives of His justice and vengeance—civil magistrates were bound to wield the sword according to God's own direction and law.

3. *Magistrates must deter evil by ruling according to God's law.*

In the Old Testament, those who showed themselves worthy were safe, but the wicked would die (for example, 1 Kings 1:52). So "the wrath of the king is as messengers of death" (Prov. 16:14). The civil magistrate was accordingly called to be a terror to evildoers. But, then, if civil rulers in Israel were ordained by God as His deputies who were to be a terror to evildoers (but no threat to the righteous), is it not obvious that they had to rule according to God's law? If they rested on their own wisdom and moral discernment, they would easily have judged with partiality, leniency, and harshness rather than the purity of God's justice. For even civil rulers among

God's chosen people were sinners who needed the guidance and correction of God's revelation, especially in official decisions they made which affected the nation and its uprightness.

Thus, the Old Testament taught that *justice is perverted whenever the law of God was slackened* (Hab. 1:4). Since judges were required to execute justice and righteousness (Jer. 22:3), God said: "And in a controversy they shall stand to judge; according to mine ordinances shall they judge it: and they shall keep my laws and my statutes" (Ezk. 44:24). Kings were forbidden to frame mischief by a law (Ps. 94:20), receiving the charge to "keep his [God's] statutes, and his commandments, and his ordinances, and his testimonies, according to that which is written in the law of Moses" (1 Kings 2:3).

Over and over again, the rulers of Israel pleased the Lord by dedicating themselves to keep His commandments (for example, Josiah and Ezra's reform). The reason why kings were to stay sober was just so they would not "forget the law and pervert judgment" (Prov. 31:5). Daily they were to read God's law (Deut. 17;19), and morning by morning they were to punish the workers of iniquity (Ps. 101:8).

It follows, of course, that those rulers who spurned the law of God in their official capacity as civil magistrates were subject to the judgmental wrath of God. Isaiah cried out, "Woe to those who enact evil statues, and to those who constantly record unjust decisions" (10:1). Psalm 82 teaches that God Himself stands in the law court of the "gods" (judges) so as to rebuke unjust judgments passed there. When those who rule for God depart from His laws, then they must be judged by God. The very foundation of the civil order was undermined when judges did not discern between good and evil (cf. 1 Kings 3:9).

The Old Testament abounds with illustrations of God's judgment upon kings, rulers, and judges in Israel who departed from the just standards of His law in their governing of society. Note especially King Ahab, who for his own selfish ends engaged in false witness, theft, and even murder (1 Kings 21:1-22). These matters were recorded by the historian for posterity and as an example, *instead of* Ahab's feats in battle which are known from secular accounts of the period! It was of crucial importance in Israel that rulers abide by the law of the Lord. Those who, like Jeroboam and Jehu, departed from God's commandments and made the people sin, had evil brought against their own houses by God, and were swept away (1 Kings 14:8-10; 16:2-3). When princes became unrighteous and rebellious, the whole city was characterized as unrighteous (Isa. 1:21-28), and God always eventually judged the injustice. When the Jews returned from years of exile and captivity, they confessed that their kings had not kept the law of God (Neh. 9:34-37), and in restored Jerusalem the magistrates determined to execute true and peaceful judgments in the law courts (Zech. 8:16).

Law and politics in Old Testament Israel revolved around God's law for the civil magistrate. But what about the Gentiles? Did their governments have *different* moral standards from Israel's? To this question we must now give attention.

24

LAW AND POLITICS IN NATIONS AROUND ISRAEL

"God did not exempt nations around Israel from the claims of His righteousness, but rather held them accountable for moral degeneration."

Law and politics in Old Testament Israel revolved around God's law for the civil magistrate. That much would be granted by virtually any Christian who takes an interest in a Christian political stand and who has read the Bible. In the "theocracy" of the Old Testament God obviously gave laws for His people to obey in the political sector of life.

Nevertheless, it is often thought, those "theocratic" laws given to Israel for her political life are of little help to Christian political theory today. Why? Were Old Testament laws about crime and punishment *less inspired* than prophecies about the coming Messiah? Well, no, we will be told. Were Old Testament laws about crime and punishment *less of a reflec-*

tion of God's unchanging holy character than commandments about the attitude of one's heart toward his neighbor? Well, no, we will again be told. Were Old Testament laws about crime and punishment *ceremonial* (or restorative, redemptive) in character like the sacrificial system, foreshadows to be replaced by the reality of the coming Messiah and his work? Well no, once again we will be told. Why then are "theocratic" laws pertaining to the political sphere thought to be of little guidance and help to Christian political theorizing today?

The answer which is offered over and over again today is that the political laws given by God to Israel as a "theocracy" were for Israel *alone* to obey. Only Israel was given a *written revelation* of these laws, to be sure. All will grant that. But that fact alone does not imply that only Israel was bound to obey the moral standards expressed in such written revelation. After all, through Paul, God wrote to the Ephesian and Colossian churches that children should obey their parents (Eph. 6:1; Col. 3:20), and nobody seriously takes that fact to imply that *only* children of Christian parents are under moral obligation to obey their parents. Therefore, the fact that only Israel was given a special revelation of certain political laws would not imply that only Israel was bound to keep such laws.

Gentiles Were Under God's Law

What God revealed in writing to His chosen, redeemed people about their moral duties was *also* revealed by God — without writing out words — to *all other* created people as well. The Gentiles who were not given the law still have the work of the law written on their hearts, thereby condemning their sinful behavior. This is Paul's testimony in Romans 2:12-16, and it is a truth which is foundational to the universal gospel of salvation which Paul goes on to elaborate in Romans. All people are under obligation to the standards of God's law — in whatever form it has been received, written or not — and thus all have sinned and are in need of Christ's redemption (Rom. 3:23). God is no respector of persons here. He has the same standard for all men whom He has created. And all men know those standards in virtue of their creation as God's image, in virtue of living in God's world, and in virtue of God's clear work of general and special revelation. Nevertheless, there are Christians who maintain that with respect to a special subclass of the laws revealed to the Jews in the Old Testament, those laws were meant for only Israel to keep. These laws were political in character. The kings and judges of Israel were bound to obey them, we are told, but not the rulers in other nations. *All* children — Jewish or Gentile — were under moral obligation to obey their parents, it is thought, but *only* Jewish rulers (not Gentile) were under moral obligation to punish crimes (for example, assaulting one's parents violently) in the way specified by the Old Testament law. That is, according to this outlook, some laws from God were universal in obligation, and other laws were localized.

Is such a delineation of universal and localized laws made in the *text* of the inspired Old Testament?

Well, no, it must be admitted. Is such a delineation of universal and localized laws made in *Paul's teaching* about the general or universal revelation of God's moral standards? Well no, it must again be admitted. In fact, the Roman epistle states quite clearly that those who commit abominable misdeeds such as homosexuality know from "the ordinances of God that those who practice such things are worthy of death" (Rom. 1:31).

There does not seem to be any *obvious* Biblical support for the opinion that political laws in the Old Testament were intended only for Israel to obey. Just about every line of theological consideration would incline us in the direction of the opposite conclusion: the Creator of all men, who has an unchanging moral character, has revealed the standards of his law to every nation of men and will hold men accountable for their behavior in all areas of life, including politics. If His standards have been given clear, written expression to a special group of men—the Jews—then it would seem reasonable for all men to pay attention to those written laws and strive to conform to them.

When we turn from theological themes to a specific reading of the Scripture, this is the viewpoint which we find definitely decreed. In special blessing God gave the Jews a written expression of His law (for all areas of life), and that written law was intended as a model for *all* nations—not simply Israel—to follow. In giving Israel God's law to be kept in the "theocratic" land, Moses was inspired to say: "Behold, I have taught you statutes and ordinances, even as Jehovah my God commanded me, that you should do so in the midst of the land whither you go in to possess it. Keep therefore and do them; *for this is your wisdom and your understanding in the sight of the peoples,* that shall hear *all* these statutes and say, surely this great nation is a wise and understanding people. . . . And what great nation is there, that has statutes and ordinances so righteous as all this law which I set before you today?" (Deut. 4:5-8). Israel's law was a *model* for all the nations round about. And it was such a model with respect to *all* the statutes delivered from God through Moses —including, then, the statutes touching on political matters like crime and punishment.

When we considered the Biblical teaching about law and politics in Old Testament Israel, we in summary found that: (1) God's appointed rulers are not to be resisted; (2) Bearing religious titles, rulers were avengers of divine wrath; and (3) magistrates must deter evil by ruling according to God's law. A survey of what the Old Testament teaches about the rulers in Gentile nations will lead us to make the same three summary points about non-Jewish magistrates. The doctrine of the civil magistrate's moral duties, therefore, is uniform in the Old Testament.

The fact that God was dealing with Israel in a redemptive and covenantal fashion, and not setting His electing love upon any other nation (cf. Amos 3:2), did not introduce a disparity or difference in moral standards between Israel and the nations. All those who wander from God's statutes—indeed all the wicked of the earth—are condemned by God, according to Psalm 119:118-119. Accordingly, there was no recognition of differing laws for differing kinds of people (Jewish, Gentile) in the Old Testament. "There shall be one standard for the stranger as well as the native, for I am the Lord your God" (Lev. 24:22). With respect to politics, as with all things, God did not have a double standard of morality. The justice of His law was to be established as a light to the Gentiles (Isa. 51:4). Indeed, the prophetic hope was that *all* nations would flow into Zion, saying "Come and let us go up to the mountain of Jehovah, to the house of the God of Jacob; and he will teach us of his ways, and we will walk in his paths: for out of Zion shall go forth the law, and the word of Jehovah from Jerusalem" (Isa. 2:2-3).

The Old Testament perspective was that God's law had international and civic relevance. Its binding character was not confined to the borders of Israel. Accordingly, the Wisdom literature of the Old Testament (for example, the book of Proverbs) made wise and practical application of the law of God, and it was written for the entire world. The wisdom of Proverbs had universal bearing, expressing axiomatic truths for all men. Rather than being localized and nationalistic, the Wisdom literature was intended for use in cultural interaction with other peoples. God's law—Israel's wisdom in the sight of others (cf. Deut. 4:6, 8)—was designed for the moral government of the *world*.

Gentile Civil Magistrates

Biblical teaching about the civil magistrate in Gentile nations during the Old Testament period, reflecting parallels with the teaching about magistrates in Israel, begins with the truth that:

1. *God's appointed rulers are not to be resisted.*

The leaders of the foreign powers around Israel were *servants of God's will.* Pharaoh had to learn the lesson that God was unsurpassed in all the earth in terms of power and authority (Ex. 19:14-16). Gentile kings were subject to God's reproof (Ps. 105:14). All civil magistrates owed their authority to God's sovereign disposition of history, and as such they were subject to His rule, being set up or brought down according to His decree (Ezk. 17:24).

God gave the earth to those unto whom it seemed right to Him (Jer. 27:5). It was God who would either break the yoke of the Babylonian king or establish it as iron (Jer. 28:1-14). He was "Most High" over the earth (Ps. 9:2; 83:18), setting the course of nations subject to His rebuke (Ps. 9:4-8; 83:9-12). Even "beastly" rulers have been *given* their authority by God (Dan. 7:6). Daniel, a Jew in exile who would gain political honor, wrote that God "removes kings and sets up kings" (2:21); "the most High rules in the kingdom of men and gives it to whomever he will" (4:25). Both Nebuchadnezzar and Belshazzar, Gentile leaders, had to learn this truth under the aweful hand of God's judgment (Dan. 4:28-34; 5:18-28). The nations round about Israel were to know that God is the one who sovereignly appoints and removes rulers. Indeed, having learned this lesson, Nebuchadnezzar sent a decree to all nations so that they might also recognize that God dominates the political affairs of men (Dan. 4:1-3). The *Old* Testament, then, taught that with respect to Gentile magistrates "the powers that be are ordained of God" (cf. Rom. 13:1).

Such rulers were to be given submission and respect. God prohibited resistance to their proper authority. Those who respected God should give honor also to the king (Prov. 24:21). Opposition to God's ordained rules will bring punishment from the ruler and from God (vv. 21-22). Peter alluded to these verses in penning 1 Peter 2:13-14 for New Testament Christians living under non-Christian rulers. Likewise, in the Old Testament, the instruction to seek political peace (Ps. 34:14) was taught as applicable even when Gentile rulers are in power over God's people: "Seek the peace of the city whither I have caused you to be carried away captive, and pray unto Jehovah for it; for in the peace thereof you shall have peace" (Jer. 29:7). Parallel to this injunction is Paul's instruction to offer prayers for kings and high officials in order that a peaceful life might be possible (1 Tim. 2:1-2). God's people in "dispersion" (1 Pet. 1:1) must seek peace even under the threat of persecution (1 Pet. 3:10-14, again citing Ps. 34:14).

So then, if God has decreed that Nebuchadnezzar come to power, "It shall come to pass that the nation and the kingdom which will not serve the same Nebuchadnezzar king of Babylon, and that will not put their neck under the yoke of the king of Babylon, will I punish, says Jehovah" (Jer. 27:8). Those who resist God's appointed rulers will receive judgment, even as Paul taught in Romans 13:2.

2. *Bearing religious titles, rulers were to avenge divine wrath.*

In Israel the titles of "My Servant" and "My Shepherd" had clear religious overtones because of their typological significance, pointing to the coming Messiah (for example, Isa. 53:11; Ezk. 34:23). What is of interest to us is that such religiously significant titles are applied to political rulers *outside* of Israel. Nebuchadnezzar was called by God "My servant" (Jer. 25:9, etc.), and Cyrus was called "My shepherd" (Isa. 44:28). Indeed, Cyrus is even designated "My annointed one" ("My Christ" in Greek translation) by Jehovah in Isaiah 45:1. Such titles show how religiously important the office of magistrate was even in Gentile lands, according to God's word.

It was appropriate, then, that Gentile magistrates be expected to avenge God's wrath against evildoers, for the magistrates were representatives and servants of the Most High. For instance, the Assyrian king was to be "the rod of My anger, the staff in whose hand is My indignation" (Isa. 10:1). God gave "charge" to Assyria to do His work of vengeance, and when Assyria overlooked its servant status under God, it was punished for its stout heart and self-sufficient arrogance in attacking Israel (Isa. 1:12-13). In Old Testament perspective, therefore, God was viewed as *enthroned* over *all* nations (Ps. 47:2, 7, 8), making all Gentile rulers the deputies of God. "The shields [rulers] of all the earth belong unto God," declared the Psalmist (47:9). Civil rule in all the nations is secondary and subordinate to God's rule. God reigns among the nations in righteousness according to the Old Testament (Ps. 93:1-2, etc.).

As appointed deputies of the Most High God, Gentile rulers were under moral obligation *to rule according to God's standards*. The Proverb indicated, "the throne is established by righteousness," and "the king establishes the land by justice" (Prov. 16:12; 29:4). Thus the throne of any magistrate is to be fashioned after God's throne, founded on righteousness and justice (Ps. 97:2). The guidance and decisions made by civil magistrates—even among Gentiles—should have reflected God's conception of justice for social affairs, and that conception was found in God's law. So it was an abomination for any magistrate among men to justify the wicked or condemn the righteous (Prov. 17:15).

3. *Thus, magistrates must deter evil by ruling according to God's Law.*

In the New Testament, Paul would teach that magistrates were to bring praise to the good and terror to evil men (Rom. 13:3). The same perspective was advanced in the Old Testament Proverb: "The execution of justice is joy to the righteous, but is terror to the workers of iniquity" (21:15). But how can this truly be the case unless the magistrate, whether in Israel or not, judges and punishes according to the standards of God's law? When tyrants rule among men, even righteous citizens need to fear the judgments of the ruler, for he does not adhere to proper standards; likewise, with a magistrate that does not honor the law of God, a wicked citizen need not necessarily fear the ruler's decisions. Gentile magistrates were thus required in the Old Testament to keep the law of God for political affairs.

One Moral Standard

God did not exempt nations around Israel from the claims of His righteousness, but rather held them accountable for moral degeneration. Proof of this statement is sufficiently found in the stories of Sodom (negatively) and Ninevah (positively). But the most dramatic proof that God's law was valid outside of Israel is found in Lev. 18:24-27. God there required His people to avoid the abominations against His law which were practiced by the Canaanites of the land, and He threatened to punish Israel in the same way as he would punish the Gentiles for these offenses. Clearly God had *one* moral standard for all societies. For that reason the indictment, "Woe to him that builds a town with blood and establishes a city by iniquity," was voiced against Israel (Mic. 3:10) as well as against the Babylonians (Hab. 2:12). It is obvious from these observations that God expected Gentile magistrates and citizens to honor his standards of righteousness and justice just as much as he expected it of Israelite magistrates and citizens. As the Proverb taught, "Righteousness exalts a nation, but sin is a disgrace to any people" (14:34).

The axiomatic political truth taught by the Old Testament was that "it is an abomination for kings to commit wickedness" (Prov. 16:12) — any king whatsoever! Correspondingly, Ezra could praise God for putting it into the heart of the pagan Emperor, Artaxerxes, to have God's law enforced (even to the point of its penal sanction of death) throughout the region surrounding Israel (Ezra 7:11-28). Indeed, David himself declared that he would take God's law for Israel and speak it before other kings (Ps. 119:46). And he warned that the kings and judges of the earth who would not fear Jehovah and serve Him would perish in the way (Ps. 2:10-12).

The Old Testament evidence is quite abundant, then, that expectations for civil rulers outside of Israel were often the same as they were for rulers in Israel. They were appointed by God to avenge His wrath by enforcing the law of the Lord. The political aspects of God's law, therefore, were certainly *not* intended for the exclusive use of the Jews in their "theocratic" situation. The political justice God required in Israel was required of all nations as well. It was not racially or geographically relative.

25

LAW AND POLITICS IN THE NEW TESTAMENT

"If no divine law is recognized above the law of the state, then the law of man has become absolute in men's eyes—there is then no logical barrier to totalitarianism."

Recent years have brought a renewed concern among evangelical and Reformed Christians for a distinctively Christian attitude and approach to all areas of life and behavior, including socio-political ethics. So we have asked what the standard of that distinctive perspective would be for a Bible-believing Christian. In the Old Testament it is evident that God's chosen people, Israel, were to govern their political activity according to the revealed law of God which was given through Moses and expounded by the prophets. Upon examination, it turned out that even the Gentile nations around Israel were held accountable by God for obedience to His law in the Old Testament era. God's law touched on all aspects of life, including criminal justice, and that law was not presented by the Lawgiver as a racist or tribal standard of right and wrong. It was God's universal and eternal standard of righteousness for human affairs.

In a sense, we have already offered an implicit answer to our question about the standard for a distinctive Christian outlook on political ethics. God has spoken to issues of social justice and public policy toward crime in His law. There is a divine point of view on politics, and it has been expressed in the law of the Old Testament. Two things are to be said about that law. First, it continues to be the general standard of ethical conduct today according to the Scripture — as we have seen many times over in previous chapters. Second, Old Testament law did not have a moral validity restricted to the Jewish race; it has intended to be the standard of conduct outside the redeemed community as well as within it. Consequently, if the Old Testament law of God expresses (among other things) God's view on political morality, and if that law has universal and abiding validity, we should expect that the New Testament perspective on law and politics would likewise affirm the standard of God's law for public policy. Differences in time and locality, differences in dispensation and race, differences in culture and redemptive status do not demand or imply differences in moral standards.

We would thus expect that the distinctive Christian approach to political ethics would be defined by the entire word of God, *inclusive of* the law of God revealed through Moses and expounded by the prophets in the Old Testament. When we turn to study the New Testament writings themselves on this question, this is precisely what we find to be the case. There is definite continuity between the political ethics of the New Testament and the political ethics of the Old Testament. There is complete harmony between what Paul says about the state, for instance in Romans 13, and what we found to be taught in the Old Testament — namely:

1. As appointed by God, rulers are not to be resisted.

2. Bearing religious titles, rulers are avengers of divine wrath.

3. So rulers must deter evil by ruling according to God's law.

These very points, made by the Old Testament with respect to Jewish and Gentile (redeemed and non-redeemed) magistrates both, are clearly expressed by Paul in Romans 13:1-6. They are premises upon which a distinctive Christian attitude toward public justice can and ought to be formulated.

Romans 13

If the three points laid out above are each taken seriously, then perhaps we can avoid falling into the unfortunate excesses of two conflicting interpretive approaches to the teaching of Romans 13 about the state. On the one hand we have Bible interpreters who contend that Romans 13 should be read *descriptively*, thus laying nearly exclusive stress upon Paul's practical exhortation to Christians. That is, when Paul says that the civil magistrate "is a minister of God, an avenger of wrath to evildoers" (v. 4), some interpreters take him to be giving an actual description of all earthly rulers in their real character and function. All statesmen would then be described as God's ministers who avenge wrath on the evil element of society — regardless of the actual quality and conduct of the particular ruler one may have in mind. Even Hitler and Idi Amin would be described as genuine ministers of God. In that case, Paul's practical thrust in Romans 13 would simply be to instruct believers that they must submit obediently to whatever magistrate God has placed over them in society (with the proviso, of course, that they cannot obey men when human rulers order them to disobey God: Acts 5:29).

On the other hand we have Bible interpreters who argue that Romans 13 should be read *prescriptively*, thus emphasizing that Paul was giving the moral standard for civil magistrates and thereby indicating *which* rules were to be given submissive obedience by the Christian. That is, when Paul says that the magistrate is "a minister of God, an avenger of wrath to evildoers" (v. 4), some interpreters see him as laying down a moral prescription for civil rulers — telling them what they ought to be. Magistrates are to be ministers of God who avenge wrath on evildoers. Consequently, the prescriptive approach to

Romans 13 does not stress practical submission on the part of the believer; it rather stands in evaluative judgment over all magistrates, showing the Christian which ones are deserving of their submission and obedience. Both of these interpretations of Romans 13 have tended toward practical consequences which are pretty clearly unacceptable, given the rest of what Scripture says to Christians about morality and politics. The descriptive view of Romans 13 has led many believers in past history to be indifferent to concrete political wrongs and even to comply passively with the injustices of political tyrants, like Hitler. On the other hand, the prescriptive view of Romans 13 has often encouraged a rebellious spirit toward the civil magistrate, leading believers to take lightly the Biblical injunctions against revolution or civil disobedience.

It can be said in defense of each approach that these practical consequences are in fact *abuses* of the respective views—abuses that do not take into account other Biblical teaching, qualifications made, and the full context. This may be, but if one keeps in mind the Old Testament background to Paul's instruction about the civil magistrate in Romans 13, it is possible to interpret the passage in a way which does justice both to the Christian's need to resist political injustice and to the Christian's obligation to be in submission to the powers that be.

When Paul says that the ruling powers are ministers of God who avenge wrath against evildoers, he is explaining what civil magistrates ought to be and simultaneously explaining why believers must maintain a submissive attitude toward their rulers. The three points outlined above demonstrate this dual explanatory role of Paul's teaching by summarizing what the apostle says in Romans 13. The Christian must not have a rebellious attitude toward the civil magistrate, because the magistrate is appointed by God. Appointed for what purpose, however? Appointed to be *avengers of divine wrath,* in which case magistrates can bear religious titles like "minister of God."

If this is true, then rulers must honor good citizens and deter evil by punishing the criminal element in society, using the standard of God's law as their guide (as to good and evil). This explains why Christians must nearly always be submissive to the civil ruler: that ruler is obligated in his public capacity to serve the Christian's Lord, and thus loyalty to the Lord requires loyalty to the king. However, when such service is repudiated by the king (or other ruling authority) and the law of the Lord is violently and persistently transgressed, so that good citizens are terrorized by the ruler and evil men tolerated or exalted, the Christian must not comply with the tyrant's policies but rather work for reform in the name of the Lord and divine standards of public justice.

The fact that God's law is binding on present-day civil magistrates explains both why the Christian should shun rebellious attitudes toward rulers and why Christians may not cooperate with unjust regimes. Absolute *submission* under any and all circumstances, or absolute *independence* of the magistrate regarding each and every decision he makes, may be simple and easy positions to understand or follow, but the more complex attitude of general submission for the sake of the Lord but resistance when God's law is outrageously violated is more faithful to Scriptural teaching and truer to political realities. It is this balanced approach which Paul presents in Romans 13 and which is summarized in the three points outlined earlier.

Romans 13:1-7 states what God requires of *believers* regarding their civil leaders, and it states what God requires of rulers regarding their civil function. Submission to superiors is essential to both statements of duty. The Lord expects His people to submit obediently to their rulers, for the Lord expects those rulers to submit obediently to His law. For conscience' sake, then, Christians can submit to their civil authorities, knowing that indirectly they are submitting to the moral order of God Himself.

1. *As appointed by God, rulers are not to be resisted.*

Paul begins with the generalization that civil government is a divine institution: "there is no power (authority) but of God" (Rom. 13:1). God has actually "ordained" the powers that be. Obviously, then, supremacy belongs to God and not to the state. Respect for the rulers of state ought never to reach such proportions that the believer gives the state that unquestioning obedience which should be reserved for God alone. Paramount in Paul's mind is the fact that, even if Christians are under orders from the state, the state itself is under orders from God above.

Since God has ordained the magistrates who rule in the state, those magistrates have been put not only in authority over others, but also under the authority of God. Magistrates are under moral obligation to the prescriptions of the Lord. John Murray observed:

> The civil magistrate is not only the means decreed in God's providence for the punishment of evildoers but God's instituted, authorized, and prescribed instrument for the maintenance of order and the punishing of criminals who violate that order. When the civil magistrate through his agents executes just judgment upon crime, he is executing not simply God's decretive will but he is also fulfilling God's prescriptive will, and it would be sinful for him to refrain from so doing.[1]

Since all civil magistrates have no power unless it has been given to them from above — as Christ declared, even while standing before Pilate (John 19:11) — *they are responsible to reverence and obey Almighty God.* When they, as with Herod, accept praise as a god, they come under the terrible wrath of God and can be deposed from power: "Upon a set day Herod arrayed himself in royal apparel, and sat upon the throne, and made an oration unto them. And the people shouted, 'The voice of a god, and not of a man.' And immediately an angel of the Lord smote

---

1. *The Epistle to the Romans,* 2 vols. (Grand Rapids, Michigan: Eerdmans, 1965), II, p. 149.

him, because he gave not God the glory; and he was eaten of worms and gave up the ghost" (Acts 12:21-23).

The proper aim of all ethical conduct is the glory of God, and civil magistrates, being ordained by God to rule, are not exempt from the moral obligation to rule for the glory of God. Those appointed by God will be answerable to God for the kind of rule they render in society. This is nothing else but the doctrine of the Old Testament, whether we consider the rulers of Israel or the rulers of Gentile nations around Israel. Paul's teaching is grounded in the Old Testament. Both the Old and New Testaments, then, begin their "philosophy of state" within the supremacy of God, to whom all rulers owe reverence and obedience.

Submission and Prayer

In *that context* Paul goes on to insist that civil rulers, as God's appointees, are not to be given resistance. "The one resisting the authority has opposed the ordinance of God, and they who oppose will receive to themselves judgment" (Rom. 13:2). The Old Testament background to this statement by Paul is the best commentary on the verse. Parallel statements are also found in the New Testament at Titus 3:1 ("put them in mind to be in subjection to rulers") and 1 Peter 2:13 ("be subject to every ordinance of man"). Throughout Scripture, we see that God does not approve of a rebellious, disrespectful, or disobedient spirit concerning those who have been ordained by God as our civil leaders. Honor is to be rendered to whom honor is due, Paul says (Rom.

13:7), and since the Old Testament law stipulated "You shall not revile God, nor curse a ruler of your people" (Ex. 22:28), Paul himself displayed a repentant spirit when he had (unwittingly) spoken evil of a ruler (Acts 23:5).

Old Testament believers were told to pray for their unbelieving, Gentile rulers (Jer. 29:7; Ezra 6:10). When captive in Babylon, they were to seek the peace of Babylon. This would clearly contrast any attitude of resistance. Likewise, in the New Testament, God's people are exhorted to pray for kings and all that are in high places (1 Tim. 2:2), and Peter writes to Christians in "Dispersion" (1 Pet. 1:1) who faced imminent persecution from the Roman high command (1:6; 4:12; 5:13) that they should imitate the godly pattern of peace-seeking as found in Psalm 34:14 (1 Pet. 3:10-14). Over and over again we find definite continuity between the Old and New Testaments regarding political ethics. Here that continuity is evident in that saints under both the Old and New Covenants were to respect civil rulers as appointed of God, praying for them, and seeking peace within their societies. God's people have always had the obligation to submit to their magistrates, knowing that those same rulers were ordained as part of God's moral rule over creation. Just because the ruler stands under the authority of God, those who profess allegiance to God must respect the ruler. It is not simply out of pragmatic expediency that the Christian obeys the civil authorities — "not simply because of the wrath" which they can express against dissenters (Rom. 13:5a). He must obey *also* "for the sake of conscience" (Rom. 13:5b). That is, out of regard for the Lord Himself who stands over the civil magistrate, His deputy, the Christian must submit to the ruler—and in so doing submit to the supreme Ruler.

Conscience

It should be obvious, despite the short-sightedness of some commentators, that the submission given to civil magistrates must be *in the context of* the magistrate ministering for God, for this submission is explicitly prescribed by Paul for *conscience'* sake. Paul frequently uses the word 'conscience,' meaning *conscience toward God* (for example, Acts 23:1; 2 Cor. 4:2; 2 Tim. 1:3). "God alone is Lord of the conscience and therefore to do anything out of conscience or for conscience' sake is to do it from a sense of obligation to God" (John Murray, *Epistle to the Romans,* vol. 2, p. 154). Moreover, Paul always qualified the obedience that must be rendered *to men* as obedience given for *godly* ends—obedience given in the context of submitting first and foremost to the moral demands of God Himself.

Charles Hodge expressed this insight:

> In like manner, Paul enforces all relative and social duties on religious grounds. Children are to obey their parents, because it is right in the sight of God; and servants are to be obedient to their masters, as unto Christ, doing the will of God from the heart, Eph. 6:1, 5, 6.[2]

---

2. *A Commentary on Romans* (London: Banner of Truth Trust, [1835], 1972), p. 408.

This is made quite clear in 1 Peter 2:13, where we read that we ought to "be subject to every ordinance of man *for the Lord's sake.*" Thus believers submit to the civil magistrate for the sake of *conscience* — which is to say, for the Lord's sake — just because *the magistrate* is to be submissive to *the Lord,* seeking His glory, and obeying His commands.

Conscience cannot permit a rebellious spirit against the *Lord's* appointed ruler, even as it cannot permit compliance with dictates of the ruler which defy the law of the *Lord.* Paul's teaching ever places Christ as *Lord over all,* even as in the first commandment of the Decalogue.

The Supremacy of God

Therefore, the supremacy of God is a key for correctly understanding the view of the state advanced by Paul in Romans 13:1-7. Just as taught in the Old Testament, Paul also teaches that believers are under strict obligation to obey the civil magistrate because the Most High God, who is supreme over all, has ordained the rule of the magistrate. Just because the ruler is conceived of as under orders from God who appointed him, the Christian must respect the ruler, as a way of showing submission ultimately to God Himself. Because God is supreme over all and has given authority to those who exercise rule in society, such civil magistrates are not autonomous agents, free to do as they wish, and answerable to nobody. As deputies of God they must serve His purposes. When and if they defy the will of God, acting in a sinful and satanic fashion with their brute power, the Christian's "conscience before the Lord" cannot go along with them.

Since the Lord is the supreme Judge, the Christian must *not resist* those who are appointed by God and minister for Him. For the *same reason,* the submission given to rulers by the Christian is *qualified* by his primary allegiance to the Lord, and by the understanding that submission to the state is for the sake of the Lord, whose will the magistrate ought to pursue.

2. *Bearing religious titles, rulers are avengers of divine wrath.*

The supremacy of God as the preconditioning assumption of Romans 13:1-7 comes to expression in the titles assigned to civil rulers by Paul. In Old Testament Israel statesmen were sometimes designated "priests," and even in the Gentile nations around Israel civil leaders were occasionally called by God "My servant," "My shepherd," and "My annointed (Christ)." This tendency to see the office bearer in the state categorized as a religious official—someone answerable to God Almighty—carries over into the New Testament, once again demonstrating the continuity which exists between the Old and New Testament regarding the powers that be.

The idea of a *secular* state, one which divorces its authority and standards from religious considerations about God and His will, is completely alien to Biblical revelation. Indeed, it was alien to much of the ancient world in general. All politics is the expression of a moral point of view, which in turn is the outworking of a theological conception of man, the world, and God. The modern world is no different; its political philosophies are simultaneously political theologies, and its civil rulers are often seen in a religious light (even if religious vocabulary is shunned).

Magistrates as Ministers

Paul, following the Old Testament, had a religious conception or understanding of the civil magistrate. In Romans 13 he twice categorized the magistrate in society as a "minister of God" (vv. 4, 6). If you ask the ordinary Christian today where one can find God's "minister," he will point you to the pastor of the local church. He will not think to point you to the city, state, or federal magistrate, for he has capitulated to the mentality of humanistic secularism. Paul had not done so, even though the Roman emperors of his day were far from "religious" in the commendable sense of that term. Whatever the Caesars may have thought of themselves, Paul thought of them as *God's ministers*. They were God's prescribed instruments for maintaining order and punishing evildoers according to God's will.

In Romans 13:6 Paul used the title of "leitourgos" to describe the magistrate as God's "minister." In the ancient world this term was used for work done to promote the social order, work performed in the service of the divine-state. So Paul used the term with a theological twist. The magistrate is not a minister of the divine-state, but rather *the state is the minister of God Himself.* In the Greek translation of the Old

Testament (the Septuagint), this term is used to describe the ministry of angels, priests, and prophets—and yet it is likewise used for civil leadership.

In Romans 13:4 Paul's term is "diakonos" or "deacon." Outside the New Testament the term is used in the title, "deacon of the city," an office which aimed at the education of good citizenship. Within the New Testament the term is clearly laden with religious connotation, being applied to the "ministry" of Christ (Matt. 20:28), of Paul (1 Tim. 1:12), and of an office within the church (Acts 6:1-6). Even as there are deacons within the church, Paul declared that there are deacons in the state: namely, men who are appointed by God to minister justice in His name.

By utilizing these two terms for "minister," and by making clear that the ruler is a minister *of God,* Paul unequivocally teaches the religious character of the civil leader's office. In the perspective of the New Testament, magistrates must be deemed *servants* of God. His rule is supreme, and their rules are subordinate. Civil magistrates must be understood to be deputies of God Himself, not free and independent despots who can simply do as they please.

The Ministry of the Sword

What is it that God requires of his ordained "ministers" in the state? How are they to render service to Him? The power of the civil magistrate, in distinction from all other authorities (the family, the church, the school, etc.), is the power of compulsion; the civil magistrate has the right to punish those who do not conform to his laws, and punish them with external afflictions: financial fines, bodily pains (labor or scourging), and even death.

Other sectors of society may in various ways impose penalties on offenders, but never capital punishment. Parents cannot execute, pastors cannot execute, employers cannot execute — but the civil magistrate's authority clearly *stands out* as the authority to execute criminals. The power of the magistrate is thus appropriately symbolized in the power of the *sword*. The most extreme penalty has been placed at the disposal of the civil magistrate, the death penalty. Paul speaks of the magistrate in Romans 13:4 as one who "carries the sword." (For the meaning of this symbol one can consult Matt. 26:52; Acts 12:2; Heb. 11:37; Rev. 13:10).

The civil magistrate, according to Paul's teaching, must be seen as a minister of God, one whose activities include the use of the sword in the punishment of offenders. Civil rulers have a God-given ministry of the sword. Is this to say, however, that God throws the blanket of His endorsement over any and all uses of the sword by any and all civil magistrates throughout history? Hardly! There have surely been men who were bloody tyrants, men who abused the power placed in their hands, men who executed capital punishment where it was immoral to do so. Power, arrogance, bribery, jealously, lust, and prejudice have corrupted the ministry of the sword as it has been expressed in the reign of many a magistrate in the course of history.

It is here that we must pay attention to Paul's wording in Romans 13:4. He does not describe any and all uses of the civil sword as the ministry of God in a society. Paul rather distinguishes (implicitly) between a proper and an improper use of the sword, speaking of "bearing the sword *in vain."* Even as common sense and historical experience would tell us, some magistrates have wielded the sword in a way which is empty of value as far as a ministry for God is concerned. Some have made a futile use of the sword, a use which God never intended it to have. Some have carried the sword in vain. Over against such vain uses of the sword, Paul describes in Romans 13 the magistrate who truly ministers for God. Paul sets before us in Romans 13:4 the model of God's civil minister, one who "bears not the sword in vain."

The Wrath of God

What is the "minister of God" who "bears not the sword in vain" to do in the service of God for society, according to Paul? Paul says that he is to be "a minister of God, an avenger for wrath to him who works evil" (Rom. 13:4). *Whose* wrath is the magistrate to avenge? Surely not his own, for it is just in such self-serving displays of wrath that the sword has been vainly used throughout history. Rather, Paul indicates that the magistrate must avenge the wrath of *God.* In his paragraph just preceding the one now under discussion, Paul had exhorted believers to be at peace with men and not to avenge themselves of wrongs suffered. Romans 12:19 said, "Avenge not yourselves, beloved, but give place unto the wrath of God: for it is written,

Vengeance belongs unto me; I will recompense, says the Lord." Two words stand out here: vengeance and wrath. God Himself will avenge wrath upon offenders, so believers need not take such a task into their own hands. But *how* will God avenge His wrath upon offenders? Romans 13:1-7 answers that natural question. God has ordained a ministry of the sword in society. Those whom He has placed in authority are to be "avengers for wrath"—that is, avengers of *divine wrath* for the One who declares that all vengeance belongs to Him. The minister of God in the state, the one who bears not the sword in vain, will work to avenge the wrath of God against offenders— against "the one who practices evil" (Rom. 13:4). This is an important part of the description of the civil magistrate. He must see to it that good citizens have nothing to fear from his rule and that the criminal element of society has much to fear. As Paul says, "Rulers are not a terror to the good work, but to the evil. . . . He is a minister of God to you for good, but if you do what is evil, be afraid" (Rom. 13:3-4). The magistrate is under obligation correctly to distinguish virtuous and vicious activities within society. He must reward the one and punish the other.

Those who are to undergo his judicial wrath as he bears the sword for God are described as "evildoers" by Paul in Romans 13:4. If we skip down just six verses to Romans 13:10, we read that *love* works *no evil* to one's neighbors. It is precisely these citizens—those who unlovingly transgress the commandments of God which are designed to protect the life, liberty, and property of neighbors — who are the "evildoers" that Paul would have the magistrate punish, even to the point of death (where appropriate). In Pauline perspective, the civil magistrate today bears religious titles, being called to be an avenger of divine wrath against law-breakers.

Old Testament Concepts

The New Testament attitude toward law and politics as it is found in Romans 13:1-7 has turned out to correspond at crucial points with the Old Testament attitude, whether pertaining to Jewish or Gentile magistrates. Paul's underlying assumption was the supremacy of God over all. Taking this for granted, Paul could portray rulers as appointed by God and therefore not to be resisted. Indeed, Paul could go on to repudiate any secularized notion of civil rule by calling those who rule in the state "ministers of God," appointed by God to avenge His wrath against evildoers who violate His laws. As seen previously, this was precisely the doctrine of the Old Testament. According to it, one can formulate a distinctive Christian view of public justice. Peter summarizes much of the Old and New Testament teaching regarding the civil magistrate when he describes rulers as "through Him [God] sent for vengeance on evildoers" (1 Pet. 2:14). Such a description can lead to only one conclusion:

3. *Rulers must deter evil by ruling according to God's law.*

This conclusion has been seen to be the consequence of the Old Testament teaching about civil rulers in Israel, as well as the consequence of the Old Testament perspective on civil rulers outside of Israel. Since civil rulers are appointed by God, since they bear religious titles, since they are sent to be avengers of God's wrath, since they must punish those who are genuine evildoers, the only proper *standard* for their rule in society — the only proper criterion of public justice — would have to be the law of God. Those who are ordained by God must obey His dictates, not their own. Those who are called "ministers of God" must live up to such a title by serving the will of God. Those who are to avenge God's wrath must be directed by God Himself as to what warrants such wrath and how it should be expressed. Those who are to punish evildoers must have a reliable standard by which to judge who is, and who is not, an evildoer in the eyes of God.

So everything points to the obvious conclusion that the civil magistrate, according to Romans 13:1-7 (even as in the Old Testament), is under obligation to obey the stipulations of God's law as they bear on civil leadership and public justice. Within its own literary context (especially 12:19 and 13:10), Romans 13:4 specifically teaches that God's law ought to be the guide for the magistrate who is not to bear his sword in vain. The law of God defines those who are truly evildoers, and it indicates those upon whom God's *wrath* must come.

What Better Standard?

Those who do not favor taking God's law as the ultimate standard for civil morality and public justice will be forced to substitute some other criterion of good and evil for it. The civil magistrate cannot function without some ethical guidance, without some standard of good and evil. If that standard is not to be the revealed law of God (which, we must note, was addressed specifically to perennial problems in political morality), then what will it be? In some form or expression it will have to be the law of man (or men)—the standard of self-law or autonomy. And when *autonomous* laws come to govern a commonwealth, the sword is certainly wielded *in vain*, for it represents simply the brute force of some men's will against the will of other men. "Justice" then indeed becomes a verbal cloak for whatever serves the interests of the strongmen in society (whether their strength be that of physical might or of media manipulation).

Men will either choose to be governed by God or to be ruled by tyrants. Because of the merciful, restraining work of the Holy Spirit in societies, we do not see at every stage *in history* these stark polarities coming to expression; most societies will to some measure strive for conformity to God's law, even when it is officially denounced. However, *in principle* the choices are clearly between God's law and man's law, between life and death for a society. If no divine law is recognized above the law of the state, then the law of man has become absolute in men's eyes—there is then no *logical* barrier to totalitarianism.

When God's law is put aside, and the politician's law comes to reign in its place, we have "the beast" described for us by the Apostle John in Revelation

13. Regardless of one's eschatological school of thought, and regardless of the overall interpretive structure one has for the book of Revelation, all Bible readers must agree that "the beast" is the *wicked* civil magistrate *par excellence*. He is the very opposite of what Paul described in Romans 13, and thus it comes as no surprise that the book of Revelation *commends* Christians for resisting the dictates of the beast — even though Romans 13 *condemns* resistance ordinarily.

It will prove insightful to note how John describes the evil magistrate known as "the beast." In Revelation 13:16-17 we read of "the mark of the beast," which must be placed upon one's forehead and hand if he is to engage in commerce in the marketplace; the mark identifies the name or character of the beast himself. In order to have a viable place in society, the beast requires that his name and authority — his law — direct the thinking and behavior (head and hand) of all citizens. Those familiar with the Old Testament will readily catch John's allusion to Deuteronomy 6:8, where God said that *His law* was to be bound upon the forehead and the hand of His people. The beast is portrayed as taking away God's law and *replacing* it with his own human law. Staying in harmony with this portrayal, Paul himself describes the beast in 2 Thessalonians 2 as "the man of *lawlessness.*"

The paradigm of a wicked political leader in the Bible, as we have seen, is one who rejects the law of God as the standard of public justice and turns to an autonomous standard instead. John makes it quite clear who can be counted upon to resist the beast, the man of lawlessness. Those who resist him are described in Revelation 12:17 as those "who keep the commandments of God and hold the testimony of Jesus," and in 14:12 as those who "keep the commandments of God and the faith of Jesus." The opposition between the saints and the beast thus clearly pivots on the law of God.

Paul's Political Morality

The magistrate who wins the approval of Paul in Romans 13 is the one who is a minister of God "for the good," but a "terror" to those who "practice evil." In saying such things Paul was clearly not departing from his pattern of defining good and evil according to the law of God. Indeed, when Paul stood before the Sanhedrin of the Jews protesting his innocence, he declared that he had done nothing *evil* (Acts 23:9 and 25:11) — nothing contrary to God's law — or else he would be quite willing to accept the justice of his execution. For Paul, political morality was to be evaluated by the norm of God's revealed law. He did not take a dispensational attitude toward social justice, seeing the standards of the Old Testament laid aside regarding matters of public policy, crime and punishment, in the era of the New Testament. God has one unchanging standard of good and evil, even with respect to political ethics.

In terms of God's one standard for political morality, it is not surprising to find that New Testament preaching and writing was *anything but* apolitical. John the Baptist preached against the unlawfulness of Herod's marriage (Mark 6:18), and Jesus called Herod a "vixen" (Luke 13:32), a cutting denunciation. John told soldiers of their obligations to God's law (Luke 3:14), and Jesus required that Zacchaeus make restitution for false tax-gathering (Luke 19:1-10). Paul preached "contrary to the decrees of Caesar, saying that there is another King—Jesus" (Acts 17:7), for which he was banished from Thessalonica. In writing back to the church there, he alluded to the city council's antagonism to him as the hinderance of Satan (1 Thes. 2:18). In all of these incidents we see that the New Testament is not silent about political wrongs, and that it weighs these wrongs in the balances of God's revealed law. At the most practical and applied level, the distinctive standard for Christian political morality was found in the well-known commandments of God.

Conclusion

Recent years have witnessed a revival of Christian political concern. However, that revival has not frequently been associated with a clear-cut, Biblical conception of socio-political morality. The distinctive *standard* of Christian politics has been overlooked. By studying the *Old* Testament regarding Jewish and Gentile magistrates and by studying the *New* Testament revelation regarding law and politics, we have discovered complete *harmony* on these three essential points:

1. As appointed by God, rulers are not to be resisted.

2. Bearing religious titles, rulers are avengers of divine wrath.

3. So rulers must deter evil by ruling according to God's law.

This provides us with a foundation for Christian involvement in political philosophy and practice. From this platform a distinctive contribution can be made.

26

CRIME AND PUNISHMENT

"If some ruler thought that stealing two pennies deserved death, while killing an innocent child deserved the fine of two cents, many Christian teachers would have no objective way to demonstrate the injustice of this arrangement."

Scripture has taught us that a distinctively Christian approach to political morality calls for recognition of the civil magistrate's obligation to rule according to the dictates of *God's revealed law.* We have likewise observed that the *key function* of the civil magistrate, as God Himself presents it in His written word, is that of bearing the sword as an avenger of wrath against evildoers. Civil rule is a ministry of justice, aiming to punish criminals in accord with the revealed will of God. When we combine this connection with the Biblically based belief that *God's law is binding in every detail until and unless the Lawgiver reveals otherwise,* we come to the conclusion that the civil magistrate today ought to apply the penal sanctions of the Old Testament law to criminals in our society, once they have been duly tried and convicted by adequate evidence. Thieves should be made to offer restitution, rapists should be executed, perjurers should suffer the penalty they would have inflicted on the accused, etc.

Quite simply, *civil magistrates ought to mete out the punishment which God has prescribed in His word*. When one stops to reflect on this proposition, it has an all-too-obvious truthfulness and justice about it. "Shall not the Judge of all the earth do right?" (Genesis 18:25). If civil magistrates are indeed "ministers of God" who avenge *His* wrath against evildoers, who better would know what kind and degree of punishment is appropriate for every crime than the Lord? And where would He make this standard of justice known but in His word? The penal sanctions for crime should be those revealed in the law of the Lord. That makes perfectly good sense.

The Necessity, Equity, and Agency of Punishment

God has not only laid down certain stipulations for how people should live in society together (for example, forbidding stealing), He has also backed up those stipulations — rendering them more serious than divine recommendations — with penal sanctions to be imposed on those who disobey His dictates (for example, offering restitution). A law without such supporting penalties would not be a law at all. Now, in the case of certain Old Testament commandments, there was laid down a *dual sanction* against the offender. A murderer, for instance, would not only undergo the *eternal* wrath of *God* after his death, but he would also need to undergo the *temporal* and social penalty which God prescribed for the *civil magistrate* to apply (in this case, the death penalty). Not all of God's commandments carried this dual sanction, for not all sins are likewise crimes within the state. It is wicked to lust after a woman, but the civil magistrate can neither convict nor punish for lust. When lust becomes adultery, however, then God has stipulated certain measures to be taken by His ordained deputy in the state.

Where God has prescribed it in His word, such civil punishments for crime are quite necessary. Indeed, Paul can say that the law of God was enacted precisely for dealing with public criminals — murderers, perjurers, homosexuals, and the like (1 Tim. 1:8-10). The destruction of the wicked is a proper goal of a godly magistrate (Ps. 101:8) so that he may root out evil (for example, Deut. 17:12; 19:19) and protect the righteous of the land (Ps. 125:3; Prov. 12:21). Such civil penalties against crime are to be executed without mercy or pity to the criminal (Deut. 19:13, 21; 25:12; Heb. 10:28), lest judges become respectors of persons, looking upon the face of criminals and deciding according to some standard other than strict justice who should pay the price of his wrongdoing. Besides, when judges let proven criminals go unpunished, they in effect punish those who have been wronged by the criminal in the first place. As Luther once wrote: "If God will have wrath, what business do you have being merciful?

. . . What a fine mercy to me it would be, to have mercy on the thief and murderer, and let him kill, abuse, and rob me!" So Scripture teaches that civil penalties are necessary. The magistrate is not to carry his sword in vain.

Not only are such penal sanctions *necessary* in society, they must also be *equitable*. The measure of punishment according to the just Judge of all the earth is to be an eye for an eye, a tooth for a tooth, a life for a life — no less, but no more (for example, Ex. 21:23-25; Deut. 19:21). The punishment must be commensurate with the crime, for it is to express retribution against the offender. Especially when one compares the Biblical code of penal sanctions with those in other ancient civilizations does it become apparent how just and wise God's laws are; they are never overweighted, lenient, cruel or unusual. Far from being arbitrary, they are laid down with a view to perfect justice in social affairs. *Indirectly,* these penal sanctions will become a deterrent to crime in others (for example, Deut. 17:13; 19:20), but they are designed to punish a person retributively, "according to his fault" (Deut. 25:2). That is why, for instance, those who commit capital crimes are said in the Bible to have "committed a sin *worthy of death*" (Deut. 21:22). God always prescribes exactly what a crime deserves; the stringency of the penalty is proportioned to the heinousness of the deed. His punishments are thus always equitable.

The agency which God enlists for executing His just and necessary penalties in society for crimes is the civil magistrate. The reason why, *by men,* the blood of offenders may be shed is given in Genesis 9:5-6, namely because man was created in the *image of God*. Men can reflect the judgments of God against criminals because men — those appointed to this task — are the image of God, able to understand and apply His standards of civic rectitude.

Paul described the civil magistrate as ordained by God, one who "bears not the sword in vain" *because* he is "a minister of God, an avenger for wrath against evildoers" (Rom. 13:1-4). Without such authorization, the punishment of one man by another would be pure presumption, the perpetration by one group of a misdeed against another individual or group. The very notion of *public justice* ("the right" surpassing considerations of "might") is rooted in the assumption that *God's direction stands behind the function of the civil magistrate in society*. Given that fact, it is only natural that the standard by which the magistrate should mete out penalties to criminals ought to be the revealed law of God.

Unwillingness to Endorse the Law

Yet not all Christian teachers are willing to grant that point. Those who deny the validity of the penal sanctions found in the revealed law of God, however, rarely have cogent and clear *alternatives* to offer. When they do, these alternatives rarely stem from a *Christian* standpoint. Moreover, those advocating criminal penalties apart from God's revealed law hardly ever show a willingness to stand behind or defend the fairness and justice of their *specific* proposals. In short, those who demur at the idea of having current day magistrates follow the penal sanctions of God's law usually leave us with the position that there are *no permanently just standards* of punishment, for magistrates are left to themselves to devise their own penal codes autonomously. If some ruler thought that stealing two pennies deserved death, while killing an innocent child deserved the fine of two pennies, many Christian teachers would have *no objective way* to demonstrate the *injustice* of this arrangement. Their failure to produce a God-glorifying, Scripturally-anchored, method of *knowing* what justice demands in particular cases of criminal activity would in principle leave us at the mercy of magistrate-despots.

When there is *no law above* the civil *law,* restraining and guiding its dictates, then human will becomes absolute and fearsome. Before any reader is tempted to turn away from the all-too-obvious proposition that God's revealed law should be followed by the civil magistrate when it comes to crime and punishment, let the reader be clear in his or her own mind just what the *alternatives* are. In many cases those who criticize the use of God's penal sanctions objectively known from the Scriptures have either *no* alternative or arbitrary *tyranny* to offer in its place.

In addition to asking for the alternative which the critic of God's law has in mind, the reader should make a point of requesting some *justifying evidence from Scripture* for this rejection of the Old Testament law's penal sanctions. This is highly important, for Jesus warned that anyone who taught the breaking of even the *least* commandment of the Old Testament (and the penal commandments are surely commandments found among the Law and Prophets) would be called least in the kingdom of heaven (Matt. 5:18-19). Unless those who advocate the abolition of these penal sanctions can offer justification for their attitude from the word of God, then their position comes under the heavy censure of Christ Himself. Moreover, Paul taught that the law of God was *lawfully used* to restrain criminals today, being the standard God expected His ministers in the state to use when they wielded their swords (1 Tim. 1:8-10; Rom. 13:4). To reject those standards would appear on the face of it to be speaking against the word of the Lord Himself on the subject.

Are the Penalties Culturally Variable?

What reason might someone offer for refusing to endorse the present applicability of the penal sanctions of God's law? It is sometimes suggested, without due reflection, that since the penal sanctions of the law are found among the case laws of the Old Testament—laws whose cultural details are not universally binding—these laws simply teach us *that* certain crimes should be punished but not *what* the punishment should be. Therefore, "You shall not allow a sorceress to live," and "Whosoever lies with a beast shall surely be put to death" (Ex. 22:18, 19) simply teach that those who practice witchcraft or bestiality should be punished in *some* way, *not* that they must be punished in a *particular* way. The underlying principle is alleged to be merely that these acts are punishable; the death penalty is but a variable, cultural detail.

As attractive as this suggestion may sound in abstract (after all, it would make it much easier to promote God's law within a secularized culture), it is clear that the suggestion cannot be defended in the face of particular textual and theological realities. For instance, the two texts rehearsed above are specifically worded so as to require *more* than just *any* kind of punishment for those who practice witchcraft and bestiality. What is prohibited in Exodus 22:18 is that a witch should be *allowed to live*. A magistrate who merely fines a witch (i.e., a genuine witch as Biblically understood) would *transgress* this prohibition, allowing thereby what the text forbids — namely, the allowing of a witch to live. Exodus 22:19 used an idiomatic Hebrew expression to communicate the *certainty* of the death penalty for someone committing bestiality: "shall *surely* be put to death." The whole point here is that this crime is so heinous that only the death penalty is its just recompense.

The arbitrariness of some commentators here is perplexing. For example, R. A. Cole writes, "Our attitude to perversions of God's natural order can hardly vary from those of the law, while our treatment of offenders will be very different today."[1] Yet the Hebrew text teaches that our *treatment* of this crime *must not* vary: "surely" such an offender is to be put to death. If that is not the justice which we en-

---

1. R. A. Cole, *Exodus* (Tyndale Old Testament Commentaries), edited by D. J. Wiseman (Downers Grove: Inter-Varsity Press, 1973), p. 174.

dorse, then indeed even *our attitude* toward the perversion *itself* has varied from that prescribed by God's law!

Someone might convincingly argue that the *method* of execution (for example, stoning) is a variable cultural detail, but the text simply will not support the thesis that the law's *penal sanctions* are culturally variable. It will not support teaching an open-ended approach to penology — that is, teaching simply that criminals should be punished, without saying *what* the punishment must be. The principle taught in such case laws is that the relevant crimes are *worthy* of this or that specified treatment.

The various alternatives for treatment may not be changed around — as though a murderer could be fined, and a thief could be executed. It is precisely the *equity* of God's penal sanctions which precludes any shifting of them around; yet this shifting of penalties is what the suggestion before us would allow (by saying that the case law teaches *no set sanction* but only that there should be *some* kind of sanction). Such shifting violates the principle of an eye for an eye, a tooth for a tooth, a life for a life, etc. We have already seen above that equity characterizes the penal sanctions of God's law. Crimes have meted out to them precisely what justice says they *deserve*. This is the Biblical approach to penology, and to depart from it is to welcome (in principle) arbitrariness, tyranny, and injustice into one's society.

No More, No Less

Biblical penalties, we are observing, are never too lenient and never too stringent for the cases which they address. Consequently, if a magistrate departs from the strict justice and equity of the Biblically prescribed penalties for crimes, then the magistrate must either require *more* or require *less* than the law of God. Either way he will depart from the norm of equity — meting out what a crime deserves — and thus will be *unjust* in his judgments, being either too hard or too easy on criminals. Hebrews 2:2 tells us, contrary to the mistaken assumption of many, that the Old Testament penal sanctions were not "heightened" or "intensified" punishments, going *beyond* what strict justice for society would dictate. The verse declares, as foundational to an *a fortiori* argument for the eternal justice of God toward apostates, that according to the Mosaic law ("the word spoken through angels," cf. Acts 7:53) "every transgression and offense received *a just recompense* of reward." God's penalties were not overbearing there, and thus His judgment must be seen as fair toward apostates as well. God never punishes in an unjust manner, one that is too lenient or too harsh; He always prescribes exactly what equity demands. He can be counted on to stipulate a *just recompense* of reward for every crime. Those who depart from God's penal sanctions, then, are the ones who are unjust.

If God says that some crime is to be punished by the magistrate with death, then the crime in question is indeed "worthy of death," to use the Biblical phrase (for example, Deut. 21:22). One of the strongest endorsements of the justice of the law's penal sanctions is found in the words of the Apostle Paul at Acts 25:11. When he was accused of many grievous things by the Jews, Paul responded: "*If* I am an *evil-doer* [cf. the same expression in Romans 13:4] and have committed anything *worthy of death* [the law's designation for a capital crime], then I *refuse not* to die." Paul did not argue that these Old Testament penal sanctions had been abrogated, nor that they were appropriate only for the Jews of the theocracy. He rather insisted that they applied at the present time, and he would not seek to avert their requirement. He was willing to submit to divine justice, the justice of God's law — provided, of course, that he had truly transgressed that law. We too endorse the justice of God's penal code, if the Bible is to be the foundation for our Christian political ethic.

Invalid Attempts to Sidestep Biblical Penology

Some Christians have attempted to escape the Biblical requirements regarding penal sanctions on crime. Without answering the positive considerations which have been laid out above, they have suggested various reasons why we should not endorse the penal sanctions of the Old Testament law. We can quickly survey some of these reasons.

Some say that the use of the death penalty would cut short the possibilities for evangelism. That may be true, but we must avoid portraying God's word as in conflict with itself (as though the evangelistic commission of the church could override the justice demanded by the state). "The secret things [for example, who will be converted] belong unto Jehovah our God; but the things that are revealed [for example, the law's requirements] belong unto us and to our children forever, that we may do all the words of this law" (Deut. 29:29).

Others appeal to emotion, saying that the penal sanctions of the Old Testament would lead to a bloodbath in modern society. Such a consideration is by its nature a pragmatic concern, rather than a consideration for truth and justice. But more importantly, it directly contradicts the *Bible's own* teaching as to what the effect would be of following God's penal code. Far from leading to numerous more executions, such a practice would make others "hear and fear" (for example, Deut. 17:13) so that few will commit such crimes and need to be punished. God's sanctions bring safety, protection, integrity, and life to a community—not a blood bath.

Some teachers have likened the Old Testament penal sanctions to the ceremonial laws of the Old Testament, no longer followed in the same way as they were previously because of the work of Christ. However, such penalties were not ceremonial in character, foreshadowing the person and work of the Redeemer (for example, like the sacrificial system); they were not redemptive in purpose or religious in character. While the New Testament shows that the sacrifices, temple, etc. have been laid aside, the New Testament endorses the continuing use and authority of the penal sanctions. They simply are not in the same theological category as the ceremonial laws.

The *social* penalties prescribed by the Old Testament law cannot be seen as fulfilled in the death of Christ, the excommunicating discipline of the church, or the final judgment—for none of these deal with social justice within history. Christ did not remove the penalties for social misdeeds, or else Christians could argue that they need not pay traffic fines! The discipline of the church does not remove the need for the state to have just guidelines for penalties in society. And far from confirming social penalties, waiting for the final judgment removes social penalties for crime altogether. Even if one could argue (with Biblical indicators) that the penal sanctions of the Old Testament foreshadowed the final judgment, it would be something else to argue that those penalties did *nothing else but* foreshadow final judgment. After all, they also dealt with historical matters of crime and punishment, and so they could continue to do so today (while still foreshadowing the coming final judgment).

May We Abrogate All but One?

If the above arguments have proven awkward in the light of Biblical teaching and logical consistency, one can understand how much more difficult it would be to defend the position that the penal sanctions have been abrogated today, except for one (namely, the death penalty for murder). Such a position fails to show that the penal sanctions have been laid aside *in general*. At best it appeals to a fallacious argument from silence, saying that such social penalties were not mentioned, for instance, by Paul when he spoke to the Corinthian church about an incestuous fornicator. Of course, neither did Paul dispute those sanctions, seeing that he was speaking to the church about *its* response to the sinner (not the magistrate's response). Does his silence challenge *or* support the validity of the sanctions? Neither, really, for a consideration of silence is logically fallacious. What is important is the *presumption* of continuing validity taught elsewhere by Christ (Matt. 5:19) and Paul (Acts 25:11; Rom. 13:4; 1 Tim. 1:8-10; cf. Heb. 2:2). Silence cannot defeat that presumption, for the presumption can be turned back only by a definite word of abrogation.

Conclusion

There is *no general* repudiation of the penal sanctions in the New Testament. And *if there were,* there would be no textually legitimate way to salvage the penalty for murder. The attempt to limit our moral obligation to the Noahic covenant (Gen. 9:6) is misconceived, not only because the New Testament recognizes no such arbitrary limitation (see Matt. 5:17-19), but also because the Mosaic law is necessary to understand and apply fairly the Noahic stipulation about murderers (for example, the distinction between manslaughter and murder is not drawn in Genesis 9). That Paul in Romans 13 was not limiting the power of the sword to the guidance of Genesis 9 is clear from the fact that Paul recognizes the right of taxation, which is unmentioned in Genesis 9. If the Old Testament sanctions have been abrogated (and we have no reason to think they have been), then there appears to be no way to salvage the death penalty for murder either. Yet very few evangelicals will be content to accept that conclusion, especially since it leaves Paul's words about the magistrate's "sword" without any application.

We must conclude that God's word, even concerning matters of crime and punishment, is dependable and unchanging. Without His guidance, the magistrate would indeed wield "the sword in vain."

27

CHURCH AND STATE

"It is in fact impossible not to have some religious presuppositions whenever a law maker takes a stand one way or another on an issue."

We have observed that a distinctively Christian position with respect to law and politics will call for promoting the comprehensive gospel advocated by the Reformed faith—a gospel which has political implications because Christ has established God's kingdom (with its influence in every area of life) and now rules as King of kings over all mankind. True believers pray that God's kingdom will more and more come to expression through history, and that God's will be done on earth as it is in heaven. Study of Scripture has shown that God's will for public justice and politics has been revealed in the permanent standards of God's law. Therefore, Christians ought to work to persuade others of their obligation to the commandments of God, including the civil magistrate of his duty to enforce the penal sanctions of God's law against criminal activity in society. Without God's law, the Christian may take an interest in politics, but he has nothing to contribute in the way of concrete guidance that could not just as well be contributed by autonomous social wisdom. God's law is the key, then, to the Christian attitude toward socio-political morality.

A complaint which is often heard in our secularized society (and even heard from Christians who have succumbed to the pressures of secularization) is that we cannot recognize God's law as the standard for political morality because of the "separation of church and state." We need to explore this complaint from many angles in order to see just how weak it is.

The Separation in the Old Testament

First of all, there are people who reject God's law as the standard for present-day political ethics because they believe that the Old Testament social arrangement did not, as we do today, recognize any separation of church and state. The thought seems to be this: since the Mosaic law was intended for a situation wherein church and state were merged, those commandments would be ethically *inappropriate* for a *different* situation like ours where church and state are separated.

This line of thought may be common, but it is invalid nonetheless. We can begin by taking note of the fact that the Old Testament surely *did* recognize many kinds of separation between the cultic-religious and civil-political aspects of life. Kings were not priests in Old Testament Israel, and priests were not civil leaders (as in the pagan cultures around Israel). Indeed, when a king like Uzziah presumed to take upon himself the religious tasks of a priest, he was struck with leprosy from God for daring to break down the recognized separation of "church" and "state" (2 Chron. 26:16-21). There was a clear difference between the office and prerogatives of Moses and Aaron, between those of Nehemiah and Ezra. The Old Testament social arrangement did not, then, "merge" the religious cult and the civil administration.

We read that Jehoshaphat set the chief priest over the people "in all the king's matters" (2 Chron. 19:11). A functional separation between king and priest—both answerable to God—was known and followed. Thus, kings and priests had different houses, different officers, different treasuries, different regulations, and different forms of discipline to impose. The alleged merger of church and state in the Old Testament is simply based on little familiarity with Old Testament realities as presented in Scripture.

Recently it has been suggested by one Old Testament seminary instructor that the membership of the Old Testament Jewish state was coextensive with that of the Old Testament Jewish church, for (he claims) circumcision and participation in the passover were required of all citizens in Israel. Despite *prima facie* force to this suggestion, we will find it acceptable only if we neglect to read the actual Biblical account of the Old Testament social situation. As a matter of fact, there were indeed citizens of Israel (members of the state) who were *not* circumcised (bearing the mark of belonging to the covenant community), namely the women. But even more importantly, there were men in Israel who enjoyed the privileges and protections of citizenship, and yet who were not members of the "church" — who were not circumcised and did not partake of the redemptive meal of passover. These were the "sojourners" in Israel. They had the same law (Lev. 24:22) and same privileges (Lev. 19:33-34) as the native Israelite, but unless they were willing to undergo circumcision and join the religious community, they did not take passover (Ex. 12:43, 45, 48).

In many ways this parallels the situation today. All men live under the same laws and privileges in our state, but only those who assume the covenant sign (baptism in the New Testament) would be members of the church and free to take the Lord's Supper (the redemptive meal). Even at this level we do not find a situation in ancient Israel that is altogether different from our own. Church and state were not merged in any obvious way in Old Testament times.

Of course there were many unique aspects to the situation enjoyed by the Old Testament Israelites. In many ways their social arrangement was not what ours is today. And the extraordinary character of Old Testament Israel may very well have pertained to some aspect of the relation between religious cult and civil rule in the Old Testament. Nevertheless, we will search in vain to find any indication in the

Scripture that the validity of the Mosaic law for society somehow depended upon any of these extraordinary features of the Old Testament social arrangement. Despite the uniqueness of Israel, its law-code was held forth as a *model* for other nations to imitate (Deut. 4:6-8). What was *not* extraordinary or unique was the *justice* embodied in the law of God; its validity was universal, applying even to nations which did not in every respect parallel the social (or church-state) situation in Israel. Consequently, even if we were to point out that today our social arrangement differs somewhat from that of Old Testament Israel's, we would not thereby be justified in concluding that the law revealed to Israel is not morally valid for our present day society. Whatever the precise church-state relation was in Israel, the law revealed to Israel ought to be obeyed even by societies which have a slightly different church-state relation today.

A consideration of the separation of church and state (or lack thereof) in Old Testament Israel does not, then, invalidate the authority of the Old Testament law for current American society. Christ taught that we should render unto Caesar the things that are Caesar's, and unto God the things that are God's (Matt. 22:21). There is a difference between Caesar and God, to be sure, and we must obey both with that distinction in mind. And yet while we owe obedience to the powers that be (Rom. 13:1-2), the *civil magistrate* owes allegiance to God's revealed will, for he is the "minister of God" (Rom. 13:4).

To admit that the church is separate from the

state is *not* the same as saying that the state is separated from obligation to God Himself and His rule. Both church and state, as separate institutions with separate functions (i.e., the church mercifully ministers the gospel, while the state justly ministers public law by the sword), serve under the authority of God, the Creator, Sustainer, King, and Judge of *all* mankind in *all aspects of their lives*.

Different Senses of This "Separation"

When people today speak of their commitment to the separation of church and state, we need to realize that this commitment can be taken or interpreted in many ways. "I believe in the separation of church and state" may be the answer to one or more logically distinct questions. For instance, we might ask whether the church should dominate the state (for example, the Pope dictating to kings) or the state should dominate the church (for example, Congress dictating church policy), and the answer might very well be that we should hold to the separation of church and state — namely, that neither institution should dominate the other. We should have a free church in a free state.

A second question might be whether the state should establish one denomination over others as the state-church (or tax the population for financial support of the ministers of one particular church or denomination), and the answer again might very well be that we should hold to the separation of church and state — namely, that all churches should be supported simply by voluntary offerings, and one denomination should not be favored above others by the state. This, as a matter of historical fact, is what the First Amendment of the U.S. Constitution laid down when it prohibited the "establishment" of religion. It did not prohibit the expression of religiously-based views by politicians or their supporters; nor did it prohibit obedience to the Bible by public officials. It merely prohibited the establishment of one denomination as the state-church.

Finally, in recent days, it has come to be asked whether a distinctive religious system or revelation should be the standard for individual lawmakers as they determine public policy. In previous ages people would have been wise enough to see through such a question, for it is in fact impossible *not* to have some religious presuppositions *whenever* a lawmaker takes a stand one way or another on an issue. The only question should be *which* religious beliefs ought to guide him, not *whether* religious beliefs should guide him! However, today those who favor the pseudo-ideal of religious neutrality when it comes to politics tend to express their position as a commitment to the "separation of church and state." By this they mean the separation of morality (or religiously-based morality) from the state; they favor instead secular or autonomous laws in society. Those who believe that magistrates are bound to the law of God are (mistakenly) accused of violating the separation of church and state — which should mean the separation of two institutions and functions.

Conclusion

We must be careful to understand how people are using their terms. The Christian who promotes obedience to the law of God within his society is not violating any *Biblical* understanding of the separation of church and state. Indeed, it is hoped that believers would strongly *advocate* such a separation — meaning that neither institution should dominate the other in any official capacity, and that no denomination should be established as the state church. However, the Christian may very well be violating "the separation of church and state" when secular humanism uses that as a catch-phrase for religious neutrality in public policy. But at that point our concern is not for loyalty to an ambiguous slogan but for loyalty to the King of kings. "Let God be true, though every man is a liar" (Rom. 3:4). We must be faithful to Scripture's requirements, including the obligation of the civil magistrate to God's law, rather than to the popular dictates of our age. In short, "we must obey God rather than men" (Acts 5:29).

28

AUTONOMY AND ANTINOMIANISM

"Autonomous reasoning may reject our
endorsement of the law of God for ethics, but
autonomous ethics has nothing finally to offer
in its place."

The theological perspective which has been advanced in these chapters has not been formulated or determined by popular opinion polls, a desire to synthesize the wise variety of human attitudes, or even by seeking a "middle of the road" position among evangelical Bible teachers and pastors. Our aim has been to be faithful to the full range of Biblical revelation concerning the validity of God's law in ethics today; we have tried to be true to the word of God and not the traditions of men. If this effort has enjoyed any significant measure of success—that is, if we have in fact taught what Scripture teaches about God's moral standards—then it would come as no surprise that there exist a number of other positions on God's law or on the norm for ethics which stand in opposition to what has been set forth herein. Many erroneous theories of ethics are flourishing today (and always have, actually). Some are *more* dangerous than others, of course, but to *some* extent all depart from what God says about His law.

The Autonomy of the Unbeliever

The most stark antagonism to the law of God which we encounter will naturally be voiced by those who do not have faith in Christ and who refuse to submit their reasoning and behavior to the revealed word of God. Unbelievers do not in principle seek to conform to the commandments of God, and they do not in principle have the conviction that they are under obligation to God's law. Yet unbelievers are never without ethical assumptions, beliefs, and attitudes. Consequently, the thoughtful unbeliever will strive to formulate a philosophy of ethics for himself (if not for others), and his ethical reasoning will be characterized as *autonomous*.

The word "autonomy" derives from two Greek words: *autos* (meaning "self") and *nomos* (meaning "law"). To operate autonomously is to become *a law unto yourself*. The autonomous philosopher presumes that he can define good and evil according to his own unaided, self-sufficient powers of reasoning. He is not subject to the authority of another (especially that of God) but rather believes that he can competently exercise his own authority in moral matters. The unbeliever seeks to set aside God's law so that he can establish self-law in its place.

Romans 1:18-32 and 2:12-26 teach that nobody who has ever lived in God's creation has been unaware of the Creator's standards of conduct. All men, even those who have never heard of the Bible, hinder the truth by means of their unrighteous lives. Yet even though they may not have been privileged to receive a written revelation of the law of God (e.g., the "oracles of God" given to the Jews: cf. 2:17, 27; 3:1-2), "the Gentiles who have not the law . . . show the work of the law written on their hearts" (2:14-15). In their innermost selves all men know the requirements of God's law, but they seek to escape that condemning knowledge and to construct substitute theories of ethics for themselves. "The natural man receives not the things of God's Spirit" (1 Cor. 2:14), and indeed the mind controlled by the sinful nature "is not subject to the law of God, and neither can it be" (Rom. 8:7). By nature the unbeliever must oppose the concept of the law of God which this book promotes. Like Adam their father, unbelievers seek to "be like God," determining for themselves what will be good and evil — setting aside God's self-attesting revelation in nature and Scripture, and proceeding down the road of sinful rebellion toward the demise of ethics.

Plato and Sartre

Plato taught that ethics is independent of religion, for the form (or essential idea) of goodness and piety exists apart from the thinking of the gods, who approve of actions by looking above themselves to the absolute, unchanging standards for goodness and piety. Such a view rescued ethical theory, thought Plato, from both skeptical relativism (since the form of goodness was unchanging and absolute, not depending upon fluctuating human experience or opinion) and dogmatic religion (since goodness or piety did not receive their character from what the gods said about them). But by securing absolute authority for ethics in this way, Plato simultaneously lost ethical relevance, for how is anyone living through the changes of history supposed to know what this absolute standard of goodness requires in day-to-day experience? We never encounter the unchanging form of goodness in our ordinary experience and so by observation can know nothing of it (and especially nothing of its concrete application to particular moral problems and questions). Plato had a "heavenly good" which was "of no earthly value." He said that men could know "the good" by rational intuition; but that only plunges ethics into chaotic relativism once we realize that men differ radically in what they "intuit" as being good or evil.

In many ways the existential philosophy of Jean-Paul Sartre is quite incompatible with ancient Platonism. Both Sartre and Plato, however, sought to free ethics from the dictates of dogmatic religion. Sartre's starting point was the non-existence of God, from which he inferred that there exist no fixed values whatsoever. Man is totally free to determine for himself what will constitute good and evil. There is no essential idea of goodness which precedes his decisions and stands in judgment over them. Whatever values come into one's life must be freely chosen and defined by him on his own. Unlike Platonism, then, existentialism makes ethics very relevant; far from being unattainable, the standard of right and wrong is immediately accessible to the individual, being completely under his voluntary control! He can readily know what to do in particular ethical situations, for he himself decides what is right and wrong in each case. Of course this ethical relevance is purchased at the extremely high price of forfeiting an absolute authority in ethics. For Sartre every choice made by man is absurd, but every choice (providing it was genuinely a free choice) is justifiable. There are not good and bad choices, only choices. What is chosen as right by one individual in a specific situation does not govern what should be seen as right by another individual in a similar situation. Everyone "does what is right in his own eyes," and consequently there is no universal, binding standard of conduct which can guide and correct our living.

Plato had ethical absolutes without relevant applications. Sartre had relevant applications without an ethical absolute. Both problems — ultimately destructive of ethics in their own ways — stemmed from a rejection of God's revelation of His divine law for human behavior. By contrast, the Christian ethic has absolute authority, being based on the revelation of the Lord's will. It also has relevance, for what the all-knowing and all-controlling God says pertains quite specifically to our day-to-day lives and problems; God has clearly revealed unchanging standards for even the most specific aspects of living. Autonomous reasoning may reject our endorsement of the law of God for ethics, but autonomous ethics has nothing finally to offer in its place. Autonomy spells the death of an absolute and relevant ethical standard.

Varieties of Antinomianism

The opponents of God's law in Christian ethics are not restricted to the world of unbelieving thought, and so we must continue our survey of antagonism to the perspective advanced in these studies. Many believing *Christians* would likewise reject the idea that the law of God is now normative for ethics. They would in one way or another, to one degree or another, and for one reason or another, repudiate the binding authority of the revealed commandments of God. Those who do this are generally known as "antinomians" because they are *against* ("anti-") the *law* ("nomos"), although we must carefully recognize that a wide variety of different attitudes (not all sharing the same problems) fall under this label. We need to draw distinctions.

Licentious antinomianism — the most serious form of antinomianism — maintains that since we have been saved by grace, apart from works of the law, we have been set free from the need to observe *any* moral code whatsoever. Laws or rules have no place in the Christian life, and thus in principle the door is open to complete license in the way a believer lives. Such thinking hardly squares with New Testament teaching. Paul not only insisted that salvation was not *by* works, he also went on to say salvation is *for*

the sake of doing good works (Eph. 2:8-10). He recognized that God's *grace* instructs us to live *righteously*
in this world (Titus 2:11-12). John pointedly said,
"sin is law*less*ness" (1 John 3:4).

Spiritual antinomianism would admit that the
Christian needs guidance for the holy living expected by God, but it would deny that such guidance
comes from a written (or verbally defined) code.
Ethical direction is rather found in the internal
promptings of the Holy Spirit. Thus this position is
against insisting upon the normativity of God's revealed law, finding such insistance a stifling of the
spontaneous work of the Spirit within us. Quite ex-
pectedly, such thinking leads quickly to *subjectivism*
in Christian ethics, with each man doing whatever
he claims "the Spirit" has prompted him to do—
despite the fact that it conflicts with what the Spirit
has prompted others to do and (worse) with what the
Spirit has revealed once-for-all in the Scriptures.
The Bible teaches us that the Spirit works through
the word, not speaking or directing from Himself
(John 16:13-15). The Spirit works to fulfill *the law* in
us (Rom. 8:4-9). The abiding of the Spirit in
believers brings obedience to God's *commandments* (1
John 3:24).

Dispensational antinomianism would freely grant
that God has revealed standards for living (contrary
to licentious antinomianism), and revealed them in
written form to be kept (contrary to spiritual antinomianism). However, it would be against the *Old*
Testament law of God as the present-day norm of
Christian conduct. This form of antinomianism is

called "dispensational" because it stands opposed to the law of the previous dispensation (the Old Covenant law of Moses); today, we are told, Christians should govern their lives by the commandments of the *new dispensation* (the New Covenant).

Such a perspective suggests some rather unacceptable theological implications: for instance, that God's holy character is not reflected in the law, or that His character has changed (so that the law has changed). Moreover, this perspective surely does not comport with the widespread practice of the New Testament writers who rely unapologetically upon the presumed authority of Old Testament commandments. Then again, we have the explicit endorsement of the Old Testament law in statements like Matthew 5:19, "whoever breaks the least of these commandments and teaches men so shall be called least in the kingdom of heaven," or in 2 Timothy 3:16-17, James 2:10, etc.

One wonders also about ethical norms of the Old Testament which the New Testament had *no occasion* to repeat; are they *no longer* definitive for good and evil (say, the prohibition of bestiality)? However, the most obvious difficulty with dispensational antinomianism is that it does not do justice to the very wording of the New Covenant which it seeks to exalt. According to God's word, the New Covenant would mean, not the replacing of God's law or its abrogation, but rather its Spiritual empowering within us. *This is* the New Covenant: "I will put my law in their inward parts" (Jer. 31:33) — *not* a *new* law, but "my law," the *well-known law* revealed and known through Moses and the other Old Testament writers.

Finally, we can mention *latent* antinomianism as an incipient brand of opposition to God's law. Latent antinomians are not explicitly antagonistic to the law; instead they would *broadly* endorse the Old Testament commandments. But at this point they would take a smorgasbord approach to the collection of laws found in the Old Testament, accepting some and rejecting others as binding today *on some other basis than specific revealed teaching*. The latent antinomian is opposed to *some* laws in the Old Testament, and he has *no Biblical warrant* to offer for his rejection of them. This is not an outright rejection of the category of law, nor of written law, nor of Old Testament law. It is only incipiently antinomian because at heart it opposes the binding authority of certain Old Testament commandments on non-Biblical grounds; if the principle of this practice were *carried out* consistently and self-consciously, it would amount to genuine antinomianism.

Latent antinomians usually want the Old Testament law, but *not* certain *categories* of it (e.g., civil) or *not* its full *details* (e.g., case laws or penal sanctions). If those who felt this way could offer some attempted Biblical justification for setting these portions of the law aside, then they might be theologically mistaken, but they would not be latently antinomian. It is the failure to let *God's word* govern which laws we take as binding and which laws we see as set aside that makes this position *latently* antinomian. Jesus said that man must live by every word that proceeds from God's mouth (Matt. 4:4).

We cannot subtract from God's law, then, without His authorization (Deut. 4:2).

Over against the unbelieving attitude of *auto*nomy, these studies have promoted *theo*nomy (God's law). Instead of being *anti*nomian (in either licentious, Spiritual, dispensational, or latent ways), they have taken a *pro*nomian stand. In ethics we *presume* that *God's law* from the *Old* Testament *remains* normative for conduct *until* the Lawgiver reveals otherwise. Self-law and opposition to God's law are both incompatible with genuine ethical theory and practice.

29

ARGUMENTS AGAINST THE LAW'S GENERAL VALIDITY

"To insist that we are New Covenant believers or that the Mosaic commandments must come to us through Christ is not to subtract anything from our obligation to the Old Testament law."

These studies have found extensive Biblical evidence for the position that God's law is fully binding for modern ethics (unless alterations have been revealed). We have seen that one must *presume* continuity of moral standards with the Old Testament, and this presumption holds for *socio-political portions* of the law as much as with personal portions of the law. Only God's word has sufficient authority to alter our obligation to previously revealed commandments from God.

Some Christian teachers or writers would contend, however, that the law of God does *not* have a *general validity* in the age of the New Testament. They would attempt to marshall arguments against the conclusions to which we have been driven by our study of Scripture. In all fairness we need to survey some of the main reasons which people offer for saying that the law of God is not generally valid in the New Covenant dispensation, asking *whether* such considerations genuinely *disprove* what we have said herein.

Matthew 5:17-19

A passage of Scripture which clearly seems to teach the presumption of moral continuity today with the Old Testament commandments is Matthew 5:17-19. Yet some write as though this passage says nothing of the sort. They argue, for instance, that verse 17 deals not with Christ's attitude toward the Old Testament law, but rather with Christ's life as the prophetic realization of everything in the Old Testament canon.

It is true, of course, that the scope of Christ's declaration here is the entire Old Testament ("the Law and the Prophets"). However, there is absolutely nothing in the context of the verse or its wording which touches on the life of Christ (in distinction from His teaching) or on prophecy-typology. The focus of attention is obviously the *moral standards* by which Christ would have us live, and in particular the question of the Old Testament commandments is taken up. Verse 16 speaks of our "good works." Verse 17 twice denies that Christ abrogates the Old Testament revelation—in which case any interpretation which makes "fulfill" imply the abrogation of the law simultaneously renders the verse self-contradictory.

Verse 18 speaks more specifically of "the law," and in verse 19 Jesus referred back to the object of His remarks in verses 17-18 as "these commandments." Verses 20 and following speak to the question of righteousness and how the Pharisees have distorted the requirements of God's commandments. It is quite evident that we find in this passage a direct statement by Jesus on the validity of the law, and what He said was that not the least commandment — not the smallest stroke of the law — had been abrogated or would pass away until the end of the spatio-temporal world.

It might be suggested that the word "but" in Matthew 5:17 need not bespeak direct contrast between "abrogate" and "fulfill." However, Greek has two adversatives, and it is the stronger of the two which appears here. Jesus does not speak merely of general contrast, but of direct antithesis between abrogating and fulfilling. It might then be suggested that the negation (the "not") in verse 17 need not be one of absolute character, for elsewhere we read phrases in the New Testament which have the same form ("*not* this, *but* that") and the obvious sense is one of *relative* negation (i.e., "not so much this as that"). However, in such cases we have something of a paradoxical introductory formula, where something is affirmed and then denied, only then to have the contradiction resolved by the relative negation (for example, "Whoever *receives* me does *not receive* me, but [even more] the One who sent me," Mark 9:37). This is not what we find in Matthew 5:17.

Instead of something being affirmed and then denied, we have something *denied twice* in a row: "Think not that I came to abrogate the Law or the Prophets; I came not to abrogate." This is not a paradoxical introduction but a downright emphatic denial of something! Matthew 5:17, along with the vast majority of instances of "not this, but that" statements in Matthew's gospel, expresses strong contrast or antithesis, not relative negation.

Others who oppose the general validity of the law in the New Testament might hope to come to terms with Matthew 5:17-19 by arguing that the subordinate clause "until all comes to pass" in verse 18 limits the validity of the law to the obedient ministry of Jesus Christ on earth. To do so, they have to read a great deal *into* a very colorless phrase with little distinctive character; the phrase in Greek says little more than "until everything happens." The structure of the verse seems to make this phrase parallel to one which went before, one which specifically stated "until heaven and earth pass away." The interpretation before us, then, would make the verse self-contradictory by saying that the law was both valid until the end of the world and valid until Jesus had kept it all (in which case it is now both set aside and not set aside). Besides, this interpretation takes "all" in the phrase "until all things happen" as referring to all of the "jots and tittles" of the law mentioned in verse 18. But this is grammatically incorrect, seeing that "all" and "jot and tittle" do not agree in gender or number according to the Greek text.

There appears to be no escape from the thrust of

Matthew 5:17-19. We must presume a general validity for the Old Testament law today. Even if someone wants to point out (quite correctly) that the teaching here must be qualified by New Testament revelation elsewhere, our point would remain. Our *presumption* is that the Old Testament law is binding *until* the New Testament teaches us otherwise. If a commandment is not altered or set aside by the New Testament, we must assume an obligation to keep it.

Alleged Dismissals of the Law in the New Testament

Although it overlooks the extensive positive evidence which has been presented in this introductory book and in my more comprehensive treatment, *Theonomy in Christian Ethics* (2nd edition, 1984), one procedure for arguing against the general validity of the law is to point to isolated New Testament passages which appear to dismiss the Old Testament law for today. The treatment given such verses elsewhere in this book demonstrate that such passages do not in fact contradict the general validity of the law; at least they *can* be understood legitimately in a non-contradictory fashion. Those who insist on reading them in another way — so that they conflict with clear endorsements of the law's validity in the New Testament — create a theological tension where one need not exist.

Acts 15

A few New Testament passages seem to appear quite often in the polemics of those who oppose the law's general validity today. Acts 15 is commonly cited, as though the Apostolic Council's decree were intended to delineate precisely those laws and *only* those laws which remained valid from the Old Testament. But such a view is incredible. According to it, since the Council did not forbid blasphemy and stealing, such behavior would be condoned today — the prohibition of these things not carrying over into the New Testament!

1 Corinthians 9:20-21

In 1 Corinthians 9:20-21 Paul says that he was "not under the law" and could behave as one "without law." However, these remarks come in the context of saying that he behaved one way among the Jews and behaved another way among the Gentiles. The difference here was surely not one which pertained to moral matters (as though Paul was a thief among some people, but not a thief among others!), but it had to be a difference pertaining to laws which separated Jews and Gentiles. Thus, Paul would be speaking here of the *ceremonial* laws which created a middle wall of partition (cf. Eph. 2:13-16).

In order to minister to all men, Paul observed such laws among the Jews, but disregarded them among the Gentiles. All the while, he declares, he was "not without law to God, but under law to Christ." Obviously, then, Paul is not dismissing the law of God. He kept the law *under the authority of Christ,* and Christ Himself — we know from elsewhere (for example, Matt. 5:17-19) — taught that every least commandment of the Old Testament was binding today.

Galatians 3 - 4

In Galatians 3 - 4, Paul speaks of an historical epoch wherein the law served as a prison-master and as a tutor until the object of faith (Jesus Christ) came and made believers mature sons who no longer need such a tutor. Some people have seized such metaphors and statements and jumped to the hasty conclusion that the entire law of God—which Paul called "holy, righteous, and good" in Romans 7:12— is nothing but "weak and beggarly rudiments" (Gal. 4:9) which have now passed away. However, a better reading of Galatians will pay attention to the *historical context:* Galatians is a polemic against the Judaizers who insisted on the keeping of the *ceremonial* law as a way of *justification* (cf. Acts 15:1, 5; Gal. 5:1-6).

The portion of the Old Testament law which Paul speaks of in Galatians 3:23 - 4:10 was a "tutor unto Christ" which taught that "we should be justified by faith" (v. 24). The *moral law* (for example, "You shall not steal") does *not* serve this function; it shows us God's righteous *demand*, but it does not indicate the way of gracious *salvation* for those who violate the demand. On the other hand, the ceremonial law was indeed an instructor in salvation by grace, typifying the redemptive work of Christ. Now that the object of faith has come, however, we are no longer under this tutor (v. 25). We are mature sons who enjoy the reality which was previously only foreshadowed. When we were but children, we were under "the rudiments"—"the weak and beggarly rudiments," (4:3, 9). Paul spoke in Colossians 2:16-23 of "rudiments" and "ordinances," explaining that they were but "a shadow of the things to come, but the body is Christ's" (cf. Heb. 10:1).

Paul was speaking of the ceremonial law which foreshadowed the work of the Redeemer, but which was weak and impoverished in comparison to the reality brought in by Christ. If this is not evident enough from the historical context (Judaizing insistence on circumcision), from the very vocabulary chosen by Paul ("rudiments"), and from the function assigned to the specific law which Paul had in mind (pointing instructively to Christ and to justification by faith), it should be obvious from the example which he immediately offered at the end of our passage. In Galatians 4:10, Paul specifies what he means by the illustration of observing the ceremonial calendar. Galatians dismisses the shadows of the ceremonial law, but it *endorses* the continuing demand of the moral law of the Old Testament, as we see in 5:13-14, 23b, where love and the fruit of the Spirit are demanded in order to conform to the law.

Hebrews 7:11-25

Another passage to which appeal is commonly made by those who oppose the law's general validity today is Hebrews 7:11-25, for it speaks in verse 12 of a *necessary* "change of the law." If we consult the passage carefully, however, it will be clear that the change which is in mind here is a particular or singular change pertaining to a requirement for the priesthood. The priesthood has been changed from the Levitical order to the order of Melchizedek (vv.

11-12), which obviously points to the fact that the
priest spoken of in Hebrews need not come from the
particular tribe of Levi, chosen in the Mosaic law to
serve the altar (vv. 13-14). Instead the great High
Priest, Jesus Christ, came in the likeness of Melchizedek — "not according to the law of a fleshly requirement [namely, Levitical family origin]" — so that
there has been "a setting aside of a foregoing commandment," in order that the better hope promised
in Psalm 110:4 might be realized (vv. 15-21). This
singular change in the law is, first, one which pertains to the *ceremonial law,* and thus it does not contradict the general validity of the Old Testament law
as presented in this book. Second, this change is said
to be a *"necessary" change,* arising from its ceremonial
character and from the Scriptural teaching that the
final High Priest would come after the order of
Melchizedek. This kind of necessity does not prove
that any other law of God has been changed unless it
too is ceremonial in nature and dictated by the word
of God Himself. Consequently, Hebrews 7 does not
stand in opposition to the presumption that the Old
Testament law is binding today until God's word
teaches us otherwise.

Theological Considerations About
Revelation and the Covenant

If we turn now from arguments against the law's
general validity which arise from consideration of
specific passages of Scripture, we come to a variety
of theological considerations which are meant to
militate against the perspective which has been

taken in these studies.

There are some who would betray misconceptions of what our position is by saying that we need to pay corrective attention to the "progress of revelation" pertaining to redemptive history. The difficulty is that our position has been formulated by studying what the *New* Testament says about the Old Testament law, along with what the whole Bible reveals about the character of ethical norms. Consequently, we have been very mindful of progressive revelation which has brought us to the conviction that Old Testament commandments must be taken as binding until changes are declared by the word of God itself. Those who vaguely appeal to "progressive revelation" as supposedly a sufficient refutation of the position taken in these studies seem to have confused progress of revelation *about* God's law with *ethical evolution* of God's standards themselves. Another theological consideration which has been advanced in the debate over the general validity of God's law is the observation that Jesus Christ is the mediator of the New Covenant, the apex of God's revelatory work, and the Lord of our lives — in which case we must listen to *Him* and pattern our lives after *His* life if we are going to have a Christian ethic. Of course, there is nothing we need to contradict in such observations. Our obligation is indeed to the word and example of Jesus Christ. The question that remains, however, is whether Christ by His word and example taught us to honor the authority of the Old Testament commandments. Since He *did,* as abundant evidence demonstrates, then the suggestion that we should follow Jesus and not Moses is a misleading and false antithesis. Since the New Testament endorses the moral standards of the Old Testament, we are not forced to choose between an Old Testament ethic and a New Testament ethic. We are to follow them both, for they constitute one unified moral standard.

Is it true, as some claim, that since we live under the *New* Covenant today we should formulate our Christian ethic on the basis of the New Testament Scriptures exclusively, seeing the standards of the Old Covenant as obsolete? If we pay attention to the very terms of the New Covenant, our answer must be No. Jeremiah 31:33 stipulated that when God made a New Covenant He would write His law on the hearts of His people — not that He would abrogate His law, replace His law, or give a new law. Consequently, to live in submission to the New Covenant is to rejoice in the law of the Old Covenant, for it is written upon our hearts, out of which are the issues of life.

Promises and Demands

Those who suggest that the establishment of the New Covenant nullifies the general validity of the Old Testament law appear to have confused the sense in which the Old has become obsolete (Heb. 8:13) and the sense in which it continues the same (Heb. 10:16). All of God's covenants are unified. They make the same moral demands and focus upon the same promises. However, the promises call for historical fulfillment — the change from anticipation to realization—in a way which the demands do not; there is a difference in perspective between Old and New Covenants regarding the promises of God, while the moral standards of both are absolute and unchanging. Thus the Old Covenant administration (sacrifices, covenant signs, temple) can be set aside for the New Covenant realities, even though the Old Covenant moral law remains fundamentally the same. Historical events are crucial regarding the promises, whereas they are irrelevant to the demands. Indeed, the need we had for Christ to come and historically fulfill God's redemptive promises arises precisely because God's just standards cannot be set aside. Hebrews specifically teaches that the New Covenant is a "better covenant" because it is enacted on "better *promises*" (8:6)—*not* a better *law.* Rather, the *Old* Covenant's law is written on the heart of the *New* Covenant believer (v. 10). Therefore, we live under the *realized promises*—the fulfilled realities—of the *New* Covenant, not the Old Testament shadows of redemption, and yet we live under the *same essential covenant* as did the Old Testament saints because all of God's covenants are one. They constitute "the covenants of the promise" (Eph. 2:12), progressive outworkings of the one promise of salvation. Within these Old Covenant administrations, the law was not against the promises of God (Gal. 3:21). This very same law is written on the heart in the New Covenant's fulfillment of the promise (cf. Heb. 8:6-12).

Therefore, the fact that Jesus Christ is Lord of the New Covenant and that His example is the model for Christian ethics, and the fact that the New Covenant is the administration of God's single promise under which we now are privileged to live, do not imply in any logical or Biblical way that the moral standards of the Old Testament have been laid aside as invalid today. To insist that we are *New* Covenant believers or that the Mosaic commandments must come to us *through Christ* is not to subtract anything from our obligation to the Old Testament law, as interpreted and qualified by the advanced revelation of the New Testament.

Remarks Relevant to the Law's Categories

Finally, we can survey a few popular arguments against the general validity of the Old Testament law, all of which relate to the categories commonly recognized by theologians (namely, moral law, judicial law, ceremonial law).

First, there is the argument that the Bible never speaks of such categories, in which case the law must be viewed as an indivisible whole. If the law has been laid aside in *any* sense, then accordingly the *whole* law has been laid aside, it is thought. Such thinking is simplistic and fallacious.

To begin with, the Bible can often be correctly *summarized* in ways which are not actually spoken of in the Bible itself (for example, the doctrine of "the Trinity"), and so the convenient categorization of the law is not unacceptable in advance. It all depends on whether the categories and their implications are true to Scriptural teaching. Secondly, there *is* a sense in which the law stands together as a unit; indeed, the Bible does not carefully classify laws for us according to some explicit scheme. We should bear this fact in mind if our temptation is *a priori* to ignore a whole segment of the Old Testament law as nullified in virtue of our own classification schemes; commandments cannot be easily pigeonholed for dismissal. Thirdly, Biblical teaching does, nevertheless, demand our recognition of a fundamental difference between moral laws and cultic-symbolic-redemptive laws. God implied that category differentiation when He declared "I desire mercy, not sacrifice" (Hos. 6:6); the differentiation is also clear from the New Testament's different handling of Old Testament commands — some are reinforced as our duty, while others are laid aside as outmoded shadows.

Some laws in the Old Testament had a *redemptive purpose,* looking forward to the work of the Savior (for example, the sacrificial and priestly codes), but it would be erroneous to assert that all laws (for example, "You shall not steal") had that character or aim. Thus, we should not repudiate the notion that there is a *ceremonial division* within the law (perhaps better called "restorative laws"). Moreover, the ceremonial laws, which in their very nature or purpose imposed a separation between Jews and Gentiles, were designated by Paul "the law of commandments contained in ordinances" (Eph. 2:15; cf. Col. 2:14,17 for "ordinances"). He recognized a system of laws "in ordinances" (a special category of commandment) which had been abolished by Christ's redemptive works.

The Case Laws

Another category-related argument against the general validity of the Old Testament law today maintains that the applications and illustrations of the Decalogue which we find in the case laws (or "judicial laws") of the Old Testament are not perpetually binding. Some people say this and mean no more than the obvious truth that the cultural examples and applications of God's standards will be different between ancient Israel and modern America. However, others seem to be claiming something further: namely, that the principles revealed illustratively in the case laws of the Old Testament must be flexibly reapplied today in a new way—in a way which is personal or geared to the new church-form of God's kingdom, and that their current application must be restricted to these domains alone.

This latter view is erroneous. Consider the following example. Keeping the sixth commandment ("you shall not kill") once meant, among other things, not being careless where human life could be endangered (for example, chopping with an ax that had a loose head). To say that this defining specification of the sixth commandment means is no longer applicable—that is, to say that carelessness when life is endangered is now morally acceptable (for example, one may legitimately drive with poor brakes)—is in fact to *alter* the very meaning and requirement of the sixth commandment. It is to tamper with what God intends by His commandments. If we change God's case-law explanations and applications (the principles they illustrate or teach), then we will have to answer for tampering with the intended meaning of His word. To say that the sixth commandment is perpetually binding, but not the related judicial or case laws, is to render "You shall not kill" an arbitrary label which covered one kind of conduct in the Old Testament but is pasted over a *different* kind of conduct in the New.

Since the case law's principles *define* the Decalogue, the case law's principles (in their full scope: personal and social, ecclesiastical and civil) are *as perpetual* as the Decalogue itself. Thus, the New Testament practice which we have previously observed is to cite the case laws of the Old Testament as readily as — and right along with — the ten commandments (for example, Christ's list of moral duties rehearsed for the rich young ruler in Mark 10:19 includes "You shall not defraud" right along with the Decalogue).

Conclusion

We have examined specific New Testament texts and have reflected upon various theological themes, but in none of them have we yet to find any convincing evidence which runs counter to the perspective formulated in this book. There may be isolated Bible verses that, when read out of literary theological context, give a passing impression that "the law" no longer binds our behavior. Upon closer look, however, not a single New Testament text says that the *standards of conduct* taught in the Old Testament law are now immoral, outdated, or incorrect in the way they define godliness. "We know that the law is good," said Paul (1 Tim. 1:8).

In a similar fashion, there may be certain concepts or theological considerations that initially suggest a passing away of "the law" of the Old Covenant. When correctly understood and Biblically analyzed, however, none of these theological themes logically implies the repeal of the *moral standards* of the Old Covenant. If they did, we could have no principled objection to situationism or cultural relativism. We would forfeit the objective, absolute, universal authority of Biblical morality. Paul's presupposition was clear: "Now we know that whatsoever things the law says, it speaks to them who are under the law in order that *every* mouth may be stopped and *all the world* may be brought under the judgment of God" (Rom. 3:19).

Cogent arguments against the goodness and universal validity of the moral standards taught in the Old Testament law have simply not been found. Critics have failed to offer us a non-arbitrary, Scripturally grounded, unambiguous *principle* by which they may *altogether* disregard the Old Testament's definition of good and bad behavior or attitudes — *or* (even tougher) by which they can distinguish between valid and invalid *portions* of the Old Testament moral instruction. The general validity of God's law for our day, apart from particular Biblically-based qualifications on it, cannot successfully be evaded.

30

ARGUMENTS AGAINST THE LAW'S POLITICAL USE

" 'Theonomists' preach and promote biblical law's authority and wisdom, praying that citizens will be persuaded willingly to adopt God's standards as the law of the land."

Even when they grant that the law of God has a general validity in the New Testament age, some Christians nevertheless believe that it is wrong to maintain that this validity and use of the law extend to the political realm. They say: "The law of God may be generally binding in personal, ecclesiastical, and interpersonal social affairs, but it should not be the standard for political justice and practice in the modern world." Since this attitude conflicts directly with the conclusions to which we have been brought by our study of Biblical teaching regarding the law, we need to listen to the reasons which are offered for a negative attitude toward the political use of God's law today. Are they of sufficient weight to overthrow our understanding of the Biblical requirements? It would not seem so.

Arguments Pertaining to God's Law and the State

1. *Directionless Revelation*

Some would have us believe that God's New Covenant revelation has no direction for political morality, for (it is thought) social reform in an unbelieving society is not a proper task for the Christian. This truncated view of Christianity, however, is what stands opposed to New Covenant revelation. Christ is now "King of kings," and in the future He will judge all magistrates for their rule. Christians are to be "holy in all manner of life," even in their relation to the powers that be. The Church has been commissioned to teach the nations whatsoever Christ has commanded, and that includes His words pertaining to socio-political morality and the validity of the Old Testament law. Christianity is to be salt that influences the earth and light which is not put under a basket. Indeed, Christianity is a complete world-and-life-view, not simply a narrowly "religious" message about the afterlife. God is not the God merely of the churches. He is the living God over all creation. So what standard for political morality should God's people adopt today, if not God's revealed law? Does not their political opposition to "the man of lawlessness" tell us where they find their guidance by contrast?

2. *The Uniqueness of Covenant Israel*

Some have argued that it is mistaken to see the

civil aspects of the Old Testament law as binding on modern states because such a view overlooks the context of the Old Testament law as given only to Israel as a redeemed nation placed in national covenant with God. Since modern nations are not in the same place or situation as Old Testament Israel (i.e., not being redeemed for a national covenant with the Lord), it is thought that "imposing" God's civil law on those who do not participate in redemptive covenant with God—on those who have not been converted or joined the church—would be to overlook the only proper context for such a law.

In reply, we need to remind those who voice this criticism that we are not advocating the forcible "imposition" of God's law on an unwilling society. "Theonomists" preach and promote biblical law's authority and wisdom, praying that citizens will be *persuaded* willingly to adopt God's standards as the law of the land. As secularists campaign and debate to see their convictions influence civil law, so Christians should work to have God's word influence civil law instead. We do not advocate any modern "holy war" or use of force to compel submission to God's standards.

Not everything about ancient Israel is to be made part of our modern political experience, as the above indicates. We are concerned simply with the *standing laws of civil justice*. "Holy war" during Israel's conquering of the promised land was by God's direct and specific command, for a set time and place, concerning particular abominable cultures of that day; it was not standing civil policy for all men (any more than was the specific order for Samuel to anoint

David king of Israel at a set time and place). The laws that God revealed in the Old Testament concerning general types of situations (for example, murder, rape, perjury) had a standing or policy character, over against special imperatives for particular occasions. Accordingly, ancient Israel experienced from time to time a variety of different kinds of political administration: tribal heads, city elders, liberator-judges, the monarchy, ruling council, etc. From this we see that God has not prescribed a particular administrative form for political government. We are not obligated today to abolish the three branches of civil government in the United States, or the British Parliament, or the monarchy of Jordan, etc. What is proposed here is that all civil governments, whatever their structure, should be encouraged to submit to and apply the standing laws of Old Testament Israel.

Still, some would criticize this proposal, claiming that even the standing laws pertaining to civil government were uniquely for Israel as a nation redeemed by God and in national covenant with Him. What such arguments imply is that modern political policy for "secular" nations ought not to be learned from the principles of the Mosaic law for "covenanted" Israel.

So then, does God's word teach that the Old Testament civil law was *restricted* in validity to Israel as a nation in redemptive covenant with God? Previous chapters have clearly shown that it does not. God judged nations outside of Israel for transgressing the standards of His law, and in His revelation to Israel

He encouraged the spreading of the law to the Gentile nations. In the New Testament, Christ endorsed *every* jot and tittle of the law of God (unless qualified by Scripture elsewhere), and Apostolic writers acknowledged the law of God as the standard for political ethics—even in the day of pagan Roman emperors.

The redemptive history and national covenant enjoyed by Israel certainly set the Old Testament Jews apart from modern nations as significantly unique. But this does not mean that Israel was *in every respect* different from her neighbors or from nations today. Paul teaches in Romans 1 and 2 that the same moral standards revealed to Israel through "the oracles of God" were more generally revealed to *all* men through general or natural revelation. Israel did not have a unique moral code, as though God operated with a double standard for Israel and the Gentiles.

Moreover, Israel was not completely different from modern nations or her Gentile neighbors, for like these others, Israel faced historical (pre-consummation) problems of crime, social justice, and punishment. The law of the Lord directed Israel as to the requirements of divine justice in such situations, and that law *ought* to be the standard of justice for crime and punishment everywhere else as well (even in nations that did not or do not have a corporate, redemptive covenant with God)—for social justice in God's eyes is not racially variable or different from nation to nation. *Justice is absolute.* If the civil aspects of God's law were meant only for Israel, as the critic says, then he should be asked to explain the New

Testament's apparent practice of taking the standards of political ethics from God's law — and asked what the New Testament standard for political justice is, if not God's commandments. Those who restrict the validity of the Old Testament law to Israel may not realize it, but their philosophic outlook is that of "cultural relativism," where what counts as justice is adjusted from culture to culture.

Those who press the argument that modern states are not bound to the civil aspects of God's law since it was given in a national and redemptive covenant with Israel, will find that they cannot long maintain with consistency *any* of the Old Testament commandments today. Not only were the civil aspects of the law revealed in the same context of a national covenant, so also were the personal and interpersonal aspects of the law. If the passing away of the national covenant means the invalidation of those moral standards revealed within it, then we would lose even the ten commandments! If the judicial laws of the Old Testament are thought to have expired when God's purposes for the Jewish nation were complete — that is, if only the "national" aspects of the national covenant have passed away — then we would be overlooking the *justice* of those laws and their *full* purpose, which included of being a *model* to *other* nations (Deut. 4:6-8). Besides, *God's word* never draws such a distinction between the "personal" aspects of the law and the "political" aspects, as though the one were any more or less a reflection of God's unchanging holiness than the other. Who are *we* to draw such a distinction on *our own,* with the *aim* of evading or laying aside a portion of those duties revealed by God? To read this *into* the text (rather than taking it *from* the text) is to lord it over the word of the Lord!

3. *Israel's "Heightened Purity"*

The direction God gave to Jewish society was not a "heightened" standard of purity and did not embody a "unique severity"—it was not an "intrusion" of the standards of Final Judgment into the course of ordinary history. Heightened and unique standards would hardly be a model of justice and could not fairly be applied to other nations, and yet the Old Testament presents God's law as such a model and applied its standards to other nations. Moreover, if the civil law of the Old Testament really were a reflection of the standards of the Final Judgment, then *all* sins would have been crimes and *all* would have been punishable by death, neither of which was true. Even if the penal sanctions of God's law are typological foreshadows of Final Judgment in some sense, they are *not merely* such foreshadows; they are *also* God's direction for justice in matters of crime and punishment *prior* to the Final Judgment. To hold that laws with a symbolic or typological aspect to them have been invalidated today would be to surrender the validity of more than certain civil commandments of the Old Testament. It would be to invalidate even the laws pertaining, for instance, to marriage and sexual purity, for they symbolize the relation of God to His people!

4. *Multiple Moral Standards*

Some who criticize the perspective taken in this book say that magistrates (past or present) who are outside of Israel's "theocracy" should rule according to the moral standards of general revelation, not those of God's law. The faulty assumption here, of course, is that God has two moral standards, one revealed through nature and conscience and a different one revealed in the Bible. The Biblical perspective is that the law revealed to the Jews in spoken form has been revealed in unspoken form to the Gentiles, and the two moral codes are co-extensive. Paul did not somehow restrict natural revelation to the Decalogue (see, for example, Rom. 1:32), even *if* we could see how the ten commandments might be understood apart from their explanations and applications in the case laws.

5. *Ignoring the Evidence*

Others who have disagreed with the perspective advanced herein have wanted to mitigate the force of subordinate aspects or observations in the arguments put forward (for example, disagreeing with the claim that Old Testament Jewish and Gentile rulers had religious titles). Even if we left such details undefended, however, the main lines of argumentation in favor of the position taken on the political use of God's law would be unaffected by these minor criticisms. Thus such details need not be defended here, for they are not crucial to the case made.

Others who have disagreed with the case made in

this book have complained that it is made "by inferences" from Scripture — apparently, instead of by direct and explicit statement of the political validity of God's law. But since the same misguided complaint could be made about major doctrines of the faith (for example, the Trinity, the hypostatic union), it is hardly a telling point against our position here on political ethics.

Another argument has been that if we temporarily set aside the major New Testament evidence that is enlisted in support of the perspective taken in these studies, and if we then read the New Testament without that evidence present, then we would not get the impression that God's law, in its political aspects, is valid today. It is thought that the purported evidence in favor of our position has been mistakenly interpreted in a way that does not harmonize with the rest of the New Testament.

This line of criticism shows how desperate some can become in trying to refute the thesis that the political use of God's law is valid today. In the first place, if we subtract the positive evidence for the thesis, the rest of the New Testament is *not contrary* to the thesis; it is simply silent on the subject. In the second place, it is hardly a legitimate complaint against a position that it has no support when its main lines of support are put to the side! A lawyer who argued for his client by merely asking the jury to ignore the evidence presented by the prosecutor would not long retain his job. Until definite *negative* evidence against the thesis can be adduced from the New Testament we should acknowledge that Scripture teaches the political use of God's law. Such negative evidence has yet to be produced by any published critic of the perspective taken in these studies. Appeals to the "New Testament emphasis" or to "the impression made by the New Testament" are simply too vague and subjective to have any critical weight in theological decisions.

Arguments Centering on Church-State Relations
1. *New Testament Differences*

Those who disagree with the political use of God's law sometimes argue that because the relation of church to state is different today from what it was in the Old Testament, the laws governing society must likewise be different. It is hard to see what rationale one could have for such a line of thought, however. Since the equity, validity, and authority of Old Testament civil laws were *not* somehow *made dependent* upon some *specific relation* of church to state (that is, Moses never conditioned the obligation of civil magistrates upon a special church-state interaction), whatever changes in that relationship have been introduced in the New Testament would be ethically irrelevant to the justice of the civil code which magistrates were required to enforce. There is not one kind of justice for a rapist when the church's relation to the state is X, and another kind of justice for a rapist when the church's relation to the state is Y. Rape is rape, and justice is justice—regardless of the intimacy of church with state or the lack thereof. Old Testament magistrates—not priests, let us be reminded—judged and punished rapists (and other

criminal offenders), even as New Testament magistrates must also deal with the criminal problem of
rape. The extraneous relation of these magistrates to
priests (or to the church) is not pertinent to their
relation to the criminal, nor does it affect what
justice demands in the case of crime; the church-
state question is really to the side.

The common claim that the religious and the
civil aspects of community life were fused in Old
Testament Israel simply will not square with a
reading of the Old Testament text, as previous
chapters have pointed out. This is not to say or
claim, as some critics have thought, that the church-
state relation in the Old Testament is identical in
every respect with the church-state relation in the
New; such a premise is not indispensable to the position taken herein. The position does stand opposed
to the inaccurate argumentation often heard, which
says that there was *no separation* of church and state in
Israel. The Old Testament cult was clearly a
separate authority and function from the Old Testament civil rule. (This observation, it must be explained to some critics, does not imply that the Old
Testament cult is taken as wholly identical with the
New Testament church; there *is* a parallel or analogy
however, as Paul indicates in 1 Cor. 9:13-14.) Kings
could not sacrifice, and priests could not execute, in
the Old Testament situation; the state and the
church had separate functions and directions.

Nevertheless, some writers have believed that
there are significant (morally significant?)
differences between our situation today and the

church-state situation in Old Testament Israel. Israel was a *priestly nation* then, whereas the church — not America — has that status today. This is correct: the religious mission of the corporate body (the priestly function of the community *as a whole*) has now been assumed by a different kind of body, the international community of faith, rather than a particular nation. However, this says nothing about the relation of church to state *within* the nation of Israel, and it certainly does not belie the legitimate separation between the two which we read of elsewhere in the text.

2. *The "Theocracy" Argument*

It has been claimed that the Old Testament church-state (the sense given to "theocracy") has now been replaced with an international church (minus state) in the New. This flounders on the *mistaken assumption that the Old Testament was a church-state*. As explained previously, priests and kings had separate authorities, and the membership of the state was not coextensive with the membership of the religious body (for example, the sojourners in Israel).

3. *The "Redemptive Community" Argument*

The claims that the Old Testament state was a "redemptive" community and that the state existed for a "religious purpose" are too ambiguous — being obviously correct on some interpretations (for example, that the state arose out of God's redemption of the people from Egypt and served the religious aim of punishing social evil), yet irrelevant to the annulment of the civil aspects of the law of God. Such a "redemptive state" viewpoint is obviously so mistaken with respect to other interpretations (for example, that the civil laws had a redemptive effect, or that the state authorities were the cultic or religious heads as well)—that it cannot be of any service as an argument. Similarly, claims to the effect that the Old Testament state punished "religious" crimes (for example, blasphemy) overlook the "religious" character of other crimes as well (for example, murder, adultery). Such arguments are based on a false notion of the *secular/sacred dichotomy* which is promoted by modern humanism, and they are therefore unhelpful in theological argumentation.

What the opponents of Biblical law need to demonstrate—but do not—is that "religious" crimes like blasphemy are of no continuing relevance or importance for social justice in the modern state. Is it contrary to the church's evangelistic mission for Christians to promote the political use of God's law, if this means the state will punish blasphemers and open idolaters? Such a conflict would be possible only if we first assumed that God's word could contradict itself (teaching one thing regarding civil ethics and a contradictory thing about evangelism). Promoting the punishment of blasphemers is no more contrary to evangelistic concern than is the promoting of punishment of murderers.

Arguments Relevant to the Penal Sanctions
1. *Only for Israel*
    Against the political use of God's law today some

urge the consideration that the penal sanctions of the law were given only to Israel. Since the Bible teaches, however, that the whole law of God was the moral obligation of nations existing outside of and prior to Israel (for example, Sodom, the Canaanite tribes), *where* is the qualifying exception revealed which says the *penal* sanctions were *excluded* from this obligation? It is not to be found. The argument before us is *read into* the Bible, not taken *from* the Bible. The Bible *praised* pagan rulers for enforcing the sanctions of God's law (for example, Ezra 7:25-27).

2. *Israel as Church Only*

Some critics claim that the Old Testament penalties were revealed to Israel *as the church,* rather than as the state, and that *only* the church today should punish "religious" offenses. Scriptural support for such reasoning is totally lacking, however. It was the *magistrates* of Israel who enforced the requirements of restitution and retribution, for those requirements were revealed for them, not the priests. So it was *not* Israel as the church, but rather *Israel as a civil state,* which punished thieves, rapists, and blasphemers. If only the "religious" crimes in the law are reserved (allegedly) for the discipline of the church today—leaving at least some offenders to be dealt with by the state—then we will need a principled, Biblically defined way of distinguishing "religious" from "non-religious" crimes. Apart from that, the argument before us is simply unworkable or arbitrary; worse yet, it is without Scriptural warrant.

The premise that *only* the church is called upon to

deal with "religious" offenses today (whatever they might be) is one that will need Biblical backing, given the New Testament endorsement of the law of God in general, as well as the New Testament doctrine that magistrates should enforce the law of God (for Whom they are a "minister," avenging wrath against evildoers). Is blasphemy less heinous in God's eyes today, or less destructive of social justice, or less relevant to the concerns of "God's minister" in the state? It is perfectly true, as some point out, that the "evil" which Paul says the magistrate should punish (Rom. 13:4) must be *restricted*, since not all sins are crimes. But the reasonable thing seems to be to restrict it *according* to the law of God, *not* to make it more restrictive *than* the law of God! The basic problem with most arguments against the position taken in this book is that these arguments have *no Biblical* warrant and authority. God's people must then set them aside as without force.

3. *The "Severity" of the Law*

To say that the penal sanctions of the Old Testament are "too severe" for a period of "common grace" is to overlook at least two important points: (1) Israel of old enjoyed God's common grace (at least as defined in Gen. 8:22), and was *still* required to enforce His law, and (2) God's political laws serve to *preserve* the outward order and justice of a civilization and thus are a sign of God's "common grace" — rather than detracting from common grace. If "common grace" really conflicts with God's law, then the critic will need to demonstrate that *what he means* by "common grace" is actually taught in Scripture and logically implies the law's abrogation. This has yet to be done. The parable of the wheat and the tares (Matt. 13:24-30, 36-43) teaches that the general execution of unrighteous unbelievers awaits the Final Judgment, not that civil magistrates ought never to execute those individuals guilty of civil crimes (more specific than general unbelief) — or else there would be *no* penal sanction of death (even for murder), and the specific purpose of the state (the power of the "sword") would vanish.

4. *The Absence of Explicit Sanctions*

It has been suggested — without due reflection — that the Old Testament penal sanctions did not render what crimes really and fully deserve punishment (namely, eternal damnation), and thus today it is acceptable for magistrates to punish in a way less than what justice of the law requires. But in the first place the Old Testament law *did* give what every offense justly deserved (Heb. 2:2) within the realm of *civil* justice. That is why thieves were punished *differently* from rapists, even though *both* thieves and rapists will suffer in Hell eternally. In the second place, *if* the law of God prescribed less than what full justice demands for criminals, how would that fact justify a magistrate requiring *even less* than what the law prescribed? Such a magistrate would simply be guilty of a failure to do what God ordered him to do, not even living up to the (allegedly) limited penal severity of the law.

5. *The Argument from Silence*

Three last arguments may be quickly mentioned, all of which are guilty of notorious fallacies in reasoning. First, there is the "argument from silence" that the New Testament does not call for us to campaign for the penal sanctions of the law, as in the case of the incestuous fornicator (1 Cor. 5:1-5). Well, there may not be a specific illustration available (given the character of the society and magistrate in those days), but the *principles* are *indeed taught* — as we have discussed in previous studies. Paul need not say anything further about the magistrate's duty regarding incest, for instance, since the Old Testament and natural revelation were already adequate. What he needed to reveal was the disciplining procedures required of the church — to whom, after all, the Corinthian epistle was written (not the civil magistrate). Given the Biblical doctrine of the law's continuing validity (Deut. 4:2; Matt. 5:17-19), we need more than silence to nullify God's commands.

6. *The Argument from Abuse*

Second, there is the argument from abuse — the argument that unsaved magistrates have abused God's law by trying to enforce it in the past, leading to such horrors as the Inquisition. But of course God never commanded these abuses in his law (for example, He did not grant the magistrate the right to judge heretics in the first place), and so this argument is actually an argument *in favor* of our thesis. Since these abuses violate God's law, God's law ought to be endorsed as valid in order authoritatively to condemn the abuses of personal freedom, dignity, and life. If abuses of law by the magistrate are corrected by removing any law to abuse, then there will be no law for the magistrate to enforce except his own, arbitrary will — which is the surest way to achieve tyranny!

7. *The Argument from Tradition*

Third, there is the argument from tradition, the claim that the perspective advanced in these chapters has never been advanced by any of our respected forefathers in theology. Such an argument is theologically futile, however, if our obligation is to believe what Scripture (only and completely Scripture) teaches rather than our fallible traditions (cf. Matt. 15:3-9). If one *cannot show* that Scripture does *not* actually endorse the position advanced herein, then he will have to choose between God's word and his theological tradition. Those who are submissive to the Lord's authority will know which one they must choose. But beyond this we can briefly indicate that there is abundant evidence that respected theologians of the past have taught and promoted the perspective taken herein toward the political use of God's law. In my other books on this subject one can pursue indications from Bucer, Calvin, Bullinger, Latimer, Cartwright, Perkins, Gillespie, Bolton, Ames, Cotton, and *many others* who have recognized the general authority of God's law and the political use of it today. It has been a mainstay of Reformed political ethics for centuries.

8. *The Last Resort*

Since none of the common or published arguments against the position which we have taken herein succeeds in disproving the general validity of God's law or its political obligation today, the only thing left for one to do, if he wants to continue to resist the position, is to point to certain "horrid examples" of what God's law requires, appealing to our emotion or autonomous reason that such things simply cannot be accepted today into our morals. That is, the critic resorts to ridiculing the moral orders revealed by God to Israel. One is left with the choice between following the wisdom and evaluations of men who have no Biblical standard (and who actually disagree with the Biblical norms) and following wholeheartedly the dictates of God's law. Shall our feelings correct the Bible, or should the Bible correct our feelings? Which will have supreme authority, the thinking of sinful men or the infallible word of the Lord? "Let God be found true, though all men are liars" (Rom. 3:4). "Choose this day whom you will serve!" (Josh. 24:15).

Conclusion

In chapter 29, we found no successful rebuttal to the general validity of the Old Testament law, and in this chapter we have seen that this general validity of the law applies just as much to political affairs as to private, family, and ecclesiastical ones. God is offended by all expressions of injustice and unrighteousness, including (if not especially) by those placed in positions of civil rule over their fellow men.

If they refuse to submit to the Lord (Ps. 2), they will eventually answer to "the King of kings" (I Tim. 6:15) for their rebellion. This means that there are standards of justice to which they will be answerable.

If those standards are not found in the Old Testament, then why not? Then where else? Such questions receive no convincing and theologically consistent answer from those who reject the political use of the Old Testament law. Do these critics of theonomy believe that political rulers are free to do whatever seems right in their own eyes?

We have seen attempts made to disprove the validity of the socio-political laws of Moses by appealing to some special feature about Old Testament Israel. However, such a special feature is never clearly defined. The segment of the law which is thought to be invalidated is never delineated on the basis of explicit principle; specific laws are rather included or excluded from the segment arbitrarily and subjectively by the person advancing such an argument. The alleged unique feature is often not even actually true about Old Testament Israel. And finally, no demonstration is forthcoming, grounded upon Scripture, that the validity of this intended segment of the Mosaic law rested entirely upon that unique feature of Old Testament Israel in the first place. Other kinds of arguments against the modern use of the Old Testament in political ethics appeal to considerations which are utterly irrelevant to the truth or falsity of that idea—arguments from silence, subjective impression, abuse, tradition, and ridicule. In short, those who have argued against the political use of the Mosaic law today have fallen into errors and fallacious reasoning which no Christian scholar can find acceptable.

In the end, one does not find good reasons being given for turning away from the moral standards for socio-political affairs found in the Old Testament law. When the poor reasoning is stripped away, what is left as the core of opposition to those standards is *personal feeling* — the personal feeling that those standards are too harsh or tyrannical for our pluralistic age.

Of course, to be intellectually honest, one is then compelled to stop and ask whether God's law should change pluralism, or whether pluralism ought to change God's law. That question should not be begged (though it usually is). If magistrates are indeed "ordained" as the public "ministers of God" (Rom. 13:1, 4), does Jehovah morally permit them to serve many gods, or does He require them to submit to His rule alone? This may seem despotic to some minds, but the alternative is just another kind of despotism, one that is infinitely worse — the despotism of those civil rulers who deem themselves free from the objective standards of God's holy law. Then we get the worst kind of tyranny imaginable, *where political might is not restrained by what is morally, objectively right.*

For this reason, we must see the failed arguments examined in this chapter as more than simply illustrations of fallacious reasoning in the intellectual sphere. We must see them as ultimately dangerous (even if unwittingly so) to the wellbeing of Christian civilization.

31

THE AUTHORITY OF
GOD'S LAW TODAY

"The question is this: by what standard are moral judgments to be made? How do we determine in any particular case what godliness requires of me or my society?"

There is much more to the study of Christian ethics than has been discussed in this book. There are foundational issues about the perception and production of godliness in ourselves and in our society which have not been touched. Nearly all of the specific moral questions which surround us have been given no applied answer. A lot has been left unsaid, and a lot more study is required. Nevertheless, the issue addressed by this book is systematically basic to Christian ethical reasoning. It asks a question which is impossible to avoid and which influences every other aspect of one's ethical theory. People may not reflect explicitly upon the question, and people may not answer it well. But everyone proceeds upon some answer or another to that inevitable question in Christian ethics.

The question is this: *by what standard are moral judgments to be made?* How do we determine in any particular case what godliness requires of me or my society? Other questions may be interesting and even important. But the Christian ethics — which is itself a reflection of the Christian faith — cannot be cogently developed and practically employed without an answer to the question of criteria. How should we live? What must we do? What kind of people should we be? It all depends upon the standard we use. Better: it all depends upon the standard that *God Himself* uses for judging good and evil. If we would know the divine norms of righteousness, then, Christian ethics will naturally depend upon God's self-revelation and the proper understanding of His word.

Has His word been correctly interpreted by those who "turn the grace of our God into lasciviousness" and argue that we may "continue in sin that grace may abound"? Not at all (Jude 4; Rom. 6:1-2). There should be no doubt whatsoever about the premise that New Testament believers, those who have experienced the grace of God, must "live soberly and righteously and godly in this present world," being "zealous of good works" (Titus 2:11, 14). God's grace has created us in Christ Jesus "for good works that God has prepared that we should walk in them" (Eph. 2:8-10). The New Testament does not eliminate the call for holiness (I Pet. 1:15). Saving faith must be a living, active, and working faith (Jas. 2:14-26). Therefore, we can assert it as beyond question that those who love the Savior must demonstrate lives characterized by obedience (Heb. 5:9; John 14:15).

Should this obedience extend to the *Old* Testament? Should those saved by grace have anything at all to do with God's *law?* And if they should, can the Old Testament commandments still be the standard of moral obligation for *society and the state* as well? If Christian ethics cannot avoid answering the normative question, as claimed above, then Christian ethics will eventually be forced to answer these questions of Biblical interpretation as well. The disturbing thing is that so many Christian teachers and writers answer them without sufficient Biblical proof or concern for consistency. It is as though personal feeling gives them a conclusion from the outset for which they subsequently seek some kind of "reason." Many Christians will just take the word of such respected teachers for granted on these matters — only later to find, upon reflection and examination, that their teachers had not been thinking clearly about the issues involved at all.

The many negative opinions about the law of God as a standard for Christian obedience in our day represent a setback from the theological insights of past generations of Christian scholarship, notably the tradition of the Puritans and the Westminster Standards. What is taken for granted today as the common and "obvious" answer to whether we should obey the Old Testament in modern civil affairs, for instance, did not always enjoy that status in the eyes of earlier Christians. The winds of common opinion have shifted. Why? Has some radical new turn or discovery in Christian scholarship, some brilliant exegesis and persuasive reasoning, intervened between the Puritan age and our own today so as to account for this shift in widespread sentiment about the use of God's law in the Christian life? If so, it is hard to point to just what it might have been. It is rather *changed social circumstances and opinions*, not advances in scholarship, which have brought about the difference.

"But the word of the Lord abides forever" (I Pet. 1:25; Isa. 40:8). If our Reformed and Puritan forefathers were basically correct in their approach to the Old Testament law of God, as I believe, then the truth of that position is still discernible in the objective revelation of God's word, even if it is an unpopular truth in a secularized age. Whether congenial to popular opinion today or not, the conclusions to which we have been driven in our study of God's unchanging word indicate that the standard by which Christians should live is not restricted to the New Testament, but *includes* the law of God revealed in the Old Testament. "Scripture cannot be broken" (John 10:35). With God "there can be no variation, neither shadow that is cast by turning" (Jas. 1:17).

Our studies have pointed to the conclusion that New Testament believers ought to maintain a *pro*nomian, rather than *anti*nomian, attitude. They should seek to purge themselves of "autonomous" ethical reasoning in favor of a "theonomic" approach to moral issues. They should presume that the com-

mandments revealed by God in the Old Testament
are definitive of righteous living for themselves and
their society, being careful not to "speak against the
law and judge it" (Jas. 4:11). Those who teach that
we may break even the least commandment in the
Law and Prophets will be least within the Kingdom
of God (Matt. 5:19).

The theonomic and pro-nomian approach which
we have taken in this book to the normative questions about Christian living and the Old Testament
law is conveniently summarized in the following ten
theses:

1. Since the Fall, it has always been unlawful to use the law of God in hopes of establishing
one's own personal merit and justification, in
contrast or complement to salvation by way of
promise and faith; commitment to obedience is
but the lifestyle of faith, a token of gratitude for
God's redeeming grace.

2. The word of the Lord is the sole,
supreme, and unchallengeable standard for the
actions and attitudes of all men in all areas of
life; this word naturally includes God's moral
directives (law).

3. Our obligation to keep the law of God
cannot be judged by any extrascriptural standard, such as whether its specific requirements
(when properly interpreted) are congenial to
past traditions or modern feelings and practices.

4. We should presume that Old Testament

standing laws[1] continue to be morally binding in the New Testament, unless they are rescinded or modified by further revelation.

5. In regard to the Old Testament law, the New Covenant surpasses the Old Covenant in glory, power, and finality (thus reinforcing former duties). The New Covenant also supercedes the Old Covenant shadows, thereby changing the application of sacrificial, purity, and "separation" principles, redefining the people of God, and altering the significance of the promised land.

6. God's revealed standing laws are a reflection of His immutable moral character and, as such, are absolute in the sense of being non-arbitrary, objective, universal, and established in advance of particular circumstances (thus applicable to general types of moral situations).

7. Christian involvement in politics calls for recognition of God's transcendent, absolute, revealed law as a standard by which to judge all social codes.

---

1. "Standing law" is used here for *policy* directives applicable over time to classes of individuals (e.g., do not kill; children, obey your parents; merchants, have equal measures; magistrates, execute rapists), in contrast to particular directions for an individual (e.g., the order for Samuel to anoint David at a particular time and place) or positive commands for distinct incidents (e.g., God's order for Israel to exterminate certain Canaanite tribes at a certain point in history).

8. Civil magistrates in all ages and places are obligated to conduct their offices as ministers of God, avenging divine wrath against criminals and giving an account on the Final Day of their service before the King of kings, their Creator and Judge.

9. The general continuity which we presume with respect to the moral standards of the Old Testament applies just as legitimately to matters of socio-political ethics as it does to personal, family, or ecclesiastical ethics.

10. The civil precepts of the Old Testament (standing "judicial" laws) are a model of perfect social justice for all cultures, even in the punishment of criminals.

These propositions highlight the essential points and distinctive features of the position developed in this book. The precious truth of salvation by grace alone (#1) is the context within which every other thesis is developed and understood. "Theonomic" ethics is commited to developing an overall Christian world-and-life-view (#2) according to the regulating principle of *sola Scriptura* (#3) and the hermeneutic of covenant theology (#4).[2] The new and better covenant established by Christ does offer Biblical warrant for recognizing changes in covenantal ad-

---

2. By contrast, dispensational theology holds that Old Covenant commandments should be deemed abrogated unless repeated in the New Testament. See Charles Ryrie, "The End of the Law," *Bibliotheca Sacra,* Vol. 124 (1967): 239-242.

ministration (#5), but not changes in moral standards, lest the divinely revealed ethic be reduced to situationism or relativism—just one tribal perspective among many in the evolutionary history of ethics (#6). Righteousness and justice, according to Biblical teaching, have a universal character, precluding any double-standard of morality.

"Theonomic" ethics likewise rejects legal positivism and maintains that there is a "law above the (civil) law" to which appeal can be made against the tyranny of rulers and the anarchy of overzealous reformers alike (#7). Since Jesus Christ is Lord over all (cf. #2), civil magistrates are His servants and owe obedience to His revealed standards for them (#8). There is no Biblically based justification (cf. #4) for exempting civil authorities from responsibility to the universal standards of justice (cf. #6) found in God's Old Testament revelation (3). *Therefore*, in the absence of Biblically grounded argumentation which releases the civil magistrate from Old Testament social norms (cf. #4, #5), it follows from our previous premises that in the exercise of their offices rulers are morally responsible to obey the revealed standards of social justice in the Old Testament law (#10).

In light of the theses leading up to it, the above conclusion does not seem so controversial after all. It makes perfectly good, ethical sense for a Christian. Besides, that conclusion has a great deal of practical value in our day. It is not accidental that the glaring socio-political and criminal problems of the late twentieth century concern matters where our society has turned against the specific directives of God's law. Humanism has been taught in our schools and media; it has been practiced in economics, medicine, politics, and our courts. And the results have been a social disaster. Human life is treated as cheap. Sexual purity is an outdated concept. Truth and honesty have little place in the "real world" of business or politics. Repeat offenders and crimes which go completely unpunished belittle the criminal justice system. Prison reform is desperately needed. In short, humanism has proven its ineffectiveness in case after case. Where can we turn for socio-political wisdom which can effectively counter the degeneration and disintegration of our culture? The only acceptable answer will be to turn to God's directives for social justice, and those are (for the most part) found in the Old Testament commandments to Israel as a nation, a nation facing the same moral problems about life, sex, property, and truth which all nations must face, including our own.

Christians who claim that our ethical standards are restricted to the New Testament cannot, if consistent, deal with the full range of moral issues in our day. Ask them whether it is now immoral to have sexual relations with animals. They will gasp at the thought, but find nothing forbidding it in the New Testament scriptures. At best they can say "fornication" is condemned, only thereby presupposing what they originally denied—namely, that New Testament morality is identical with the standards of the Old Testament (in which case "fornication" applies to the same outlawed acts in both dispensations).[3] Ask them whether it is now immoral for a woman to marry her father. They may say yes, but they will not find that specific case of incest dealt with in the New Testament scriptures. Ask them whether rape is a punishable crime. Again, no New Testament directive covers it. Ask them what the equitable punishment should be for rape. No New Testament answer. Ask them whether they can even show that murder should be a capital crime today. Once more they will find no specific New Testament answer to that question, despite the fact that many conservative believers assume that it is there.

It becomes ever so clear that it is easy to *say* one holds only to "New Testament ethics," but nearly impossible to systematically and consistently *maintain* that position. In actual fact, Christians do not find it a workable policy to follow, departing from the espoused position whenever it seems convenient or necessary to do so. But that simply opens the door to arbitrariness.

The preceding book has attempted to provide a principled, systematic, and consistent approach to the question of whether and how the Old Testament law constitutes a standard for making moral decisions today.

---

3. Cf. treatment of this issue in "The Bahnsen-Feinberg Debate," a tape available from Covenant Tape Ministry (4155 San Marcos Lane, Reno, NV 89502). The debate was sponsored by the Evangelical Theological Society at its annual meeting for 1981 in Toronto.

GLOSSARY

ABROGATE — to abolish or nullify a law by authoritative action

ABSOLUTE — unconditioned by qualifications or limitations

AD HOC — only for the particular case at hand, not systematically taking into account other relevant issues or wider application

A FORTIORI — drawing an inference with even greater force or conviction than in a lesser case

ALTRUISM — the ethical view that one ought to act out of regard for the interests of others

AMILLENNIALISM — the eschatalogical view that on earth before the return of Christ there will be no age of military rule by Christ (contrary to premillennialism) nor an age of great blessing and success for the gospel (contrary to postmillennialism); at Christ's return the general resurrection of the righteous and unrighteous will take place, followed immediately by the final judgment

ANTINOMIANISM — a view which is in some fashion against the law

APOLITICAL — without interest in or consequences for civil government

ASCETICISM — the ethical view that holiness or purity is achieved by mandatory abstinence from bodily comforts and material pleasures (e.g., food, alcohol, sleep, sex, money)

AUTONOMY — the state of being a "law unto oneself," independent of outside authority

AXIOMATIC — characterized as a primary conviction from which all other conclusions are drawn or proven

CEREMONIAL LAW — those Old Covenant commandments which regulated rituals and symbolic actions pertaining to the redemption of God's people and their separation from the unbelieving world, rather than prescriptions about matters which were intrinsically moral

CONSEQUENTIAL PERSPECTIVE — a distinctive approach to ethics which emphasizes and makes decisions in terms of the consequences, goals, or situational factors of one's conduct

CONTINUITY — the relation between two things of

essential identity similarity, coherence or harmony; the lack of change from one principle or regime to another

COVENANT — a mutually binding compact between God and His people, sovereignly transacted by the Lord, wherein a promise is made by God which calls for trust on the part of His people and entails obligations of submission which are sanctioned by blessings and curses

COVENANT THEOLOGY — the position that all of the post-fall covenants made by God are essentially one, centering on God's gracious promise in Jesus Christ, with each successive covenant expanding on previous ones, rather than disgarding them or running parallel to the others; the covenants prior to Christ were marked by anticipation and administered by foreshadows, while the fulfillment or substance was found in Christ's person and redemptive work, establishing the New Covenant today

CULTIC — (as used here) pertaining to special religious ritual

CULTURAL MANDATE — God's authoritative order for man to replinish and subdue the earth, developing and governing the created order under God's dominion, and thus working to make every area of life serve the glory of God

DISCONTINUITY — the relation between two things of difference, dissimilarity, incoherence or disharmony; the change from one principle or regime to another

DISPENSATION—a distinct administration of God's covenantal relation with man or the age characterized by such

EGOISM—the ethical view that one ought to act out of regard for his own benefit or welfare

EGOTISM—the sinful, personal trait of behaving as though one's own interests were of supreme or sole importance

ESCHATOLOGY—the doctrine of the "last things" pertaining to the individual (death, afterlife) or to redemption (the coming, course, and consummation of Christ's kingdom, the millennium) or to the world (Christ's return, the resurrection, final judgment, the eternal state)

EVANGELICAL MANDATE—God's authoritative order for His people to preach the gospel to lost sinners, seek their conversion, bring them into the sacramental fellowship of the church, nurture them in the Christian life, and thus make the nations to be disciples of Christ; the "Great Commission"

EXEGETICAL—pertaining to the detailed analysis and linguistic meaning of specific texts of Scripture

EX POST FACTO—applied "after the fact," thereby disregarding the previous circumstances, status, or legal character of an event

GENERAL EQUITY — (expression used by Reformed or Puritan theologians to denote:) the underlying substance, principle, or point of a law — over against the specific case or cultural setting mentioned by it

GENERAL REVELATION — God's revelation of His person, glory, and attributes to all men in all ages through nature, conscience, and history, so that they are without excuse for not worshipping Him correctly and leading righteous lives; unlike special revelation, it is not verbal in character or redemptive in content

HERMENEUTIC — a method of interpreting Scripture or the principles for doing so

INDUCTIVE — characterized by studying particular cases (factors, evidences) one by one in order to arrive at a generalization

JUDAIZERS — a Jewish heretical party in the early church which held that, in addition to faith in Christ, one must conform to Jewish customs (e.g., the ceremonial law of circumcision, the Old Covenant festivals) in order, through such self-effort and law-works, to be justified and sanctified

JUDICIAL LAW — (tradition theological expression for:) those commandments in the Mosaic law which deliver judgments on cases pertaining to socio-political relations, policy, or rule (e.g., Exodus 21-22)

JUSTIFICATION — God's gracious act of forgiving sinners and treating them as if they had never sinned, based on the imputation of Christ's righteousness, and appropriated by living faith

LEGALISM — the view that one is saved by the merit of his own efforts to performs works of the law

LEGAL POSITIVISM — the imperative theory of law which claims that all laws are merely commands of a human sovereign, so that there is no conceptual or necessary connection between law and justice; in this case those within a legal system are unconditionally obligated to obey its laws, however immoral they may be

MOTIVATIONAL PERSPECTIVE — a distinctive approach to ethics which emphasizes and makes decisions in terms of personal motivation and character traits

NORMATIVE PERSPECTIVE — a distinctive approach to ethics which emphasizes and makes decisions in terms of duty, rules, or moral standards

OBJECTIVE — the quality of having a public nature, independent of our thoughts or feelings

PEDAGOGIC — pertaining to teaching, instruction, or education

PENAL SANCTION — a coercive, civil punishment which honors and enforces a law by being imposed on those who violate it

PENOLOGY — the study or theory of punishment,

especially the punishment of criminals by the state

PHARISEES — a separatist and self-righteous sect in Judaism which prided itself in strict adherence to the Mosaic law, but which attended only to external and trifling details and actually nullified the law by adding to it human traditions

PLURALISM — the view that civil policy should balance the rights of various social spheres (e.g., family, school, church, business) and protect the rights of all conflicting viewpoints within the society, thereby not being based upon or favoring any one distinctive religion, philosophy, party, or sphere of life

POSTMILLENNIALISM — the eschatological view that Christ will return "after the millennium"; Christ has established His Messianic kingdom on earth, it is growing in numbers, area, and influence by means of the preaching of the gospel and Christian nurture, and it will have visible, worldwide, and blessed success before Christ returns at the general resurrection for final judgment

PREMILLENNIALISM — the eschatological view that Christ will return "before the millennium" in order to resurrect the saints (the "first resurrection"), establish a military rule from Jerusalem over the rebellious nations (the battle of Armageddon), and usher in a thousand year period of material peace and prosperity; at the end of this period the nations (still in natural bodies) will rebel and make war against Christ and the resurrected saints (the battle of Gog and Magog), who will be saved by fire from heaven, followed by the second resurrection — now of unbelievers — and the final judgment

PRIMA FACIE — on first appearance

PRO-NOMIAN — characterized by favoring, supporting, or defending the law

PURITY PRINCIPLES — those truths taught or symbolized by ceremonial laws of outward cleanliness, such as the pollution of sin and its repugnance to a holy God, so that only one untainted by defilement may approach Him (e.g., laws dealing with purification for priests, issues of blood, disfigurement, leprosy)

REDEMPTIVE HISTORY — the special, unified course of historical events by which God prepared, accomplished, and applies redemption for His people and thereby advances His saving kingdom

REDEMPTIVE LAW — ceremonial laws which taught or symbolized the way of atonement or God's saving presence among His people (e.g., laws dealing with sacrifice, the priesthood, the temple)

REFORMED — (as used in theology:) characterized by agreement with or adherence to the doctrine, worship, ethic or polity of the Protestant Reformation, more particularly the Swiss or Calvinist branch thereof (in distinction from Lutheranism, Anabaptism)

RELATIVISM, CULTURAL — the view that what is

morally right or wrong is not absolute, but internally adapted to a specific culture, being determined by that particular society's attitudes, folkways or tribal values; thus "justice," for instance, actually changes from culture to culture (not simply *beliefs* about justice) and cannot be defined transculturally

RESTORATIVE LAW — those Old Covenant commandments which regulated rituals and symbolic actions pertaining to the restoration of sinners to God's favor and their separation as God's redeemed people from those still under His wrath (see "ceremonial law")

RETRIBUTIVE — pertaining to recompense to a guilty party according to what the offense deserves

SACRIFICIAL PRINCIPLES — regulations on sacrifices, offerings, and priests or the underlying general truths taught or symbolized by them (e.g., there is no atonement for sin without shed blood)

SANCTIFICATION — God's gracious and powerful work of making sinners holy in heart and conduct through the internal ministry of the Holy Spirit, applying the death and resurrection of Christ to them, so that they increasingly die to sin and live unto righteousness in the whole man

SEPARATION PRINCIPLES — those truths about the separation of God's people from sin and the unbelieving world which were symbolized or taught by certain ceremonial laws of the Old Covenant (e.g., the distinction between clean and unclean meats, the prohibition of mixing seeds or types of cloth)

SITUATIONISM — the ethical view that right and wrong cannot be defined in advance for general types of circumstances and actions, so that moral decisions should not be based upon laws; the "loving" thing to do must be determined by the situation itself, using a utilitarian approach (seeking the greatest pleasure or happiness for the greatest number of people)

SOJOURNERS — those who are alien to the people of a land but reside with them

SOLA SCRIPTURA — (Latin expression meaning:) Scripture alone

SPECIAL REVELATION — God's verbal and (usual) redemptive revelation of Himself to specific people at specific times; special revelation is communicated to us today through its inscripturation in the Bible

STANDING LAW — policy directives applicable over time to classes of individuals (e.g., do not kill; children, obey your parents; merchants, have equal measures; magistrates, execute rapists), in contrast to particular directions for an individual (e.g., the order for Samuel to anoint David at a particular time and place) or positive commands for distinct incidents (e.g., God's order for Israel to exterminate certain Canaanite tribes at a certain point in history)

SUBJECTIVISM — the view that truth or morality is a

matter of the individual's personal feelings or attitudes and do not have an objective nature

SYMBOLIC LAW — pedagogic laws which communicated certain truths by symbolic means, rather than (or not primarily) in explicit fashion (e.g., sacrifical laws, purity laws, separation laws)

TELEOLOGICAL — pertaining to a goal, aim, or purpose; teleological ethics emphasizes and makes decisions in terms of the proper goal of man or the kingdom of God as man's highest good, etc. (cf. "consequential perspective")

THEOCRACY — literally "the rule of God," however this is thought to be expressed (e.g., by His revealed principles, by His chosen leaders, by Himself in the person of the Son, etc.); the word is variously used by writers for different intended conceptions, some using it as a code word for uniqueness of Old Testament Israel, others using it for any social system where the church rules the state (or is not separated from it), and still others for a civil government which strives to submit to the socio-political standing laws revealed by God (in Old or New Testaments)

THEONOMY — literally "God's law," but recently applied to a particular view of its normativity for today

TRANSCENDENT — pertaining to what "goes beyond" man, the creation, or ordinary experience (thus used in theology to stress the mysterious, sovereign, or unique character of God)

TYPOLOGICAL — pertaining to a "type," something intended to foreshadow a later historical reality

UNREGENERATE — not born again or spiritually renewed by the power of the Holy Spirit; pertaining to the "natural man" who is lost in sin, unable to do God's will or to understand the things of the Spirit

WESTMINSTER STANDARDS — the Westminster Confession of Faith and Catechisms (Longer and Shorter) which were composed 1643-1647 at the request of the English Parliament and which, since that time, have served as subordinate doctrinal standards in presbyterian churches; deemed a model of "Reformed" doctrine

INDEX

Theonomy in Christian Ethics

Greg L. Bahnsen

This profound and challenging work created a sensation among evangelical scholars and pastors when it was first published. Regarded by many as the definitive work on the subject of Biblical law, it has set the agenda for debate around the world. Bahnsen argues: "The biblical Christian knows that society's crying demand for 'love' as well as 'law and order' is only satisfied in a genuine sense by the law of God. . . . As obedience to it is empowered by the Holy Spirit, the law of God establishes righteousness in human affairs and human hearts. The ethical dilemmas facing individuals and nations are resolved by the Christian, not by searching for answers based on his autonomous reason, but by going to the authoritative law of God; there alone are adequate answers found for the moral anarchy of the day."

In this thoroughgoing defense of "the abiding validity of God's law [*theonomy*] in exhaustive detail," Bahnsen begins with a lengthy, closely reasoned exegetical examination of Jesus' most crucial statement about His own relationship to the law: the Sermon on the Mount. Bahnsen goes on to explain how the Christian's obedience to the law is related to faith, love, and the work of the Holy Spirit. Concluding with a clear exposition of God's laws for state and society, Bahnsen points out the inevitable blessings which will follow a consistently theonomic approach to ethics in every area of life.

652 pp., indexed, appendices, hb., $17.95
Presbyterian and Reformed Publishing Co.
P.O. Box 817, Phillipsburg, NJ 08865

The Institutes of Biblical Law

Rousas John Rushdoony

In this magnificent work, Dr. Rushdoony has laid the foundation for what may well become the flowering of a Christian civilization. The *institutes* — meaning *first principles* — of the Bible's divinely-ordained social order are clearly set forth, categorized under the general headings of each of the Ten Commandments. Here are practical, workable expositions of what God's word says about work, marriage and the family, criminal law, the arts and sciences, civil government, the church, and much more.

Rushdoony emphasizes that it is impossible to understand either the Bible or the development of Western civilization apart from a solid grasp of biblical law. In fact, he points out, *all law is religious in origin*, in every culture; and "in any culture *the source of law is the god of that society.*" But there is only one true God, and this means that the Bible is the only source of true law; the nations are required to be Christian. The Bible is our final standard in *everything*.

If we believe the Bible, we cannot escape the fact that God requires universal obedience. His law governs us in every area of life, and He commands that He be glorified in all creation. The Christian can do no less than to become educated and adept in the worldwide application of biblical principles. All things, large and small, are to be placed under the dominion of Christ.

The Institutes of Biblical Law is helping Christians around the world fulfill this mandate. It has become *the* standard reference work for scholars and activists in every field.

890 pp., indexed, appendices, hb., $24.00
Presbyterian and Reformed Publishing Co.
P.O. Box 817, Phillipsburg, NJ 08865

The Dominion Covenant: Genesis

Gary North

This is the first volume of a multi-volume commentary on the Bible. It is specifically an *economic* commentary—the first one ever published. What does the Bible require of men in the area of economics and business? What does the Bible have to say about economic theory? Does it teach the free market, or socialism, or a mixture of the two, or something completely different? Is there really an exclusively Christian approach to economics?

The Dominion Covenant: Genesis answers these questions, and many others, by setting forth the biblical foundations of economics. It offers the basis of a total reconstruction of economic theory and practice. It specifically abandons the universal presupposition of all modern schools of economics: Darwinian evolution. *Economics must begin with the doctrine of creation.*

The Dominion Covenant: Genesis represents a self-conscious effort to rethink the oldest and most rigorous social science in terms of the doctrine of creation. Every social science requires such a reconstruction. The "baptized humanism" of the modern Christian college classroom must be abandoned by all those who take seriously God's command that Christians go forth and subdue the earth (Gen. 1:28).

The message of this groundbreaking work is that God has given us clear, infallible standards of righteousness—practical guidelines by which Christians are to reconstruct civilization.

496 pp., indexed, bibliography, hb., $14.95
Institute for Christian Economics
P.O. Box 8000, Tyler, TX 75711

Moses and Pharaoh: Dominion Religion Versus Power Religion

Gary North

In the fifteenth century before the birth of Jesus, Moses came before Pharaoh and made what seemed to be a minor request: Pharaoh should allow the Israelites to make a three-day journey in order to sacrifice to their God. But this was not a minor request; given the theology of Egypt, *it was the announcement of a revolution*—an anti-humanist revolution.

The conflict between Moses and Pharaoh was a conflict between the religion of the Bible and its rival, the religion of humanism. It is not common for scholars to identify Egypt's polytheism with modern humanism, but the two theologies share their most fundamental doctrines: the irrelevance of the God of the Bible for the affairs of men; the evolution of man into God; the impossibility of an infallible word of God; the nonexistence of permanent laws of God; the impossibility of temporal judgment by God; and a belief in the power of man.

What Bible commentators have failed to understand is that the conflict between Moses and Pharaoh was at heart a conflict between the two major religions in man's history, *dominion religion* and *power religion*, with the third major religion—*escapist religion*—represented by the Hebrew slaves. What they have also failed to point out is that *there is an implicit alliance between the power religion and the escapist religion*. This alliance still exists.

This book is a detailed study of the conflict between Moses and Pharaoh. It discusses the implications of this conflict in several areas: theology, politics, sociology, and especially economics. This book is Part One of the second volume of a multi-volume set, *An Economic Commentary on the Bible*. The first volume, *The Dominion Covenant: Genesis*, was published in 1982.

432 pp., indexed, pb., $12.50
Institute for Christian Economics,
P.O. Box 8000, Tyler, TX 75711

God and Government

Gary DeMar

These two volumes together comprise the most comprehensive treatment available on the biblical principles of government. Beginning with the proper foundations in self-government and the structure of the family, Gary DeMar develops a well-rounded view of the purpose and function of civil government in Scripture.

The first volume, subtitled *A Biblical and Historical Study*, contains a concise but excellent introduction to the U.S. Constitution and the problems connected with the relationship between Church and State. "While there is a *functional* separation between Church and State found in the Bible, there is certainly no absolute separation. Both institutions have a common authority; they are both under God and accountable to His revealed word."

The second volume, subtitled *Issues in Biblical Perspective*, begins with an exposition of the biblical world view, and shows its practical outworking in questions of sovereignty, dominion, and ownership. DeMar then turns to a more in-depth look at the biblical view of economics and the issues of poverty and care for the poor.

God and Government is a valuable work on several levels. First, it is an important work in its own right, as a much-needed, enlightening, and superbly written contribution to an increasingly significant area of discussion. Second, it constitutes a marvelous summary of other Reconstructionist works, studded with helpful references. Finally, its workbook format makes it absolutely ideal for in-depth study by individuals and groups alike.

Two vols., 435 pp., bibliography, large paperbacks,
$21.90 for the set
American Vision Press
P.O. Box 720515, Atlanta, GA 30328

Unconditional Surrender: God's Program for Victory

Gary North

There is a war on. The war is between God and Satan. In our day, we see it most clearly in the conflicts between Christian institutions and the institutions of secular humanism. It is a war that is not going to go away. There will be a winner.

Unconditional Surrender is an introduction to this conflict. It covers the fundamental issues of the war: 1) What is the nature of *God*? 2) What is the nature of *man*? 3) What is the nature of *law*? If we can begin to answer these questions, then we will be able to recognize the nature of the battle.

Does Christianity make a difference in life? Does Christianity offer real-life solutions to the basic issues of life? Unquestionably, the answer is *yes*. But if we answer in the affirmative, then we have to start getting specific. Exactly how does Christianity make a difference? What kind of society would Christianity bring forth? In what ways would such a society be different from the society we live in today, the society of humanism? Is there a specifically biblical system of social ethics? What *practical* difference should Christianity make in the life of a ruler, businessman, judge, teacher, or scientist?

This book introduces people to the fundamentals of Christianity, including *applied* Christianity. It is thoroughly biblical. It provides evidence taken directly from the Scriptures. It offers suggestions for further reading, as well as the names and addresses of independent Christian organizations that are equipping Christians for the battles they face today.

264 pp., indexed, bibliography, pb., $9.95
Geneva Ministries
P.O. Box 8376, Tyler, TX 75711

Backward, Christian Soldiers?
An Action Manual for
Christian Reconstruction

Gary North

Jesus said to "Occupy till I come." But if Christians don't control the territory, they can't occupy it. They get tossed out into cultural "outer darkness," which is just exactly what the secular humanists have done to Christians in the 20th century: in education, in the arts, in entertainment, in politics, and certainly in the mainline churches and seminaries. Today, the humanists are "occupying." But they won't be for long. This book shows why.

For the first time in over a century, Christians are beginning to proclaim a seemingly new doctrine, yet the original doctrine was given to man by God: *dominion* (Genesis 1:28). But this doctrine implies another: *victory*. That's what this book is all about: *a strategy for victory*.

Satan may be alive on planet earth, but he's not well. He's in the biggest trouble he's been in since Calvary. If Christians adopt a *vision of victory* and a *program of Christian reconstruction*, we will see the beginning of a new era on earth: the kingdom of God manifested in every area of life. When Christ returns, Christians will be occupying, not hiding in the shadows, not sitting in the back of humanism's bus.

This book shows where to begin.

320 pp., indexed, pb., $4.95
Institute for Christian Economics
P.O. Box 8000, Tyler, TX 75711

Paradise Restored: A Biblical Theology of Dominion

David Chilton

In recent years many Christians have begun to realize a long forgotten truth: God wants us to have dominion over the earth, just as He originally commanded Adam and Eve. By His atonement, Jesus Christ has restored us to Adam's lost position, guaranteeing that God's original plan will be fulfilled. God will be glorified throughout the world: *"The earth shall be full of the knowledge of the LORD, as the waters cover the sea." Isaiah 11:9.*

In order to demonstrate this truth from Scripture, David Chilton begins at the beginning, in the Garden of Eden. He shows how God established basic patterns in the first few chapters of Genesis—patterns which form the structure of later Biblical revelation. In the course of this book on eschatology, the reader is treated to an exciting, refreshingly *Biblical* way of reading the Bible. Avoiding the pitfalls of speculation, Chilton shows how even the most obscure prophecies can suddenly come alive with meaning to those who have grasped the Paradise Theme.

Building on a solid foundation of New Testament eschatology, the author deals at length with the message of the Book of Revelation—often with surprising results. Throughout the volume, the reader is confronted with the fact that our view of the *future* is inescapably bound up with our view of *Jesus Christ*. According to the author, the fact that Jesus is *now* King of kings and Lord of lords means that His Gospel must be victorious: the Holy Spirit will bring the water of life to the ends of the earth. The Christian message is one of Hope. Christ has defeated the devil, and we can look forward to increasing triumphs for His Kingdom in this age. Pentecost was just the beginning.

352 pp., indexed, bibliography, hb., $14.95
Reconstruction Press
P.O. Box 7999, Tyler, TX 75711

Productive Christians in an Age of Guilt-Manipulators

David Chilton

One of the most insidious attacks upon orthodox Christianity has come from the so-called "Christian Left." This book answers the "bible" of that movement, *Rich Christians in an Age of Hunger*, by Ronald Sider.

David Chilton demonstrates that the "Christian Socialism" advocated by Sider is nothing more than baptized humanism—the goal of which is not charity, but raw, police-state power.

The debate between Sider and Chilton centers on one central issue: *Does the Bible have clear guidelines for every area of life?* Sider claims that the Bible does not contain "blueprints" for a social and economic order. The catch, of course, is that Sider then provides *his own* "blueprints" for society, calling for a taxation system which is completely condemned by God's infallible word. Chilton answers that the socialist "cure" is worse than the disease, for socialism actually *increases* poverty. Even when motivated by good intentions, unbiblical "charity" programs will damage the very people they seek to help.

Combining incisive satire with hard-hitting argumentation and extensive biblical references, Chilton shows that the Bible *does* have clear, forthright, and workable answers to the problem of poverty. *Productive Christians* is most importantly a major introduction to the system of Christian Economics, with chapters on biblical law, welfare, poverty, the third world, overpopulation, foreign aid, advertising, profits, and economic growth.

458 pp., indexed, bibliography, pb., $9.95
Institute for Christian Economics
P.O. Box 8000, Tyler, TX 75711

The Law of the Covenant: An Exposition of Exodus 21-23

James B. Jordan

How relevant are the laws of the Old Testament for today? God said that Israel was to be a light to the nations (Isaiah 42:6). That someday all nations would come to Jerusalem to receive the Law (Micah 4:2). That in His Law, "every transgression and disobedience receives a just recompense" (Hebrews 2:2). That all peoples would marvel at the wisdom and justice of Israel's laws (Deuteronomy 4:6-8).

Yet, with the change from the Old to the New Covenant, there are clearly changes in the Law, "for when the priesthood changes, there must also take place a change of law" (Hebrews 7:12). How, then, are we to approach the many laws found in the Old Testament? Do they apply to Christians? If so, how?

In this book, Mr. Jordan provides four introductory chapters on the nature of Biblical law, on the redemptive historical context in which the law was first written, and on the overall changes in the law system which the New Covenant brings. Then, moving to the concrete, Mr. Jordan provides the first truly in-depth commentary on the case laws of Exodus 21-23, the Book of the Covenant. The laws are taken up one at a time. In each case, the question is asked, "What did this law mean to the people of the Old Testament age?" Then the question is asked, "What relevance might this law have for the Christian faith today?" Finally, the question is asked, "How does this law shed light on the work of Jesus Christ, of whom all Scripture speaks? That is, how can we preach Christ from this law?"

In his preface, Mr. Jordan states that he has not tried to say the last word on these chapters of Scripture, but that he has tried to say a first word, and to challenge the Church to look further into these verses to find wisdom for today. No preacher and no student of the Word can afford to be without this study.

310 pp., indexed, hb., $17.50
Institute for Christian Economics
P.O. Box 8000, Tyler, TX 75711

Judges: God's War Against Humanism

James B. Jordan

The lessons of the book of Judges come to us through stories, stories known to every Christian child. The stories of Deborah, of Gideon, of Jephthah, and of Samson are, however, not just captivating stories of faith. They are also, and primarily, theological revelations of the ways of God and men.

In this book, Rev. Jordan examines each story with a view to its theological and practical meaning. What is the command and promise of God? How do men respond? What is the evaluation of the Lord? What are we to learn from this, as we face similar situations today? How does this story display the work of Christ and the work of His Church? These questions, and the answers to them, enable the reader to see the stories of the judges in a new and thrilling light.

Nor does Rev. Jordan shrink from the hard questions. Should the Church today sing the bloodthirsty Song of Deborah? Did Jephthah really burn his daughter? Was Samson in sin when he offered marriage to the Philistine girl? Was it right for Israel virtually to destroy the tribe of Benjamin? These and other difficult questions are thoroughly explored, and the ways of God are vindicated in the face of the criticisms of men.

Written in a non-technical, highly readable style, *Judges: God's War Against Humanism* is an absolute must for the library of every pastor and Christian worker.

355 pp., hb., $16.95
Geneva Ministries
P.O. Box 8376, Tyler, TX 75711

75 Bible Questions Your Instructors Pray You Won't Ask

Gary North

Unless you're "one in ten thousand" as Christians go, you've been misled. Maybe it hasn't been deliberate on the part of your Bible teachers, but it's true. In Christian college classrooms, pulpits, and Sunday Schools throughout the land, people are being misinformed about Christianity, year after year.

Subtitled *How to Spot Humanism in the Classroom or Pulpit*, this hard-hitting little volume of pointed questions exposes many of the doctrinal compromises which modern Christian leaders are making with currently popular forms of Baal worship. People who think they are hearing "the good, old-time religion" are being indoctrinated by well-meaning (and sometimes not so well-meaning) teachers who are either outright humanists or who have been compromised by some of humanism's most important doctrines.

75 Bible Questions covers three crucial battlefields in the war between Christianity and humanism:

1. Sovereignty: God's or Man's?
2. Law: God's or Man's?
3. Kingdom: God's or Man's?

Warning: This is probably the most controversial Christian book you will ever read. Some humanist/Christian colleges would expel a student for even owning a copy. Packed with Scripture references and helpful suggestions about organizing study groups, this valuable book also contains special sections on how to stay out of trouble while reading it. *75 Bible Questions* will change your thinking—permanently!

300 pp., appendices, bibliography, pb., $4.95
Spurgeon Press
P.O. Box 7999, Tyler, TX 75711

Dr. Gary North
Institute for Christian Economics
P.O. Box 8000
Tyler, TX 75711

Dear Dr. North:

I read about your organization in Greg Bahnsen's book, *By This Standard*. I understand that you publish several newsletters that are sent out for six months free of charge. I would be interested in receiving them:

☐ *Biblical Economics Today, Tentmakers, Christian Reconstruction,* and *Preface*

Please send any other information you have concerning your program.

_____
name

_____
address

_____
city, state, zip

☐ I'm enclosing a tax-deductible donation to help defray expenses.

WHY IS THIS
TEAR-OUT SHEET
STILL IN THIS BOOK?

Tear-out sheets are supposed
to be torn out and mailed in.

STOP
PROCRASTINATING!